Rāmāyaṇa
A Critical Appraisal

Other books by the same Author

1. *Mahabharate Goenda — Safalya*-o-*Byarthata* (in Bengali)
   (A detailed analysis of the role of secret agents in the *Mahābhārata*).
2. *Chakraved* (in Bengali)
   (A detective story based on the shadow of a true incident).
3. *Martyabhumi Anandabhumi* (in Bengali)
   (A depiction of the future blissful world).
4. *Jaha Dekhiyachi Jaha Shuniyachi* (What I have seen what I have heard) (in Bengali)
   (A narration of interesting events including those happening during the author's service in the Police and the Intelligence Bureau).
5. *Spy Network in Mahabharata* (in English).
6. A compilation of one ghost and two detective stories entitled *Chakraved* (in Bengali).
7. The Autobiography of an unknown Indian Policeman (in English) (soon to be published).

Rāmāyaṇa
A Critical Appraisal

Ramendra Narayan Sanyal

D.K. Printworld (P) Ltd.
New Delhi

Cataloging in Publication Data — DK
[Courtesy: D.K. Agencies (P) Ltd. <docinfo@dkagencies.com>]

Sānyāla, Ramendra Nārāyaṇa, 1926-
Rāmāyaṇa : a critical appraisal / Ramendra Narayan Sanyal.
p. cm.
Includes index.
ISBN 13: 9788124605516
ISBN 10: 8124605513
1. Vālmīki. Rāmāyaṇa. 2. Rāma (Hindu deity) in literature. I. Title.

DDC 294.5922046 22

ISBN 13: 978-81-246-0551-6 ISBN 10: 81-246-0551-3
First published in India in 2010

Published and printed by:
D.K. Printworld (P) Ltd.
Regd. Office: 'Srikunj', F-52, Bali Nagar
New Delhi – 110 015
Phones: (011) 2545 3975; 2546 6019; *Fax*: (011) 2546 5926
E-mail: indology@dkprintworld.com
Website: www.dkprintworld.com

To the sacred memory of
my elder brother

Late Lt.-Col. Ranajit Narayan Sanyal

whose constant help, guidance and encouragement
helped me to establish in life

Preface

My first book in Bengali entitled *Mahābhārate Goenda* (Intelligence operators in *Mahābhārata*) received wide appreciation from the readers, many of whom requested me to compose a similar book on the other Indian epic *Rāmāyaṇa*. Accordingly I have prepared a book in Bengali on the *Rāmāyaṇa* on similar lines. For the benefit of the English-speaking people, this English version of the book has been prepared. The book is a critical appraisal of the events in the *Rāmāyaṇa* as also of its principal characters particularly Rāma and Rāvaṇa with special emphasis on intelligence collection, *rājadharma* and the relevancy of the teachings of Rāma and the *Rāmāyaṇa* in our present society.

Rāma got all information about Sītā and Rāvaṇa on her abduction by the latter from some of his well-wishers like Jaṭāyu and *rākṣasa* Kabandha in the course of his search for her in the forest along with brother Lakṣmaṇa. On Kabandha's advice Rāma entered into an alliance with *vānara* hero Sugrīva and this alliance in fact set in force all efforts for the search and rescue of Sītā. Rāma killed Vālī, Sugrīva's elder brother who had driven him away from the kingdom, and installed Sugrīva on the throne. That Sītā had been held in captivity by Rāvaṇa in Laṅkā was also known from Sampāti, Jaṭāyu's brother, by the group of *vānara* leaders who were deputed by Sugrīva to the south for the search of Sītā. In this group was Hanumān, Sugrīva's prime minister. He was a learned person possessing supernatural power on the strength of boons bestowed on him by Lord Brahmā and other gods.

Hanumān on reaching the seashore along with his group climbed the nearby Mahendra hills and assuming a huge form rose to the sky reaching Laṅkā by the aerial path after crossing the vast sea. In the course of search in Laṅkā after assuming a diminutive form, he ultimately found Sītā at Rāvaṇa's Aśoka garden and met and talked with her after proving his credentials. He, thereafter, again assumed a huge form and destroyed the ramparts and some of the palace buildings. He even killed the *rākṣasa* army deputed against him. Later he set the city on fire causing considerable damage. In course of his activities Hanumān collected useful information on Laṅkā's defences, strength of the *rākṣasa* army, its deployment, war tactics and strategies, weaponry, etc. Vibhīṣaṇa, Rāvaṇa's brother who sided with Rāma, was the repository of many vital secrets about war tactics of the *rākṣasa* warriors. In fact Indrajit, the valiant son of Rāvaṇa was killed by Lakṣmaṇa on the basis of information furnished by Vibhīṣaṇa.

Rāma thus had all the information about the enemy though he had no organized intelligence set-up of his own. Hanumān and Vibhīṣaṇa were his principal intelligence operators. The royal army of Ayodhyā and its secret agents had no role to play in the war.

Rāvaṇa had a strong band of trained secret agents from whom he obtained detailed information about the advancing *vānara* army. Śuka and Sāraṇa were Rāvaṇa's principal intelligence operators. In the *Rāmāyaṇa* we find, *vānara* king Vālī had also under him a band of efficient intelligence agents. His son Aṅgada collected from them advance information about the alliance between Rāma and Sugrīva. It was indeed a very difficult intelligence operation as the mountains where Sugrīva lived with his companions were out of bounds of Vālī and his men because of the curse of Sage Mātaṅga.

In the matter of intelligence gathering about each other's army, both Rāma and Rāvaṇa were equally matched. In valour and strength the principal warriors of the rival armies were equally competent. They were all armed with various divine weapons. In the terrible battle between Rāma and Rāvaṇa, victory or defeat remained undecided for a long time. It appeared, Rāma and Rāvaṇa were invincible to each other. Even the gods at one time declared both Rāma and Rāvaṇa as jointly victorious. At last Rāma killed Rāvaṇa with the *brahmāstra* sent by Devarāja Indra, his own weapons having failed to do the needful. Rāvaṇa's death at the hands of Rāma was a divine inevitability. With Rāvaṇa's death, the purpose of birth of Rāma on earth as the incarnation of Supreme God Viṣṇu to destroy the sinful Rāvaṇa, was fulfilled. The good ultimately triumphed over the evil.

On ascending the throne of Ayodhyā, Rāma established a righteous rule faithfully adhering to the principles of *rājadharma* where the people lived in peace, happiness and prosperity. In his Rāmarājya there was no widowhood. Everybody lived a long and healthy life. The rainfall was plenty and the agricultural fields grew food grains in abundance. The people lived a virtuous life. The governance was strong and impartial. With strict enforcement of the laws, the good remained ever protected, while the bad were punished with an iron hand. Mahatma Gandhi, father of the nation enamoured of Rāma's Rāmarājya, wanted to establish in India such a righteous society. Though such an ideal state is practically inconceivable, there is no gainsaying the fact that if the kings or the rulers imbued with the lofty principles of *rājadharma* as enshrined in the *Rāmāyaṇa* run the administration impartially and honestly, substantial improvement can be brought about in the society ensuring the well-being of the people.

Despite his controversial acts like killing of Vālī stealthily when he was engaged in combat with his brother Sugrīva, humiliation and ordeal of fire of Sītā at Laṅkā on her rescue, abandonment of Sītā and her eventual entry into *pātāla*, killing of Saṁbuka, a low caste śūdra for observing religious austerities, etc. Rāma is held in high esteem and devotion by the countless people for his nobility of character, achievements and establishment of a righteous society ensuring for all peace, prosperity and happiness. The religion, culture, customs and traditions, thinking and belief and in fact the very existence of the vast sections of the Hindus, centre around the teachings of Rāma and the *Rāmāyaṇa*. We hope and pray for the advent of leaders like Rāma to establish in the coming days a righteous and peaceful society in our country for the good of all.

I have composed my book on the basis of the events as described in the *Vālmīki-Rāmāyaṇa*. For this I have mainly followed the faithful Bengali translation of the original *Rāmāyaṇa* by Sri Tarakanta Devasarma published by M/s K.P. Bagchi & Company Private Limited, Kolkata. Other helping books, I have consulted are *Ramayana* by C. Rajagopalachari, *The Rāmāyaṇa* by R.K. Narayan, *Śrī Rāmacaritamānasa* by Hindi poet Tulsīdāsa, *The Rāmāyaṇa* by Bengali poet Kṛttivās, *The Vālmīki-Rāmāyaṇa* by the famous Bengali writer Rajsekhar Basu and *The Rāmāyaṇa Kathā* by Bengali writer Amalesh Bhattacharya. I have also consulted various books on Vyāsadeva's *Mahābhārata* from which I have given some relevant references in my book. From the websites and the various journals and papers I have also collected some relevant materials for the book. All comments, analyses, assessments and interpretations are, however, exclusively mine.

My wife Smt. Krishna Sanyal, my daughter Smt. Sanjukta Maitra and my daughter-in-law Smt. Devolina Sanyal helped me in various ways in the writing of the book. I convey my grateful thanks to them. I also thank my friends and well-wishers for their valuable suggestions which proved very helpful to me. I regret, I could not mention their names individually.

Written in simple and lucid language with a new outlook, the book containing all the major events of the *Rāmāyaṇa* including those in the Uttara-Kāṇḍa with detailed analyses and interpretations, will no doubt be found interesting to the reading public.

Ramendra Narayan Sanyal

Contents

1

Preliminary Observations

THE *Rāmāyaṇa* is known to be the first epic and its composer Sage Vālmīki the first poet. It is the established belief that Vālmīki composed the *Rāmāyaṇa* during the very lifetime of Rāma. Historical experiences, however, indicate that the story of the *Rāmāyaṇa* in rudimentary form was in vogue in the different parts of the country long before Vālmīki through the then current narratives, village ballads, songs and dramas during religious and other social functions and discussions among the people. Vālmīki has only collated all these current episodes and gave them a cohesive form in one composition in his wonderful language and poetical metre and rhythm. In the *Vālmīki-Rāmāyaṇa* also there have been many interpolations. In fact, the Uttara-Kāṇḍa, the last episode of the *Rāmāyaṇa*, was a later addition, and this has now become an integral part of the epic. These interpolations perhaps explain the various controversial incidents like banishment of Sītā and the killing of Vālī.

According to the research scholars, the original text of *Rāmāyaṇa* was perhaps composed some time in the fourth century BCE. Though Vālmīki in some verses mentioned Rāma as the incarnation of God, he mainly described him as a supreme powerful person. It is, however, true that during the lifetime of Vālmīki himself, Rāma was believed to be the incarnation of God by many people. After many centuries, the north Indian poet Tulsīdāsa (1540-1629) and the Tamil poet Kamban (eleventh century) introduced Rāma among the people as the incarnation of the Supreme God Viṣṇu. According to them Rāma and Kṛṣṇa were synonymous and Viṣṇu was actually Rāma and Kṛṣṇa. Subsequently many poets and devotees started worshipping Rāma as the incarnation of Viṣṇu by installing his image in the temples.

There is an interesting story behind the origin of the *Rāmāyaṇa*. One morning Sage Nārada appeared at the hermitage of Vālmīki, and in the course of discussion, Vālmīki asked the sage, "Nārada, you are omniscient. Nothing is unknown to you. Can you tell me of an all-pervading virtuous person who is strong and powerful, full of gratitude, truthful, resolute, compassionate, learned, universally popular, calm in temperament, exquisitely handsome in appearance, even-minded and free from malice, but at the same time ruthless to his enemies like the terrible destroyer Yama, the God of Death." Nārada said in reply, "It is rare to find all these qualities together in one person. Yet I have noticed all such qualities in Rāma, the eldest son of King Daśaratha of Ayodhyā." Saying this Nārada narrated Rāma's life and achievements, which had a deep impact on the mind of Vālmīki. After the departure of Nārada, Vālmīki, engrossed in the thought of Rāma, proceeded to the nearby Tamasā River for ablution accompanied by his disciple Bhāradvāja. As he entered the adjoining forest, he saw a pair of *krauñca* birds on the branch of a tree happily singing and making love. Suddenly the male bird being pierced by the arrow of a hunter, fell down on the ground tossing about in severe pain and died soon after, while the female bird was wailing by its side in a piteous tone.

Vālmīki afflicted with grief at the cruelty of the hunter, cursed him spontaneously uttering the following verse:

mā niṣāda pratiṣṭhāṁ tvamagamaḥ śāśvatiḥ samāḥ ।
yat krauñcamithunādekamavadhīḥ kāmamohitam ॥

> O hunter, you shall never receive any recognition (you shall remain ever degraded), because you have killed a *krauñca* while engaged in love-making.

Vālmīki told disciple Bhāradvāja, "My words spoken in symmetrical metre out of *śoka* (grief) will be known as *śloka* (verse)."

On return to his hermitage, Vālmīki continued to brood over the verse. Then suddenly Lord Brahmā appeared before him and said, "Vālmīki, the words uttered by you will actually be renowned as verse. It is on my wishes, these words in wonderful metrical rhythm have come out of your lips." Brahmā asked Vālmīki to compose Rāma's story in this poetical metre and disappeared. Thereafter Vālmīki composed this wonderful story of the *Rāmāyaṇa*. Composed in pure Sanskrit in twenty-four thousand verses, five hundred cantos and seven main chapters including the Uttara-Kāṇḍa, the *Rāmāyaṇa* is one of the best books in the world.

The *Rāmāyaṇa* is the story of the Tretā-yuga (age). According to the Hindu mythology, *kāla* (time) is divided into four *yuga*s viz. Satya, Tretā, Dvāpara and Kali. The Mahābhārata war occurred during the Dvāpara-yuga. We are now living at the later part of Kali-yuga. According to traditional calculation, the duration of the *yuga*s is as follows:

1. Satya-yuga — 1,728,000 years
2. Tretā-yuga — 1,296,000 years
3. Dvāpara-yuga — 864,000 years
4. Kali-yuga — 432,000 years

These *yuga*s move in cycle and the Hindu devotees believe that the Satya-yuga, i.e. the age of truth and virtue, will again be established under the influence of Kalki, the tenth and the last incarnation of Viṣṇu. In the scriptures, characteristic features of the four *yuga*s are mentioned. In the Satya-yuga religious austerities were observed only by the brāhmaṇas. In the Tretā-yuga the kṣatriyas occupied a high position in the society by dint of their power and strength and by observing religious austerities. Gradually they became equal to the brāhmaṇas. The kṣatriyas and the brāhmaṇas then collectively divided the ancient Hindu society into four main classes of brāhmaṇa (the class devoted to religious austerities); kṣatriya, (the warrior class); vaiśya (the class engaged in trade and commerce); and śūdra (the class devoted to the service of others). The brāhmaṇas were likened to the head of the human body, the kṣatriyas to the arms, the vaiśyas to the belly and the śūdras to the two feet.

At the initial stage of the establishment of the four classes, as described in the scriptures, the influence of religion was quite pronounced, but gradually irreligious activities began to creep into the society. Slowly a section of the people under influence of *rajoguṇa* (the quality of activity and spiritedness) fell pray to violence, malice and untruthfulness. At the end of the Tretā-yuga, the population of the brāhmaṇas and the kṣatriyas was almost equal. Irreligion and untruthfulness increased further. In the Dvāpara-yuga, the vaiśyas were also engaged in religious activities like the brāhmaṇas and the kṣatriyas. The śūdras did not have any such right. Only in the Kali-yuga they got this right. In the Kali-yuga, it is said, the people will be devoid of religion, truth and righteous conduct. The society will be gripped with disorder as a result of moral degradation of the people marked by their violent temper, and people will indulge in conspiracy and falsehood and various other negative activities. There will be severe food shortage and the general people will pass their days in a state of deep fear. The ruling class will be solely guided by self-aggrandizement in complete disregard of the welfare of the people. Today we are actually witnessing such a pathetic picture of the human society. Many people believe, predictions of the Śāstras are coming true.

2

Birth of Rāma

In the Tretā-yuga, there was a large empire in India by name Kosala with its capital at Ayodhyā (Ayodhyā means that which cannot be conquered by war). With artistically designed palaces, beautiful buildings, wide roads, well-maintained parks and water fountains, Ayodhyā was then a prosperous city comparable only to Amarāvatī, the capital of Indra, the king of the gods and Alakāpurī, the capital of Kubera, the God of Wealth. Under the just and compassionate rule of Daśaratha, peace and prosperity prevailed throughout the empire. The people who were religious, truthful and free from greed, lived happily. Himself a great hero, Daśaratha maintained a large well-trained army. No enemy ever dared to cast an evil eye on his empire. Daśaratha himself was, however, unhappy in his mind. He was issueless having no heir to succeed him.

During this time a strange incident took place in *Devaloka* (abode of the gods). On the attainment of great might with the boon of Lord Brahmā, Rāvaṇa, the king of Laṅkā started terrorizing the gods. For their protection, the gods appeared before Brahmā and requested Him to devise some means for destroying Rāvaṇa. Brahmā informed them that on the prayer of Rāvaṇa, he had bestowed on him the boon that he would remain unconquered by the *deva*s, *gandharva*s, *yakṣa*s, *rākṣasa*s and others and the boon once bestowed could not be revoked. Brahmā disclosed that Rāvaṇa, out of contempt for the humans, did not ask for any boon concerning them. He, therefore, could be destroyed at the hands of the humans. Suddenly the

Supreme God Viṣṇu appeared there. The gods praising Viṣṇu in hymns requested Him to be born of the wives of the king of Ayodhyā to destroy Rāvaṇa for the good of the three worlds. Viṣṇu gave his consent and disappeared.

In the meantime at Ayodhyā, at the request of King Daśaratha, sage Ṛṣyaśṛṅga organized a special *yajña* (oblation of fire) for obtaining sons for him. As the ceremony ended, a divine person came out of the sacrificial fire holding in his hands a golden bowl containing sweetened rice-porridge. He handed over the bowl to King Daśaratha with direction to distribute the divine porridge among the queens and departed. Accordingly Daśaratha gave half portion of the porridge to the first queen Kausalyā and the half of the remaining portion to queen Sumitrā. He was about to give the other remaining portion to queen Kaikeyī, but stopped after a little thought. He again divided this remaining portion and gave one portion to Sumitrā and the other portion to Kaikeyī. Thus in this distribution of the divine porridge, Kausalyā got 8 portions out of total 16, Sumitrā 6 and Kaikeyī only 2.

Why was this discrimination in the distribution of rice-porridge among the queens? Daśaratha indeed consciously made this discrimination out of deep political consideration in order to safeguard the interest of his empire. It was foretold by Sage Sanatkumāra that he would be blessed with four sons. Naturally one of the queens would give birth to twins. Though Kaikeyī was dearest to him amongst the queens, he did not want her to have twins as this would strengthen her position *vis-à-vis* the other queens. This was why he gave the smallest portion of the rice-porridge to Kaikeyī. He actually wanted either Kausalyā or Sumitrā to have the twins. This was the reason for his giving larger portions of the rice-porridge to them. We could justify Kausalyā getting the half portion of the rice-porridge being the first queen. But what could be the rationale for King Daśaratha to discriminate between Sumitrā and Kaikeyī?

Daśaratha was a far-sighted experienced king who did not want any complication to arise in the future affecting the stability of his empire out of possible rivalry among the brothers. Kaikeyī was the princess of Kekaya, then a strong independent kingdom comprising the modern Kashmir and other adjoining territories, out of the domain of his Koṣala empire. Daśaratha's fear was that Kaikeyī's son might be influenced by her father, the king of Kekaya to fulfil any evil design against his empire. With Kaikeyī having twins, this fear might prove very serious. No such fear, however, was there in respect of Kausalyā and Sumitrā. Kausalyā hailed from Kosala, a semi-independent kingdom within the large Kosala empire. In the *Rāmāyaṇa* there was no mention of the parentage of Sumitrā. But in some ancient writings, Sumitrā was mentioned as the princess of Magadha, which was also like the Kosala kingdom, a semi-independent kingdom within Daśaratha's empire. Both the kingdoms being under his influence, the sons of Kausalyā and Sumitrā with the twins of one of them, could then, he thought, stand united against any possible adventurism of Kaikeyī's son with the support of the mighty Kekaya empire. That Daśaratha's assessment was not entirely wrong was proved by subsequent events (details later) when Kaikeyī tried to install her son as the crown prince and banished to the forest Kausalyā's son, the rightful claimant to this position being the eldest among the brothers.

On taking the rice-porridge, the queens became pregnant. After 12 months Kausalyā gave birth to Rāma, Sumitrā twins Lakṣmaṇa and Śatrughna and Kaikeyī Bharata much to the relief and joy of King Daśaratha. Although all the brothers were born in close proximity, Rāma was the eldest followed by Bharata, Lakṣmaṇa and Śatrughna. While Rāma and Bharata on birth lay quietly in their cots, Lakṣmaṇa and Śatrughna, it was said, started crying. Despite all efforts they could not be quietened. Then a senior maid, as the story goes, placed Lakṣmaṇa by the side of Rāma and Śatrughna by the side of

Bharata. Then immediately they stopped their cries and lay quietly. Since then Lakṣmaṇa became deeply attached to Rāma and Śatrughna to Bharata. This was believed to be due to some divine reasons. With the attainment of age, the princes under the guidance of the royal preceptors, learned the art of warfare and various other subjects befitting the royal scions. Soon they attained high proficiency in all the branches. Rāma was, however, ahead of the other brothers. The brothers had the best of relationship amongst themselves. In all matters the other brothers unhesitatingly followed Rāma's guidance and advice. For his various noble qualities like gentle nature, sense of respect to the elders, sympathetic outlook, etc. Rāma became very popular with the general public. Daśaratha was very happy with the accomplishments of the princes. At the proper age he was thinking of the marriage of the princes.

3

Rāma with Brother Lakṣmaṇa Accompanies Sage Viśvāmitra to Janasthāna and Destroys the Rākṣasas

AT this time one day the great ascetic Viśvāmitra visited Ayodhyā to meet the king. Previously Viśvāmitra was a kṣatriya king of a large empire. Once in the course of a tour he visited the hermitage of sage Vasiṣṭha where he and his army were lavishly entertained by the sage with food and drinks produced with the help of his Kāmadhenu (cow that grants all wishes). Later when Viśvāmitra on being refused the holy cow, tried to forcibly take her away, a battle ensued between his army and that of Vasiṣṭha produced on his command by the cow. On being defeated in the battle, Viśvāmitra realized that the power of a brāhmaṇa was much superior to that of a kṣatriya. He immediately gave up his throne, and surmounting various impediments obtained all the attributes of a brāhmaṇa after engaging himself for long years in religious austerities first to seek the blessings of Lord Mahādeva in the Himalayas and then of Lord Brahmā at Puṣkar (Rajasthan). Sage Vasiṣṭha also recognized him as a brāhmaṇa.

This great ascetic Viśvāmitra was now before the king. Daśaratha received him with great honour and wanted to know the purpose of his visit assuring him he would gladly obey his command. Happy at the assurance of the king, Viśvāmitra said, "Two very powerful *rākṣasa*s (man-eating demons) by name Mārīca and Subāhu have been desecrating the sacrificial ground of my hermitage by showering meat and blood making it impossible for me to perform my *yajña*. I myself can destroy them; but as it is improper to utter any curse at the time of *yajña*, I have refrained from doing so. I have come to take with me your valiant eldest son Rāma. He is the only person capable of destroying the *rākṣasa*s so as to enable me to perform my *yajña* undisturbed."

King Daśaratha on hearing Viśvāmitra became unconscious for a few moments. Later he said, "Rāma is only a boy. He is not yet 16. He is still not proficient enough in the art of warfare. On the other hand the *rākṣasa*s are very strong and powerful. Moreover they are capable of creating illusions while fighting. It is impossible for Rāma alone to defeat them in the battle. If you permit, I shall myself go with my well-trained army to destroy the *rākṣasa*s. And if you absolutely require Rāma's services, he can accompany you along with me and my army. Kindly apprise me of all the details about the *rākṣasa*s."

Viśvāmitra said in reply, "Rāvaṇa, son of Sage Viśravas, by dint of the boon obtained from Lord Brahmā is terrorizing the three worlds. He has sent the two *rākṣasa*s to create obstacles in the performance of my *yajña*."

Daśaratha on hearing everything said, "*deva*s, *gandharva*s, *yakṣa*s and others cannot withstand Rāvaṇa's attacks. What can then the humans do against him? In the circumstances myself and my sons with our army can do nothing against Rāvaṇa and his army. I cannot allow Rāma to proceed with you alone to face of this inevitable disaster. Kindly give up your desire to take Rāma with you."

At this Viśvāmitra became very angry. He told Daśaratha, "Mahārāja, you are going against your promise. This is unbecoming of a king of the Raghu clan. If this is your decision, I am returning to my hermitage."

The gods became frightened to see the angry mood of Viśvāmitra. The royal preceptor Vasiṣṭha then advised

Daśaratha to hand over Rāma to Viśvāmitra. He explained, "Mahārāja, you need not worry at all. The great ascetic Viśvāmitra is a very powerful person. He is in possession of innumerable divine weapons. Rāma will always be protected by him. It is for the good of your son that he has himself sought his services."

At the assuring words of Vasiṣṭha, Daśaratha became pacified and he gladly allowed Rāma and also his younger brother Lakṣmaṇa to accompany Viśvāmitra with instruction to always follow his advice.

After bidding farewell to all, Rāma and Lakṣmaṇa armed with their respective weapons, left the palace in the company of Viśvāmitra. Reaching the right bank of river Sarayū (a tributary of the river Ganges), Viśvāmitra taught Rāma and Lakṣmaṇa two *mantra*s by name *bala* and *atibala*. Explaining the power of the two *mantra*s, he said, "You shall remain free from fatigue, fever and other ailments by chanting the *mantra*s. You shall not even suffer any impairment of your physical appearance. Under no circumstances the *rākṣasa*s will be able to harm you. You shall be second to none in good fortune, skill, knowledge and in the correct understanding of the facts. In the matter of argument and counter-argument you shall be able to establish your superiority over others. Theses *mantra*s will also help quench your hunger and thirst."

That night they stayed at the bank of the river. The next day they reached a beautiful hermitage at the confluence of the Jāhnavī and Sarayū rivers. Viśvāmitra explained, this was previously the hermitage of Kandarpa, the God of Love. Once when Lord Mahādeva was proceeding by the side of the hermitage, Kandarpa tried to pervert his mind. Mahādeva became enraged and as he cast his eyes towards Kandarpa, he was burnt into ashes. Since then Kandarpa had been known as Anaṅga, i.e without any body, and this place was known as Aṅgadeśa. Now the disciples of Anaṅga were living here.

After passing the night in the hermitage, Viśvāmitra with Rāma and Lakṣmaṇa crossed the Ganges by boat the next morning. While crossing the river, Rāma heard a tremendous sound and on being asked about its reason, Viśvāmitra said, "Lord Brahmā has created Manasā Sarovara out of his mind and the river Sarayū flows from this Sarovara. The Sarayū here has joined the Jāhnavī and the collision of the currents of the two rivers has caused this huge sound." On Viśvāmitra's direction the two brothers paid obeisance to the two rivers. After crossing the river, they entered a large forest. Explaining the history of the forest, Viśvāmitra said, "Previously there existed two prosperous habitations in this area. In the ancient times Indra killed Vṛtrāsura. This Vṛtrāsura was previously a brāhmaṇa and as such Indra being guilty of a great sin for killing a brāhmaṇa, was besmeared with dirt. Besides he also became very hungry. In this forest the gods and the sages removed the dirt from Indra's body with water from the Ganges and also satisfied his hunger. On being absolved of the sin, Indra had two prosperous habitations built here. Both these habitations have been destroyed by Tāḍakā Rākṣasī who lives in this forest." After narrating the history of the forest, Viśvāmitra asked Rāma to kill this irreligious *rākṣasī*. He explained, for the protection of the people a king sometimes had to commit cruel and sinful acts and he should have no hesitation in killing a woman. "My father has asked me to always obey your command" — saying this Rāma made a penetrating sound with a twang of his bow-string. On hearing the sound, Tāḍakā Rākṣasī came out of the forest and attacked all of them with a shower of stones. Rāma immediately severed her two arms, and Lakṣmaṇa her nose and the ears. Even in this condition, by creating illusion, she assumed various forms in order to infatuate them. Simultaneously she resorted to a shower of stones on Rāma and Lakṣmaṇa from all sides. Viśvāmitra asked them to immediately kill her, warning that the *rākṣasas* became very ferocious in the evening. Accordingly Rāma pierced the chest of Tāḍakā Rākṣasī with a sharp arrow and she fell down dead on the ground. Happy at her death, Indra and other gods asked Viśvāmitra to hand over to Rāma all the divine weapons which had been kept under his custody.

That night they all stayed in the forest. The next morning Viśvāmitra sat in meditation and soon after, various divine weapons like *daṇḍa cakra* (punishing discus), *viṣṇu cakra* (Vṣṇu's discus), *vajra* (Indra's weapon), *śaiva śūla* (Śiva's trident), *varuṇa pāśa* (Sea God Varuṇa's noose), *vāyavyāstra* (Wind God Vāyu's weapon) and *śoṣaṇāstra* (weapon with power of absorption) appeared before Rāma and humbly announced they were his servants always willing to obey his command. Rāma with a cheerful mind touched the divine weapons and asked them to appear before him whenever he would remember them. The weapons nodded in agreement and departed.

Viśvāmitra with Rāma and Lakṣmaṇa again began his journey and reached a beautiful place. Rāma thinking the place to be the hermitage of some sage requested Viśvāmitra to narrate its history. He also wanted to know the asectic's acrificial ground.

Viśvāmitra said, "At this place the Supreme God Viṣṇu obtained divine grace by undergoing religious austerities. For this the place is known as *sidhāśrama* (holy place where divine grace was obtained). While God Viṣṇu remained engaged in such austerities, Bali, son of Virocana defeated the gods and occupied Indra's kingdom. The gods then requested Viṣṇu to take birth as a dwarf and to reinstall Indra in his kingdom after banishing Bali by using His *māyā* power. They informed Viṣṇu that Bali who was now engaged in performing a great *yajña* in heaven was giving away everything for the asking. Accordingly God Viṣṇu took birth as the son of Aditi, daughter of Lord Kaśyapa, as a dwarf and appeared before Bali. There Viṣṇu on the plea of asking for only *tripāda bhūmi* (earth measuring only three human feet) got for himself the entire world from Bali by dint of his *māyā* power and made him a captive. Viṣṇu then reinstalled Indra in his kingdom. I live in this hermitage. The *rākṣasas* are trying to desecrate my sacrificial ground here. O Rāma, during your stay here, you shall have to kill the *rākṣasas*."

Viśvāmitra on entering the hermitage, got himself initiated to the *yajña* that very day and abstained from speech. As the *yajña* started, Rāma and Lakṣmaṇa remained on guard near the sacrificial ground. One by one five days passed off peacefully. On the sixth day as the fire of the *yajña* was ignited, suddenly *rākṣasas* Mārīca and Subāhu along with their followers who were hiding in the nearby forest, rose to the sky with a huge sound and started vomiting blood on the sacrificial ground. Rāma who was alert, threw Mārīca to the ocean about 100 *yojanas* (1 *yojana* = nearly 12 kms) away after seriously wounding him with his arrow. Thereafter Rāma killed Subāhu and other *rākṣasas* with other powerful arrows. At the death of the *rākṣasas*, the disciples of Viśvāmitra burst into shouts of joy. With the completion of the *yajña,* peace was established in the entire area. Viśvāmitra lavishly praised Rāma for his deed and said, "Rāma, you have accomplished a very difficult task assigned to you by your preceptor. For your heroism, the name of *siddhāśrama* stands justified."

The above are the armed clashes between the rival groups we come across for the first time in the *Rāmāyaṇa*. We are aware in any war prior information of the enemy, his strategy and tactics, weapons, allies, etc. are a must for its successful conduct. Here we find in the incidents of destruction of Tāḍakā Rākṣasī and of Mārīca and Subāhu with their followers at the hands of Rāma and Lakṣmaṇa, the *rākṣasas* did pay no importance to this vital fact of prior intelligence collection about their enemy. We are to keep in mind that the *rākṣasas* are not ordinary living beings akin to wild animals. They are actually all humans, but extremely ferocious possessing immense physical strength and the power of illusion. This is because of their excess of *rajo-guṇa* (quality of activity and spiritedness) and absence of *sattva-guṇa* (quality of virtue and goodness). They are actually totems described by the poet in various physical appearances in conformity with their qualities. In fact, no such living beings ever existed anywhere, nor do they exist today. In the epics we come across similar characters in various animal forms behaving like the humans. All these are the poet's imagination.

Tāḍakā Rākṣasī, Mārīca, Subāhu and the *rākṣasa* warriors belonged to Rāvaṇa's huge *rākṣasa* army deputed specifically to prevent the brāhmaṇas from performing their *yajña*s as he was against the Brāhmanical social order. In fact, they were the advance group of the large *rākṣasa* army contingent stationed under the command of his two very powerful warrior brothers in Daṇḍakāraṇya (Daṇḍaka forest) in which *siddhāśrama* was located, for the purpose of terrorizing the sages living in their hermitages in this forest. Rāvaṇa's local commanders despite having all the resources under their control including a strong intelligence apparatus, failed to correctly assess the prevailing situation. Their agents, if at all any were engaged, had apparently no understanding of the significance of Viśvāmitra's temporary absence from his hermitage and his visit to Ayodhyā to seek Rāma's services from Daśaratha. They also did seem to have no information about the divine powers of Viśvāmitra and Rāma's acquisition of the divine weapons. They were perhaps even oblivious of the presence of Rāma and Lakṣmaṇa in the forest in the company of Viśvāmitra till they started the fighting. It appears the *rākṣasa* army mainly depended on their physical strength and the power of illusion to fight the enemy. In contrast Viśvāmitra had all the information about the *rākṣasa*s and constantly guided Rāma during the fight.

Rāvaṇa who had ten heads, we know, was a great devotee of Lord Brahmā. The method of his worship was unique as also grotesque. He showed rare devotion, courage, determination and perseverance to obtain Brahmā's grace. In front of the blazing sacrificial pit he started his worship by chanting the prescribed hymn and this continued for years together. When Brahmā did not appear or send any divine message, Rāvaṇa severed one of his heads with the sword and threw the head in the sacrificial pit as his offering to Brahmā. Still having no response from Brahmā, he severed all the heads one by one except one, and offered them in the fire. Even in that condition, Rāvaṇa with his body besmeared with blood, continued his prayer with single-minded devotion. Even then Rāvaṇa did get no response from Him. He then raised his sword to severe his last remaining head to offer it in the sacrificial fire for Brahmā. At this moment Brahmā appeared before Rāvaṇa and gave him the boon prayed for. With the boon Rāvaṇa, we know, became invincible to the *deva*s, *gandharva*s and others and easily conquered the three worlds. The gods were driven away from the heaven and even Indra was brought to Laṅkā as a captive by Rāvaṇa's son Meghnāda. For his rare bravery Meghnāda was named Indrajit. Though a virtuous person, Rāvaṇa soon fell prey to the lust for wealth and worldly pleasure paying virtually no attention to the governance of his vast empire. Many of his ministers and army commanders, following him, succumbed to similar vices. In the circumstances Rāvaṇa remained completely in the dark about the happenings in Daṇḍakāraṇya.

After peace was established with the destruction of the *rākṣasa*s, Viśvāmitra told Rāma, "King Janaka of Mithilā is presently performing a *yajña* in his capital. We shall all go to Mithilā to attend the *yajña.* At Mithilā you will see a strange bow which is known as *Haradhanu* (bow of Lord Mahādeva). This bow is a gift of God Varuṇa to King Janaka. None — even the gods — could string the bow. The king worships the bow everyday with flowers and incense."

Viśvāmitra along with Rāma and Lakṣmaṇa and some of his disciples, in the course of the journey towards Mithilā, reached the bank of the Sone River. On being asked by Rāma about the history of the area, Viśvāmitra said, "One virtuous king by name Kuśa reigned here in the past. His four sons on his direction built four cities in the region. One of the cities was Girivraja (near Rājgir in Bihar). His second son King Kuśanāva had 100 beautiful daughters by wife Ghṛtāci. One day the Wind God appeared before the daughters when they were engaged in dance and music in the royal garden and expressed his desire to have them as his wives. As the princesses refused to marry him without the knowledge of their father, the Wind God made them physically crippled by a curse and departed. King Kuśanāva later married the princesses to King Brahmadatta when by his touch they all got back their former physical appearance.

"King Kuśanāva on performance of the prescribed *yajña* got a son by name Gādhi. This Gādhi is my father. As I belong to the Kuśa clan, another name of mine is Kauśika. I normally live in the Himalayas. Only for the performance of the *yajña* have I come to *siddhāśrama.* Now my wish has been fulfilled because of your might."

4

Descent of Gaṅgā on Earth

THE next day Viśvāmitra with all reached the bank of the river Jāhnavī. Here on being asked by Rāma to narrate the story of descent of the Jāhnavī (Ganges) from the heaven on the earth, Viśvāmitra said, "The king of the Himalayas had two daughters named Gaṅgā (Ganges) and Umā. On the request of the gods, Gaṅgā was sent to the *devaloka* (heaven), while Umā was married to Lord Śiva.

"In the meantime Sagara, the king of Ayodhyā by the grace of Sage Bhṛgu was blessed with a son Asamañja by name by his first queen and 60,000 sons by the second queen. Asamañja who turned up as a cruel young man, used to kill small children by throwing them into the river. The royal subjects hated him for his cruelty. The king ultimately banished him from the kingdom. Aṁśumān, the son of Asamañja was, however, of a different nature. He was brave, popular and sweet-spoken.

"After a long time King Sagara organized an *Aśvamedha Yajña* in his capital and entrusted his grandson, Aṁśumān to ensure its peaceful performance. The horse of the *yajña* under escort went out to traverse different areas and the date of its sacrifice on return was also fixed. The horse, however, did not return before the due date. Later it was learnt Indra had carried off the horse in the guise of a *rākṣasa* as he thought the performance of the *Aśvamedha Yajña* by a human might adversely affect his supremacy. As a great sin would accrue to him for not completing the *yajña*, Sagara sent out his 60,000 sons in search of the horse. The sons ultimately found the horse in the hermitage of Sage Kapila located in the *pātāla*.

Thinking the sage had seized the horse, they were about to attack him when he out of anger raised a menacing cry which burnt into ashes all the 60,000 sons of Sagara.

"Even after a long time when his sons did not return, Sagara became very much worried and sent Aṁśumān in search of his uncles. After searching many places, Aṁśumān ultimately arrived at the hermitage of Sage Kapila in the *pātāla* and found the horse there. He also noticed there a heap of ashes. Soon Garuḍa, the king of the birds who happened to be the maternal uncle of his uncles, appeared before him and said — 'Sage Kapila has burnt Sagara's sons into ashes. If Jagatpāvanī Gaṅgā (Ganges who is the purifier of the world) floods the ashes, your dead uncles will have the privilege of departing to heaven. You better return to Ayodhyā with the horse and complete the *yajña*.'

"Accordingly Aṁśumān returned with the horse and the *yajña* was duly performed. On the death of Sagara, Aṁśumān ascended to the throne. After a few years he abdicated in favour of his son Dilīpa and went to the Himalayas for religious austerities. Dilīpa deeply thought over the means to bring about the descent of the Gaṅgā; but failed to find any. After him, his son Bhagīratha, a highly religious person, became the king. For his deep religious pursuits, he was known as *rājarṣi* (king who leads a life of an ascetic). After handing over royal duties to the ministers, he went into deep religious austerities praying for the descent of the Gaṅgā on the earth. Satisfied with his devotion, Lord Brahmā granted him, on his prayer, two boons: (1) the blissful living of the sons of Sagara in the heaven on their ashes being flooded by the water of the Gaṅgā and (2) the continuity of the Ikṣvāku dynasty. Brahmā, however, warned, the force of the descent of the Gaṅgā could not be withstood by anyone else other than Lord Mahādeva and advised Bhagīratha to seek Mahādeva's blessings.

"Lord Mahādeva on being satisfied with the prayer of Bhagīratha, agreed to bear the Gaṅgā on His head. Then the

Gaṅgā fell on the head of Mahādeva with a terrible force. In her mind the Gaṅgā had the pride she would descend on the earth taking Mahādeva along with her. Mahādeva on realizing her motive became angry and kept the Gaṅgā confined in the mass of His matted hair preventing her descent. Bhagīratha again sat in prayer of Mahādeva, who on being satisfied with his devotion, released her. The Gaṅgā then started flowing in as many as seven currents. The Gaṅgā was herself the seventh current. Bhagīratha followed the Gaṅgā in his divine chariot. The humans of the earth on having ablution in the sacred water of the Gaṅgā were liberated from sin.

"At one place the sacrificial ground of Sage Jahnu was washed away by the current of the Gaṅgā. Annoyed at her boastful behaviour, the sage drank the entire water of the Gaṅgā. The people everywhere burst into loud lamentation. On the prayer of the *deva*s, *gandharva*s and the saints, Sage Jahnu accepted the Gaṅgā as his daughter and released her through his ears. Since then the Gaṅgā being the daughter of Sage Jahnu is known as Jāhnavī.

"The Gaṅgā thereafter flooded the ashes in the *pātāla*. The sons of Sagara on being liberated from the curse, went to the heaven. As Bhagīratha has brought the Gaṅgā to the earth, she is also known as Bhāgīrathī. Another name of the Gaṅgā is Tripathagā as she flowed along three paths through the heaven, the earth and the *pātāla* making them purified.

"At his unprecedented achievements, Lord Brahmā showered blessings on Bhagīratha. On His direction, Bhagīratha performed the last rites of the sons of Sagara with the sacred water of the Gaṅgā and became himself purified. He then returned to Ayodhyā and took up the reins of the government of the kingdom ending all the sorrows and sufferings of the subjects."

The wonderful story of the descent of the Gaṅgā on the earth had a deep impact on the minds of Rāma and Lakṣmaṇa.

5

Fight for the Nectar of the Sea between Devatās and Daitya-Dānavas

AFTER spending the night at the river bank, they all proceeded on their journey the next morning and reached a beautiful habitation. On being asked by Rāma to narrate its history, Viśvāmitra said, "I have previously heard its story from Indra. The story is like this. The *devatās* (gods), the *daityas* (demons hostile to gods) and the *dānavas* (demi-gods similar to the demons also hostile to the gods) are all sons of the same family. Prajāpati (protector of all living beings) Kaśyapa married all the thirteen daughters of Prajāpati Dakṣa. From amongst the daughters, the *devatās* were born of Aditi, the *daityas* of Diti and the *dānavas* of Danu. Because of similarity of the character of the *daityas* and the *dānavas*, a close friendship developed amongst them. At one time the *devatās* together with the *daityas* and the *dānavas* decided, they would avoid old age and become immortal by drinking the nectar of the sea. For this purpose, they began to churn the Kṣīroda Sāgara (sea by name Kṣīroda) by using the Mandāra Mountain as the churning rod and the serpent king Vāsuki as the churning rope. The churning work continued for thousands of years. Due to extreme exhaustion, Vāsuki started vomiting poison which threatened to burn the entire world. Stricken with fear the gods sought the protection of Lord Mahādeva. Indra, the king of the gods told Mahādeva, O the Greatest Soul, you are the greatest of the gods. Therefore, kindly accept as the first offering whatever has come out first on churning the sea. On seeing the frightened gods as also at the request of Indra, Mahādeva drank the entire poison as if it was the nectar. Peace descended on the world. Mahādeva then came to be known as Nīlakaṇṭha (blue-throated) as His throat turned blue on taking the poison.

"Again the churning work was resumed and the churning rod gradually entered into the *pātāla*. At the request of the *deva*s and the *gandharva*s, the Supreme God Viṣṇu as the incarnation of Kūrma (tortoise) then replaced the churning rod at the bottom of the sea. The churning work started afresh. First the great Dhanvantari, the physician of the heaven, came out followed by the *apsaras*es (voluptuously beautiful women — courtesans of the heaven). None of the *deva*s or *daitya-dānava*s accepted them and as such the *apsaras*es became available to all for enjoyment. Thereafter along with many valuable objects, purest nectar came out of the sea. Immediately a battle ensued between the *deva*s and the *daitya-dānava*s for the possession of the nectar. Viṣṇu by dint of His enchanting illusion, however, carried off the nectar for the *deva*s who after drinking it became immortal. All those who attacked Him were destroyed. On the death of the *daitya-dānava*s, Indra occupied the *Svargarājya* and established his supremacy over the three worlds.

"Diti then with a heavy heart at the destruction of her sons, requested husband Kaśyapa for a son, capable of killing Indra. Kaśyapa agreed. In dụe course Diti became pregnant and surprisingly the same Indra was engaged for her attendance and nursing. One day Indra by using his *māyā* power entered into the womb of Diti when she was asleep and with his *vajra* cut into pieces her son, his future destroyer. Indra later was pardoned by Diti when he explained he had to do this sinful act because she was sleeping in an unholy state in the opposite direction."

Narrating this story, Viśvāmitra told Rāma, "This was the place where Indra attended to and nursed Diti. The name of one son of Diti was Ikṣvāku. He was the first king of Ayodhyā.

The palace you see here has been named Viśālapurī after the name of Ikṣvāku's virtuous son Viśāla. Sumati, the son of great Kakutstha of this family, is living here at present."

That night they all stayed in the palace of King Sumati as his guests and left for Janaka's capital Mithilā the next morning. On the way they reached a beautiful hermitage without any habitation. On being asked by Rāma about its history, Viśvāmitra said, "This is a pathetic story. This was previously the hermitage of great Sage Gautama. Once during his absence, Indra in the guise of Gautama, came to the hermitage and had union with Ahalyā, Gautama's wife. Ahalyā (one having no flaws) who was created by Lord Brahmā out of His mind, was exquisitely beautiful. Indra wanted to marry her, but Brahmā refused. He instead married Ahalyā to Sage Gautama. Indra, however, could not forget Ahalyā and he was seeking an opportunity to meet her.

"Ahalyā who had also weakness for Indra, consented to this illicit union with him. In the meantime Sage Gautama returned to the hermitage and came to know of the whole incident. He flew into a rage and on his curse Indra lost both his testicles. Later, on the wishes of the gods he became normal with the testicles of a bull. Sage Gautama also cursed his wife Ahalyā saying — O wicked woman, you for your sin shall live in this hermitage only on air without food for thousands of years without being seen by others. You shall meet me with your former appearance on being liberated from the sin when you shall entertain Rāma, the eldest son of King Daśaratha, with devotion having no greed or attachment in your mind. On entering the hermitage Rāma saw an exquisitely beautiful woman standing nearby though she remained invisible to the others and immediately recognized her to be Ahalyā. At this time Ahalyā came to the sight of Viśvāmitra. Ahalyā touched the feet of Rāma and worshipped him with water and other offerings and led him with others to her hut where he was entertained with great devotion. On being liberated from the sin, Ahalyā was united with her husband Sage Gautama."

The story of Ahalyā is indeed a reflection of our own life. We many times fall prey to lust and greed as happened to Ahalyā. Only through repentance and acceptance of punishment we can expiate such deviations. Constant alertness is the key to our healthy life. This is the basic lesson of the story of Ahalyā's deviant conduct.

6

Rāma Breaks Haradhanu and Wins Sītā

THE next day Rāma-Lakṣmaṇa along with Viśvāmitra entered Mithilā, capital city of King Janaka and proceeded along the main road towards the sacrificial ground. As described by the Tamil poet Kamban, Mithilā was then a beautiful city with many ornamental buildings, wide roads, well-maintained parks and fountains. The people were wealthy and culturally advanced. Even roads remained strewn with pieces of gold ornaments thrown from inside the buildings. None cared to misappropriate them as everybody was well-to-do. As Rāma and Lakṣmaṇa were proceeding along, they heard melodious sounds of dance and music coming from the nearby buildings. Rows of shops stocked with various precious articles came to their notice on the two sides. They also saw horse-racing being held in some places in the midst of wide exultation of the assembled crowd. In this way, after witnessing many wonderful sights, they crossed the protective trench around Janaka's huge beautiful palace adorned with its golden domes.

While walking along the road by the side of the palace, Rāma suddenly noticed Sītā, Janaka's daughter in the balcony playing with her female attendants and became enamoured of her charm and beauty. Sītā also saw Rāma walking majestically with Viśvāmitra and Lakṣmaṇa and at one time there was even the meeting of the four eyes. Though Rāma and Sītā, as described by poet Kamban, were gracefully present before as Viṣṇu and Lakṣmī in the Vaikuṇṭha (celestial abode of Supreme God Viṣṇu), they could not recognize each other in their present human incarnations. Yet they felt having a deep spiritual attachment to each other. Sītā was eagerly looking at Rāma in the company of Viśvāmitra and Lakṣmaṇa. As soon as Rāma went out of sight, Sītā became restless. As she fell unwell with signs of abnormality in the face and the eyes, her attendants took her inside and laid her on a soft bed. But Sītā found the bed too hard and rebuked the attendants. Sītā who was always cheerful, was now having tears in her eyes. The attendants were bewildered at the sudden change of Sītā's mental state.

At this moment, as the story goes, a rare bird by name "Anreel" in a sweet voice called its mate. In normal condition, the cooing of this bird was very pleasing to Sītā's ears. Today this sounded to her very harsh. In her mind she asked the bird to stop calling her mate as she was unable to tolerate it. The very cool light of the moon was also unbearable to her. She covered her eyes with the palms and thought the entire nature had conspired against her. The attendants were worried understanding her mental agony. They arranged some soft light in the room and prepared for her a separate flower bed on the cool *candrakāntā* stone. Even on this bed Sītā's uneasiness did not subside. At one time she thought, all this was her mental illusion. Again she thought no such illusion could weaken her mind so deeply as this. Engrossed with the thoughts of Rāma, she passed the night without sleep.

Rāma, in the meantime, lying on his bed in the royal guest house, was thinking about the young girl he saw in the palace balcony. His mind was disturbed. Because of his natural mental discipline and sense of restraint, this, however, remained undisclosed to others. In his mind he felt a deep longing to see the girl again. Realizing he had fallen in the trap of the Love God Madana, he began to laugh within himself. Rāma passed the night almost without sleep.

The next morning also Sītā's condition did not improve. The attendants tried to make her as comfortable as possible. Suddenly there was a huge sound outside. The attendants rushed out and immediately brought the news of breaking of the *Haradhanu.* Some of them began to sing and dance in joy announcing, Sītā's marriage was imminent. Everybody in the palace was aware of the vow of King Janaka that he would hand over Sītā to the person who would be able to string the *Haradhanu.* The bow had broken down after it was strung and the string was pulled. The person who performed this miracle, would now be eligible to marry Sītā. The news of her marriage, however, had no impact on Sītā's mind. She was thinking whether the young man she saw yesterday had actually broken the bow. Soon all anxiety and uncertainty ended when Sītā was apprised of the identity of the person who had broken the *Haradhanu.* He was the same young man she saw yesterday and he happened to be the eldest son of King Daśaratha of Ayodhyā. He had come to Mithilā along with sage Viśvāmitra and younger brother Lakṣmaṇa to attend the *yajña* ceremony. Rāma also came to know he was going to marry the same girl he saw on the palace balcony the day before, and she was Sītā, the daughter of King Janaka. With all these revelations, peace came to the minds of both Rāma and Sītā. They were now waiting for the date of marriage to be announced. In the book entitled *The Rāmāyaṇa* of the famous writer R.K. Narayan this wonderful pre-marriage Rāma-Sītā's love story, as described by the Tamil poet Kamban, is mentioned. This is perhaps one of the first stories of love at first sight occurring in the early human society. The story does not find mention in Vālmīki's *Rāmāyaṇa.*

We shall now return to the main story. On arrival of Viśvāmitra along with Rāma and Lakṣmaṇa at the sacrificial ground, he was cordially received by King Janaka. After arranging for their stay at the royal guest-house, Janaka returned to the palace saying, they would meet again the next morning when detailed discussions would be held on various matters. Viśvāmitra with Rāma and Lakṣmaṇa met King Janaka at the royal court in the morning. Janaka received Viśvāmitra with due respect and said, "O Great Sage, order me what service I can do for you. I am ever ready to carry out your order." Viśvāmitra, after introducing Rāma and Lakṣmaṇa to the king, said they were very eager to see his *Haradhanu.* Narrating the history of the *Haradhanu,* King Janaka said, "This bow was first placed in the hands of our ancestor King Devarāṭa. This Devarāṭa was the eldest son of the great King Nimi of our clan. In ancient times Lord Mahādeva proceeded to kill the gods during Lord Dakṣa's *yajña* with this bow built by the heavenly architect Viśvakarmā. On being pacified with the worship of the terrified gods, Mahādeva handed over the bow to Devarāṭa. The bow now in my custody, is being worshipped by me everyday.

"During ploughing of the land I got a beautiful girl. Since then she is being brought up as my daughter. She is named Sītā. When she became marriageable, I decided to hand over her only to that person who is capable of stringing the bow of the *Haradhanu.* Many kings came to marry her, but none could even lift the bow. I have refused them. Since then Sītā has remained as a *vīryaśulka* (one who can be won by valour). The disappointed kings then attacked my kingdom and destroyed my army. Later with the help of the army of elephants, horses, chariots, and foot-soldiers (*caturaṅga* army) sent by the gods, I defeated the kings and established peace in the kingdom. I shall produce the *Haradhanu* for the inspection of Rāma and Lakṣmaṇa as desired by you. If Rāma can string the bow, he will get Sītā."

Then on the orders of King Janaka, a large army contingent brought on an eight-wheeled chariot a huge chest containing the *Haradhanu* to the royal court. The king told Viśvāmitra, none amongst the *devas, gandharvas, asuras, rākṣasas, yakṣas* and others were able to string the *Haradhanu.*

On the direction of Viśvāmitra, Rāma lifted the bow from the chest and easily fitted the string to it. As he pulled the string, the bow, to the astonishment of everybody, broke down into two pieces. At the huge sound of the breaking of the bow, all the dignitaries present, except King Janaka, Sage Viśvāmitra, Rāma and Lakṣmaṇa, fainted. When they regained their consciousness, Janaka told Viśvāmitra, "O Great Sage, I am now free from any anxiety as to the marriage of Sītā. Rāma with rare power and strength, has accomplished an impossible task. Sītā by having Rāma as her husband will no doubt glorify our lineage. Today there is no end to my happiness."

With the consent of Viśvāmitra, King Janaka then sent a messenger to King Daśaratha at Ayodhyā with the marriage proposals of Sītā with Rāma narrating all the details and inviting him to Mithilā with the members of the royal family, the courtiers and other dignitaries. Daśaratha was very happy at the news and soon arrived at Mithilā with a large entourage escorted by a strong army contingent. At Mithilā, besides the marriage of Rāma and Sītā, marriages of Lakṣmaṇa with Urmilā, second daughter of Janaka, and of Bharata and Śatrughna with Māṇḍavī and Śrutakīrti, respectively, the two daughters of Janaka's brother Kuśadhvaja, were also settled. Then on an auspicious day in great pomp and grandeur marriages of all the four sons of Daśaratha were solemnized at Mithilā.

The next day Viśvāmitra left for his hermitage in the Himalayas. King Daśaratha with his sons, their newly married wives and the others also left Mithilā for Ayodhyā under due army escort. On the way some bad omens came to Daśaratha's notice. Suddenly a deep darkness descended all around and the soldiers were covered with ashes making them unconscious. In the midst of this catastrophe, Daśaratha saw Sage Jamadagni's terrible-looking son, Paraśurāma, the destroyer of the kṣatriya clan, coming towards them with his axe on the shoulder and the bow and arrows in the hands. The accompanying priests apprehending that Paraśurāma had again come out on his expedition to annihilate the kṣatriyas, sought to pacify him with worship. After accepting the worship, Paraśurāma arrogantly told Rāma, "I have heard the news of your breaking the *Haradhanu*. Now show your valour by stringing my bow. If you are successful, I shall fight a duel with you." Daśaratha and others were terrified at the challenge of Paraśurāma. But Rāma accepted the challenge and said with restraint, "You are showing disrespect to me thinking I am weak and incompetent. This I shall not tolerate. Now see my valour." Saying this, Rāma with ease strung Parśurāma's bow and twanged the string. He then said, "You are a brāhmaṇa. Moreover you are known to Sage Viśvāmitra. You are, therefore, worthy of worship also by me. I shall not kill you. All your powers obtained through religious austerities will, however, be blocked by me." Rāma then shot an arrow sanctified by *mantra*s depriving Paraśurāma of his divine powers. Paraśurāma — now an ordinary person on losing his divine powers — accepted Rāma as the Imperishable Eternal Being, the Lord of the three worlds. On his prayer, Paraśurāma was allowed to proceed unharmed to the Mahendra mountains.

The bow held by Paraśurāma is known as *Vaiṣṇavadhanu*. Viśvakarmā prepared two very strong bows — one for Supreme God Viṣṇu and the other for Lord Mahādeva. Once during a combat with Mahādeva over some differences, Viṣṇu holding His bow raised a terrible roar and immediately Mahādeva's bow got loosened from his hands and it fell down on the ground signifying His defeat. Viṣṇu, thereafter, handed over His bow (*Vaiṣṇavadhanu*) to Sage Ṛcīka of the Bhṛgu clan. From him it came to Paraśurāma's father Sage Jamadagni. After Jamadagni this famous bow remained in the possession of Paraśurāma. As Rāma was the incarnation of Supreme God Viṣṇu, it was not at all difficult for him to string the bow. Rāma later handed over Paraśurāma's *Vaiṣṇavadhanu* to Sea God Varuṇa. We know how the *Haradhanu* of Lord Mahādeva came in the possession of King Janaka.

The convoy of King Daśaratha, thereafter, reached Ayodhyā safely.

7

Rāma's Exile to the Forest

At Ayodhyā Daśaratha happily remained engaged in the performance of his royal duties. In this way 12 years passed when he, in view of his old age, thought of installing Rāma as the crown prince. Rāma was his eldest son. Besides he was endowed with all the virtues. He was also very popular with the general public, who were eager to see him as their king. At a high-level meeting of the ministers, sages, kings and the wise men of the empire, Daśaratha expressed his desire to install Rāma as the crown prince and sought their opinion. They all wholeheartedly endorsed his suggestion.

Thereafter Daśaratha called Rāma to him and said, "You are my eldest son. In virtues you are superior to everybody. You are also dearest to me. By dint of your virtues you have conquered the hearts of the people. It is my wish you be installed as the crown prince in the coming auspicious conjunction of *Puṣya* star. Out of affection I am giving you some advice. Listen carefully. You are by nature modest. Even then your modesty and self-restraint will grow further if you follow my advice. Be free from anger and attachment. Always keep your granary, treasury and armoury full so that you can successfully deal with any internal and external danger. Always remember, a king's main duty is to keep the people happy. Perform your duties with complete self-restraint. Engage only trusted agents to collect information on various developments and take action on the basis of your independent assessment." Rāma nodded in agreement and departed. It may be recalled we have come across in the *Mahābhārata* similar pronouncements from the wise men on the attributes of the kings and their duties and responsibilities and on the need to build-up a strong intelligence service to help decide their plan of action.

On Daśaratha's direction, a long list of invitees was prepared for the ceremony. Surprisingly the list did not include either the father of Kaikeyī or the father of Sītā. After giving necessary instructions to the ministers, Daśaratha departed to the inner apartments. After some time he again summoned Rāma there and told him, "My son, today I had some ominous dreams. I saw there were showers of meteors on the earth during day time with huge sound. Meanwhile, the astrologers have predicted my birth star has been attacked by Ravi, Maṅgal and Rāhu. As a result I may die or fall into a great danger. I have accordingly decided to install you as the crown prince on the auspicious *Puṣya* star conjunction tomorrow itself. Human mind is restless. Under the present evil influence of the stars, I may be victim of mental derangement. This is why I want to bring forward the date of your installation as the crown prince. This night you shall have to sleep on the bed of grass in observance of the traditional religious rites. I am warning you in another matter. In such royal functions there is always certain danger. You should remain properly guarded during the night. Your brother Bharata is now in the house of his maternal uncle at Kekaya. In fact, I am preoccupied with the thought of completing your coronation ceremony ever since his departure from Ayodhyā. Bharata is no doubt a saintly person and devoted to you. Even then nothing can be said with certainty about human mind which is prone to change any moment. Remember, even the persons always engaged in religious practices, can be overtaken by mental perversion." Rāma attentively listened to father's advice and departed.

It is clear from the words of Daśaratha, he wants to hold Rāma's coronation ceremony during the absence of Bharata from Ayodhyā. Why is he so afraid of Bharata? Rāma being his eldest son possessing all the virtues, is justifiably entitled to be installed as the crown prince. Is Bharata also a rightful claimant to the throne? On royal affairs King Daśaratha has wide experience. He must have certain very strong and valid reasons to look upon Bharata, though known to be a saintly person, with suspicion. Details later.

Rāma then came to his mother Kausalyā's apartments. Kausalyā had already got the happy news and brought Sumitrā, Sītā and Lakṣmaṇa to her apartments. On Rāma's request she gave necessary instructions to the royal functionaries for tomorrow's coronation ceremony. Wishing him all success, she told him, "Rāma, be a great king and bring happiness to the relatives of Sītā and of mine." Rāma turned to Lakṣmaṇa and told him, "Lakṣmaṇa, govern this world along with me. You are my second soul." After paying obeisance to Kausalyā, Rāma returned to his own apartments with Sītā. It may be noticed Kausalyā did not call Kaikeyī to her apartments along with Sumitrā and others on getting the news of Rāma's coronation. As a result Kaikeyī remained in the dark about this important development. Apparently Kausalyā's jealousy of Kaikeyī, because of her unusual endearment of Daśaratha, was behind this discrimination.

Kaikeyī had a maid by name Mantharā whom she had brought from her father's place. She was hunch-backed. She noticed, the capital city was being decorated with a lot of activities among the people. On enquiries she came to know that Rāma's coronation as the crown prince was being held the next day and the decorations were going on for this occasion. Immediately she gave the news to Kaikeyī and said, "O Kaikeyī, a great calamity has befallen you. The king's love for you is only an outward show. He actually hates you. He has already sent Bharata to your parents' house so that Rāma can peacefully enjoy the kingdom. There is still time. Take steps to protect your own interest." Kaikeyī, however, expressed her happiness at the news and said, "I find no difference between Rāma and Bharata. The king has rightly decided to install Rāma, who is the eldest amongst the brothers and virtuous, as the crown prince."

Kaikeyī's words were intolerable to Mantharā. She flew into a rage and after throwing away her ornaments said, "My heart is burning at your stupidity. Who is that intelligent woman who can be happy at the good fortune of her inimical stepson? By birth Bharata's claim to the throne is just after Rāma. This is why Rāma is afraid of Bharata. You may remain assured, however virtuous Rāma might be, he after being installed as the crown prince unopposed during the absence of Bharata, will not hesitate either to banish him from the kingdom or even to get him killed. Do not forget, Kausalyā is your husband's co-wife. You have so long treated her with disdain emboldened by the pride that you are the king's most favourite queen. Now as the mother of the king, she will certainly take revenge on you. Today Bharata and you are in the midst of a great danger. The only course open to you now is to ensure the banishment of Rāma and installation of Bharata as the king."

Mantharā's vituperation against Rāma and Kausalyā had its desired effect on Kaikeyī. Expressing her determination to banish Rāma to the forest today itself and to install Bharata on the throne, she asked Mantharā to devise some means for the success of her decision. Mantharā, happy at the change of her mind, said, "Kaikeyī, listen to me carefully. You are aware King Daśaratha long ago fought alongside Devarāja Indra with a large army against the *asura*s when they attacked his kingdom. You were then with the king. From the battlefield, you remember, you rescued the wounded and unconscious king to the camp and brought him round by careful nursing. When the king on being satisfied with your services, offered you two boons, you told him you would ask for the same later. Now, Kaikeyī, the time has come for you to ask for the boons from the king. Against his promise, you shall pray for two boons — (1) banishment of Rāma to the forest for 14 years and (2) installation of Bharata as the crown prince. Feigning to be angry, you may immediately remain lying on the ground at the *krodhāgāra* (room where a wife shuts herself when displeased with husband) wearing dirty clothes. You must not talk with the king when he will come to meet you or accept any gifts that may be offered to you to pacify you."

As instructed by Mantharā, Kaikeyī removed all her ornaments from her person and remained lying on the ground at the *krodhāgāra* in dirty clothes.

It may be mentioned here that Mantharā, as described by poet Kamban, disclosed at this time a very significant information to Kaikeyī regarding the real claimant to the throne of Ayodhyā. This is not mentioned clearly in the *Vālmīki-Rāmāyaṇa*. According to this information, the king of Kekaya was initially unwilling to marry his young beautiful daughter Kaikeyī to Daśaratha. The main reason was the difference in age between Daśaratha and Kaikeyī. Daśaratha was then said to be as old as Kaikeyī's father. But Daśaratha, as the report goes, was so enamoured of the youthful beauty of Kaikeyī that he was determined to get her as his wife on any condition. He ultimately agreed to make Kaikeyī's son the king of Ayodhyā as suggested by Kaikeyī's father. Only then Kaikeyī's marriage with King Daśaratha was solemnized. Mantharā claimed to have heard from behind the screen about this promise given in private to Kaikeyī's father by Daśaratha. None else either at Kekaya or Ayodhyā was aware of this promise of Daśaratha. Mantharā while disclosing this information to Kaikeyī asked her not to refer to it now as it would be difficult to prove it in the absence of her father, the only person who, other than Daśaratha, was privy to this promise as he was then at far-away Kekaya kingdom. Rather, she said, Kaikeyī should bank on the two boons promised by Daśaratha during the *devāsura saṁgrāma* to ensure Rāma's banishment and Bharata's installation as the crown prince. Agreeing with Mantharā, Kaikeyī, as described, waited for the king in the *krodhāgāra*.

We do not feel inclined to give credence to the statement of the schemer Mantharā. But doubt arises when we analyse the developments at that time. Daśaratha's decision to send Bharata with Śatrughna to his maternal uncle's place at Kekaya, arrangements of Rāma's coronation during the absence of Bharata from Ayodhyā, Daśaratha's suspicion towards Bharata and his warning of Rāma, non-invitation of Kaikeyī's father to the coronation (non-invitation of Sītā's father seems to be apparently an attempt to show it in a lighter vein), discrimination against Kaikeyī in the distribution of the rice-porridge and similar other actions of Daśaratha seem to suggest there is some truth in Mantharā's statement. Daśaratha, it appears, actually promised Kaikeyī's father that her son would inherit the throne after him. But later he found it difficult to keep the promise. Rāma was his eldest son — virtuous and universally popular. He actually was the rightful claimant to the throne. All sections of the people were eager to see Rāma as their king. Daśaratha himself wanted Rāma to inherit him. He accordingly thought it prudent to install Rāma as the crown prince. He even got his decision approved in a meeting of his council of ministers, sages, kings and other elders. To avoid any complications, he decided to hold the coronation at a very short notice when Bharata was absent from Ayodhyā. He could not be expected to hold Rāma's coronation in the presence of Bharata and Kaikeyī's father whom he had earlier promised to make her son the king. The presence of Kaikeyī's father as also of Sītā's father together at the coronation, Daśaratha thought, would certainly further complicate the situation following possible disclosure of his earlier promise. This fear seems to be the real cause behind the non-invitation of both of them to the coronation. The subsequent events would, however, show Daśaratha's plan of action went awry and the mischievous scheme of things of

Mantharā was successful.

In the context of the decision to install Rāma as the crown prince disregarding his own promise earlier given to Kaikeyī's father, Daśaratha, apprehensive of some move by Bharata against Rāma, warned the latter to take suitable precautions. Daśaratha with his wide experience was aware that any move by Bharata, then at Kekaya, could not but be backed by the mighty Kekaya empire. In these uncertain circumstances, Daśaratha must have taken some counter-measures by alerting his army and the intelligence agents at the border to thwart any adventurism by the king of Kekaya. There is, however, no mention of such a development in the *Rāmāyaṇa*. Daśaratha persistently made efforts to prevent any foreign interference in the affairs of his kingdom. His discriminatory distribution of rice-porridge is a pointer in this direction. Ever-conscious about the sovereignty and integrity of his kingdom, Daśaratha, dictated by his sharp common sense, must have taken necessary precautionary measures in self-defence as described. Subsequent events, we shall see later, show that his suspicion on Bharata was without any basis.

Daśaratha had thirty-six wives. Of them Kausalyā was the senior-most and the principal queen. Kaikeyī was sometimes mentioned by Vālmīki as the second queen and sometimes the third. From the narration of the events it, however, appears Sumitrā was the second queen and Kaikeyī the third. We are aware that Kaikeyī, who was young and beautiful, was the dearest queen of Daśaratha who used to stay mostly with Kaikeyī in her apartments. During tours and excursions also Kaikeyī accompanied Daśaratha. Kaikeyī alone, we know, was with Daśaratha during the *devāsura saṁgrāma*.

To come to our main story, Daśaratha in the evening came to the apartments of Kaikeyī and was surprised to see her in the *krodhāgāra* weeping and sobbing. Despite his repeated queries about the cause of her distress, Kaikeyī first remained silent as advised by Mantharā. Later while still lying on the floor, she said, "Mahārāja, I have a wish and this can be fulfilled by you only. I shall disclose my wish only after you solemnly promise to fulfil the same." When Daśaratha gave the promise in the name of his "dearest" Rāma, Kaikeyī said, "Mahārāja, you promised two boons to me during the *devāsura saṁgrāma*. I told you then, I shall ask for the boons later. Now I am asking for the two boons. I shall commit suicide if you refuse me the boons. My prayer, you kindly install my son Bharata as the crown prince and banish Rāma to the forest for fourteen years. I want Rāma to leave for the forest today itself."

Daśaratha was dumbfounded at the terrible words of Kaikeyī. For some time he remained speechless. Later after gaining composure he harshly rebuked her and said, "Kaikeyī, Rāma is the eldest among my sons. In religious pursuits also he is superior to others. Rāma is even more devoted to you than Bharata. Give up your sinful design against Rāma who is endowed with all the virtues and is universally popular. Any other thing most precious in the world will be gifted to you. Do not compel me to commit any irreligious act." Kaikeyī flew into a rage at the words of Daśaratha and angrily said, "O King, how will you introduce yourself as a virtuous person if you repent after offering the boons? You shall be utterly defamed in the entire royal clan if you now go back on your promise. I shall die in your very presence by drinking poison if you proceed to install Rāma as the crown prince. I shall not be satisfied with anything else other than the installation of Bharata as the crown prince and the banishment of Rāma to the forest." Daśaratha and Kaikeyī were involved in prolonged arguments and counter-arguments. None could convince the other. Daśaratha while talking fainted several times. At the end he stricken with fear even fell at the feet of Kaikeyī fervently requesting her to have pity on him. Kaikeyī remained defiant as before and even taunted Daśaratha for claiming himself to be a virtuous person. As Kaikeyī continued to insist on the grant of the two boons, Daśaratha remained lying at her feet almost unconscious. Thus passed the entire night with Daśaratha realizing he had no escape from Kaikeyī's drag-net.

Meanwhile, all preparations for Rāma's coronation as the crown prince were complete. In the morning prime minister Sumantra on the direction of Sage Vasiṣṭha, appeared at the apartments of queen Kaikeyī to request King Daśaratha to get prepared for the ceremony. In his wretched condition, Daśaratha could not speak anything to Sumantra. Kaikeyī then told Sumantra, the king was feeling drowsy as he was very tired. He had asked him (Sumantra) to bring Rāma here urgently. On Sumantra seeking specific permission from the king, Daśaratha feebly said, he was very eager to see Rāma.

Rāma who in the meantime got ready with new clothes and ornaments for the coronation, soon appeared with Sumantra at Kaikeyī's apartments. He was utterly surprised to see Daśaratha in a morose state sitting by the side of Kaikeyī. Daśaratha only uttered his name and remained silent with tears in his eyes. His usual exuberance at the sight of Rāma was no more. Then Kaikeyī told Rāma, "The king is well. But he has got a wish which he is unable to disclose out of fear for you. You are very dear to him; it is very difficult for him to tell you any unpleasant truth. Your father earlier promised me two boons. Now he is repenting for this. Rāma, you are aware, it is the responsibility of the virtuous people to protect the truth. You should see that the king, for your sake and out of anger towards me, does not forsake the truth. If you promise you shall act according to the wishes of the king, I shall disclose them." On Rāma giving the promise, Kaikeyī disclosed, "Against the two boons the king promised me for my services during the *devāsura saṁgrāma*, I have now prayed for installation of Bharata as the crown prince and your banishment to the forest for fourteen years. You shall have to leave for the forest today itself. It is incumbent on you to ensure the fulfilment of the truth of your father's promise. This unpleasant truth your father is unable to speak to you. Now, save your father by protecting the truth."

Rāma calmly heard the unpleasant words of Kaikeyī and, virtuous as he was, felt no sorrow in his mind whatsoever. He told Kaikeyī, "I assure you, I shall fulfil the promise of my father. I shall leave Ayodhyā for the forest today itself for fourteen years. You may summon Bharata from his maternal uncle's place and arrange his coronation. But I am surprised, why my father is not telling me anything about Bharata's coronation. This is burning my heart. And why is he shedding tears in a downcast look?" Satisfied at the promise of Rāma, Kaikeyī said, "I am sending a messenger to bring Bharata. Out of shame the king is unable to tell you anything. Until your departure to the forest he will not take bath and food."

On hearing Rāma's words, Daśaratha began to cry loudly. Rāma left the place after paying obeisance to Daśaratha and Kaikeyī and returned to Kausalyā's apartments. On hearing the terrible news, Kausalyā fell down on the ground and fainted. After recovery, she went into wild lamentations and said, her humiliation and sufferings at the hands of Kaikeyī would have no bounds after Bharata became the crown prince. She expressed her desire to accompany Rāma to the forest. Rāma took a lot of pains to dissuade Kausalyā.

Lakṣmaṇa flew into a rage on hearing the news. He could not conceive how any father could forsake a son like Rāma who was god-like, simple-natured, self-restrained and praised even by his enemy. He told Rāma, "Before the news spreads out, you may immediately capture the throne of Ayodhyā. I am with you. I shall kill Bharata with all his associates. By depriving you of the kingdom, the king has also gone against you. It will not be improper to kill him either. Your deprivation of the kingdom at the machinations of the evil-minded Kaikeyī can never be supported." Lakṣmaṇa then in a fit of excitement turned to Kausalyā and said, "Mother, I am devoted to Rāma.

I am ever ready to sacrifice my life for him. I am determined to remove all your sorrows. I shall not hesitate to kill the king who, having lost his sense of right and wrong due to his deep attachment to Kaikeyī, has deprived Rāma of his rightful claim to the throne. Rāma and you may now witness my valour."

Kausalyā then told Rāma, "You have heard Lakṣmaṇa. Do what you think best. Rāma, you must not go to the forest leaving me in such a danger. I shall give up my life by fasting if you disobey me. In the event of my death you shall go to the hell." Rāma said in reply, "Mother, in the past many saintly persons obeyed the commands of their father with glory without raising any question about their justifiability or otherwise. I too shall follow their path." Rāma thereafter told Lakṣmaṇa, "Brother, I am aware how sincerely you are devoted to me. Your valour is also not unknown to me. I fully realize mother's mental agony. But she is suffering without realizing the significance of *dharma* (virtue) and peace. In this world *dharma* is supreme; truth is embedded in *dharma*. It has been entirely justified for our father to grant the boons to our mother Kaikeyī and it will be an irreligious act on my part if I now disobey the command of our father. For the sake of truth, I must leave for the forest. Lakṣmaṇa, you give up your resolve for the path of conflict though worthy of a kṣatriya and follow the path of peace as adopted by me." Turning to Kausalyā, Rāma again explained the tenets of religion and ultimately obtained her consent for his departure to the forest.

As Lakṣmaṇa appeared unconvinced, Rāma patiently told him, "Brother, give up your anger and grief. Have patience. Take immediate steps to stop these arrangements for my coronation. Our father is virtuous, truthful and solemnly true to his vow. He is now gripped with the fear of death. If the arrangements are not stopped, he will think that my promise given to him has no meaning. With the boons granted by him to mother Kaikeyī remaining non-implemented, our father's good name will be tarnished and he will be denounced by the society. I shall not do anything which brings disrepute to our father. Let me proceed to the forest and let the wishes of mother Kaikeyī be fulfilled with the installation of Bharata as the crown prince. You know, I look upon all our mothers with equal honour and respect. Mother Kaikeyī also loves me like her own son. Though I felt hurt at her words, I bear no ill-will towards her. I believe everything has happened due to divine ordain. None has any hand in it. I bear no regret for not being installed as the crown prince. To me banishment is now more beneficial than the acquisition of the kingdom. Lakṣmaṇa, refrain from using any harsh words against our father and mother Kaikeyī. "

Rāma's words had no impact on Lakṣmaṇa. He grew more excited and angrily told Rāma, "O great soul, being the noblest among the manly kṣatriyas, how could you explain away such dangerous developments in the name of providence? Don't you know there are many people who seek their own interest in the name of religion? The king and his dearest queen Kaikeyī, out of sheer selfish motive, have planned, through deceitful means, to banish the son who possesses the highest moral qualities and is endowed with all the virtues, by depriving him of his rightful claim to the throne. It appears, they have been nursing this motive since long. If not, why has such an old issue of grant of boons been raised now? Kaikeyī could have easily obtained the boons immediately on offering. She by taking advantage of the king's weakness, has at the opportune moment sought the boons to install her own son Bharata on the throne. I shall foil this ugly conspiracy. Kindly remain ready for your coronation."

Saying this, Lakṣmaṇa remained standing with tears in his eyes. Without having any argument, Rāma with his own hands wiped Lakṣmaṇa's tears. He later said in a soft voice, "I shall obey the commands of my parents. This is my decision.

I am sure, any virtuous person will also take the same decision." Lakṣmaṇa, mellowed by the affectionate words of Rāma, was convinced he (Rāma) could in no way be dissuaded from his declared intention. He thus gave up his path of conflict and got reconciled with Rāma's path of peace.

On getting the news of Rāma's banishment, Sītā expressed her desire to accompany Rāma to the forest. Disregarding Rāma's insistence on her staying back at Ayodhyā, Sītā angrily said, "Rāma, you are talking like an ordinary person. This is unbecoming of a royal prince like you well-versed in the Śāstras (scriptures). The father, the mother, the brother, the son and the daughter-in-law — all enjoy happiness and suffer misery according to their *karmaphala* (result of one's actions). Only the wife suffers the fate of her husband. Thus the banishment has also been imposed on me. I shall, therefore, accompany you to the forest. I am ardently devoted to you. To live with you is actually my dwelling in heaven. To live without you will be my suffering in hell. I shall give up my life by drinking poison if you refuse to take me with you. I shall never be subservient to my enemy." On Rāma accepting her plea, Sītā in a happy mind distributed her ornaments and food stuff to the brāhmaṇas and others and prepared for her journey to the forest.

On hearing Sītā's decision, Lakṣmaṇa too expressed his desire to accompany Rāma to the forest. He said, "I am always with you. Any separation with you is intolerable to me. Apart from your company, I do not want even immortality not to speak of the wealth of all the three worlds." Rāma first tried to dissuade Lakṣmaṇa. He argued, Lakṣmaṇa's presence at Ayodhyā was imperative to ensure protection and livelihood of the mothers. On this Lakṣmaṇa said, "I shall not hesitate to kill Bharata if he does not properly look after the mothers. It will not be prejudicial to religion if I accompany you. I shall with my bow and the arrows try my best to ensure safety and security of Sītā and you during your stay in the forest." Satisfied at the words of Lakṣmaṇa, Rāma agreed to take him to the forest. Sumitrā wholeheartedly supported Lakṣmaṇa's decision and told him, "My son, always remember, allegiance to the elder is the *dharma* of the virtuous people. Remain constantly vigilant to ensure protection of Rāma who is sinless. Treat Rāma as your father Daśaratha, Sītā as your mother like me and the entire forest as Ayodhyā. You may now happily go to the forest."

To cut the long story short, Rāma, Lakṣmaṇa and Sītā after bidding farewell to King Daśaratha, mothers Kausalyā and Sumitrā and other elders in the midst of heart-breaking scenes, left Ayodhyā in a chariot accompanied by Sumantra on the wishes of the king on way to the forest. Rāma took with him all his divine weapons. Lakṣmaṇa also took his own weapons. They were dressed as ascetics wearing the deer-skin and covering the body with tree-bark. As they came out of the royal compound, innumerable residents of the capital followed the chariot requesting Rāma to return. Rāma unsuccessfully tried to pacify them explaining it would not be possible for him to go back on his solemn promise given to the king. He even praised Bharata saying he would make a better king than him and asked them to extend Bharata all co-operation on his installation as the crown prince.

As the chariot carrying Rāma, Sītā and Lakṣmaṇa went out of sight, Daśaratha fell down on the ground while lamenting. When Kausalyā and Kaikeyī hastened to lift him, he angrily asked Kaikeyī not to touch him. He told her, "I do not like to see the face of such a sinful woman like you. From today I am cutting off all relations with you. If Bharata proceeds to act according to your direction, he will lose the right to perform the last-rites on my death. I am depriving him of the right." He then looked at the face of Kaikeyī and tauntingly said, "Be happy at your achievement and enjoy a long happy life of a widow." Daśaratha without going to the apartments of Kaikeyī, then came to Kausalyā's apartments where she consoled him as best as possible. But grief-stricken Kausalyā herself soon went into lamentation when Sumitrā consoled her saying, "O Gracious Aryan lady, your son is a great person endowed with all the virtues. He has given up the kingdom only for the sake of his father's honesty, respect for truth and protection of *dharma.* This protection of *dharma* by Rāma will certainly prove beneficial to you all in the other world. You should not, therefore, harbour any grief for Rāma at all. Lakṣmaṇa who is kind and sinless is engaged to look after Rāma in the forest. This is also a big gain for Rāma. Sītā who always lived a life of comfort, has gone with Rāma fully knowing the hardship of the forest life. What can be more important than this? By sharing the joy and sorrow of the forest-life together, I am sure, they will pass their days happily. You rest assured, no harm will touch the virtuous Rāma. There is no doubt Rāma on return from the exile, will be crowned as the king when all your sufferings will come to an end. Now it is your duty as the senior-most queen to assure all others who are still in the palace. This is not the time for you to remain in grief." At the just words of Sumitrā, Kausalyā was relieved of her grief.

That night Rāma and Sītā lay on the bed prepared with grass at the bank of the river Tamasā, while Lakṣmaṇa and others remained awake on guard. At a certain distance the citizens who followed them, fell into a deep sleep underneath a big tree. At dead of night Rāma with Sītā and Lakṣmaṇa silently left the place without the others' knowledge while they were still asleep and entered into a deep forest. On awaking the citizens went into lamentation without seeing Rāma. When they did not find Rāma anywhere, they returned to Ayodhyā sad and morose. Ayodhyā then had turned into a ghost city without Rāma. There was sadness all around.

In the meantime Rāma with Sītā and Lakṣmaṇa proceeded further by the chariot and reached the bank of the Ganges. Rāma decided to stay at this place for the day. Guhaka, the king of the local hunters who happened to be the friend of Rāma, on getting the information of his arrival, immediately appeared before him along with his ministers and friends. He embraced Rāma and said, "Friend, I am blessed to get the opportunity of entertaining a guest like you." Saying this, he brought various items of delicious foodstuff and drinks for Rāma and others as also fodder and water for the horses of the chariot. Rāma in reply said, "Friend, I am unable to accept any of these articles you have brought. Now I am to live in the forest only on fruits and roots wearing deer-skin and the tree-bark. I only require fodder and water for the horses." In the night Rāma and Sītā slept on the bed prepared on the ground, while Lakṣmaṇa, Guhaka and Sumantra remained on guard underneath a nearby tree. The next day Rāma, Sītā and Lakṣmaṇa crossed the Ganges by the boat arranged by Guhaka. Rāma asked Sumantra to return to Ayodhyā. He also bid farewell to Guhaka thanking him for his services.

As soon as Sumantra reached Ayodhyā in the empty chariot without Rāma, the citizens burst into a wide lamentation. He straightaway went to the king and reported, Rāma with Sītā and Lakṣmaṇa had entered the forest. On hearing Sumantra's words, Daśaratha fainted. Kausalyā and the other royal inmates began to weep. On recovery, Daśaratha expressed his eagerness to know where Rāma stayed in the night, what food he took and what he told him before entering the forest. Narrating all details Sumantra overwhelmed with emotion with tears in his eyes said, "Mahārāja, the virtuous Rāma has asked me, — O Sūta (Sumantra was a Sūtaputra), pay on my behalf my respectful obeisance to our learned father on touching his feet and convey my greetings to all the inmates of the palace after enquiring about their welfare. Convey my obeisance to mother Kausalyā and request her on my behalf to devote herself to the service of father. Tell her to treat mother Kaikeyī in the same way as she is treating father. Convey my welfare to Bharata and tell him to treat all the mothers equally. Request him on my behalf to govern the kingdom on being installed as the crown prince by retaining our father on the throne. Under no circumstances our father's prestige and authority should be undermined. Particularly tell Bharata to look after mother Kausalyā as his own mother.

"Rāma was full of tears when he was speaking to me. Lakṣmaṇa, however, remained adamant. Heaving a big sigh he angrily said — "for what crime has the virtuous Rāma been banished to the forest? If this has been done for greed or grant of the boon, I shall say hundred times, this has been a contemptible misdeed. This speaks of utter foolishness on the part of the king. I have lost all faith in him. To me Rāma is all in all. How will the king carry on his royal duties after banishing the universally popular Rāma against the public opinion?" — Mahārāja, at this time Sītā stood silently at one corner with tears in the eyes. As I was preparing to leave for Ayodhyā, Sītā while looking at Rāma began to profusely weep with tears continuously rolling down her cheeks. Mahārāja, a strange incident happened when I left the place after Rāma with Sītā and Lakṣmaṇa had entered the forest. The horses of the chariot remained firmly standing and did not move. I could understand, the horses were equally grieved and did not want to leave without Rāma. With great difficulty I could persuade them to move. On the way I stayed with Guhaka, for a few days with the hope of being summoned by Rāma. But my waiting went in vain. During the return journey, I noticed the entire nature with trees, rivers, animals and birds immersed in grief for Rāma. On entering the capital I saw sadness prevailing all around."

On hearing the details from Sumantra, Daśaratha said with great regret, "Because of the evil counsel of the sinful Kaikeyī, I have suddenly decided to banish Rāma to the forest without consulting my wise ministers, friends, senior royal officials and responsible citizens. Sumantra, I have myself invited this trouble at the words of a woman. I am unable to live without Rāma. Immediately take me to Rāma in the forest." Saying this, Daśaratha went into wide lamentation. At one time he fainted. When Kausalyā also expressed her desire to join Rāma, Sumantra told her, "Rāma has no affliction in his mind over the banishment to the forest. Sītā is her devoted wife. She is happy with Rāma in the forest. You need not worry at all for them." Even at the just words of Sumantra, Kausalyā's mind remained disturbed. She then turned to Daśaratha who by now had regained his composure and said in an accusing tone, "Mahārāja, as a result of your order of banishment without consultation with others, my children have been deprived of the comfort of the royal palace. I am in great doubt whether Bharata will hand over the kingdom and the treasury to Rāma on his return from the forest after long fourteen years." Kausalyā immediately realized she had spoken very harshly against Daśaratha and begged to be excused. Consoling Kausalyā, Daśaratha again admitted, he himself was responsible for the present catastrophe.

8

Death of Son of Blind Sage and Death of Daśaratha

THE next morning Daśaratha told Kausalyā, "Man's happiness and sorrow depend on his own actions. I am myself the example. I was then a young prince. One night I went to the bank of the river Sarayū for hunting when I heard a sound which seemed to me the sound of an elephant drinking water and discharged a *śabdabhedī bāṇa* (arrow that pierces the target by its sound) towards it. Immediately there came a heart-rending cry of a human from the river bank. As I hastened to the bank, I saw a sage boy groaning in agony being pierced by my arrow. He told me, he was the only son of his old blind parents and had come to the river to fetch water for them. A pitcher was also seen floating in water. I could understand I mistook the sound of filling the pitcher with water as that of the elephant drinking water. I felt a terrible repentance for the mistake. The boy asked me to inform his parents about the incident. He died as soon as the arrow was extricated by me from his body. Overwhelmed with grief and fear at the death of the boy, I came to his parents at the hermitage. Thinking their son had returned, they asked for the water immediately as they were thirsty. Stricken with fear I then slowly narrated the incident after introducing myself and prayed for the mercy of the sage for killing their son out of ignorance. Immersed in grief over the death of their son, the sage said, "O king, your head would have split into thousand parts had you not brought the news to me personally. As you have committed this murder out of ignorance, you are still alive. Now, you take us to the river bank. We want to see our son for the last time."

At the river bank the sage couple lamented for a long time by touching the dead body of their dear son. I remained standing with folded hands. The sage then turned to me and said, "O King, you have killed our only son out of ignorance. Even then you shall have to die in grief for your own son." Saying this, Daśaratha concluded, the sage couple got into the burning pier of their dead son and departed to heaven.

After narrating the incident, Daśaratha told Kausalyā, "O *devī*, it appears the curse of the blind sage on me is going to materialize. I am also going to die in grief for my own son." Saying this, he went into lamentation for Rāma. At the dead of night Daśaratha while still in lamentation, breathed his last. The palace inmates on noticing the pale body of Daśaratha raised an alarm. Kausalyā and Sumitrā on being roused from sleep touched the body of the king and realized he was dead. They fell down on the ground out of grief and panic. On getting the information, Kaikeyī hastened to Kausalyā's apartments and fainted on seeing the dead king. A pall of gloom descended on the palace.

9

Analysis of Rāma's Exile

In this episode of unprecedented events, what strikes us most is the firmness of Kaikeyī in sticking to her twin demands of installation of Bharata as the crown prince and the banishment of Rāma to the forest. Though the entire plan was the brainwave of maid Mantharā, it is Kaikeyī who executed it meticulously without wavering in the face of allurements, persistent entreaties and even threats of King Daśaratha. She fully exploited his infatuation towards her and acted without any flaws from the beginning to the end as instructed by Mantharā. We cannot but praise her for her steadfastness and determination, however immoral her purpose might be. The mental strength shown by Kaikeyī in the face of terrible odds, is indeed rare.

What did actually prompt Kaikeyī to take such a terrible course of action? She loved Rāma as her own son. She expressed her happiness when she first heard the news of Rāma's coronation as the crown prince. Her mind got vitiated when Mantharā depicted a terribly bleak future for her at the inevitable revenge of Kausalyā and Sumitrā on their change of fortune following installation of Rāma as the crown prince. She was aware how disdainfully she looked upon them taking advantage of the king's unusual weakness for her. As a way out, Mantharā advised Kaikeyī to ask for the two boons promised long ago by the king. She also reminded her of the promise given by the king to her father before their marriage that her son would be made the king of Ayodhyā. We know Kaikeyī as instructed demanded installation of Bharata as the crown prince and the banishment of Rāma against the two promised boons. She did not refer to the king's promise given to her father before the marriage as no immediate evidence was available. It appears Kaikeyī's actions were prompted by sheer self-interest. She realized, her domination would remain undisturbed only if her own son Bharata was installed as the crown prince and subsequently as the king. As the decision was taken at the spur of the moment, there was no prior consultation with Bharata in this regard as he was away at Kekaya. Subsequent events showed (we shall see later) Kaikeyī's scheme of things was only partially successful. While Rāma went to the forest as desired by the king, Bharata refused to accept the crown. In fact, the entire situation changed completely following the death of the king.

Lakṣmaṇa rightly denounced as dishonest Kaikeyī's prayer — for the boons offered by the king long ago, at this crucial moment when Rāma's coronation as the crown prince had been announced — and the king's acceptance of the same apparently with great reluctance. The offer of boons on the part of kings and sages in those days was very common. Here also there was a limit beyond which the beneficiary should not ask for anything. Many incidents of refusal of impossible demands are mentioned in the *Mahābhārata*. Why then did Daśaratha, a king of wide knowledge and experience, concede such a rather terrible demand of Kaikeyī? We know Daśaratha took the decision to install Rāma as the crown prince with the approval of his council of ministers, sages and other wise men of his kingdom. It was in fact a joint decision. Yet he took such a vital decision of Rāma's banishment and Bharata's installation as the crown prince, unilaterally without any consultation with his council of ministers and others. Daśaratha, of course, before his death regretted his decision. The question arises, how far was he sincere? Circumstances seem to indicate Daśaratha could have easily wriggled out of the impasse had he referred the whole matter to his council of ministers and others. There is a suspicion Daśaratha's inaction was intended to facilitate Bharata's ascendancy to the throne in compliance of his promise given to the father of Kaikeyī that her son would be made the king. Daśaratha harboured a guilty conscience in respect of Bharata on his decision to install Rāma as the crown prince. We know he even warned Rāma to remain vigilant against any possible move by Bharata. In between the just claims of both Rāma and Bharata to the throne, Daśaratha, it seems, was in a double mind to take a correct stand. Ultimately he preferred to concede the demands of Kaikeyī without consulting anyone else. For him it was indeed a very hard decision causing him immense mental agony from which he did never recover. He died while lamenting for Rāma thus fulfilling the curse of the blind sage. We are sad at the tragic end of a great king. It has been rightly said Daśaratha was a successful king, but a failed father.

The events brought into the open the characteristic differences between Rāma and Lakṣmaṇa. Rāma was calm and quiet having sublime intellect and knowledge. To him father's honour and his own promise were supreme. Lakṣmaṇa was, however, impulsive and haughty. His devotion to Rāma was so deep he was prepared to kill even his father to safeguard Rāma's interest. He was no doubt virtuous and honest in purpose. Because of these basic qualities he ultimately reconciled himself to Rāma's path of peace. The contrast between the characters of Kausalyā and Sumitrā also strikes our mind. Kausalyā was emotional. To her separation from Rāma was unbearable. No arguments, however plausible, were acceptable to her. Sumitrā, on the other hand, was unperturbed and firm in mind. She, we have seen, gladly approved of Lakṣmaṇa's decision to accompany Rāma to the forest and happily bid farewell to him. Her patient consolation to grief-stricken Kausalyā as also her advice to Lakṣmaṇa regarding his duties and responsibilities in the forest, reminds us of the great sayings of the sages. Our head bows down in respect to this virtuous and selfless woman. Perhaps only in the sacred land of India the advent of such a gracious woman is possible.

Unfortunately for reasons unknown, the poet made no mention of any subsequent role of her in the epic. This total disregard to such a great character is indeed painful.

Because of her unusual closeness to Daśaratha, Kausalyā and Sumitrā, we know, bore a deep hatred for Kaikeyī, who too looked upon them with disregard. Circumstances seem to suggest there was a system of watch through secret agents on the developments and activities in the rival camps. Kaikeyī's personal maid, Mantharā, shrewd and intelligent as she was, was her principal intelligence operator. She had under her a number of other maids who were deployed under the cover of their normal duties to collect the required information particularly about the visits of the outsiders and their discussions and decisions in the apartments of Kausalyā and Sumitrā. The king's visits to their apartments, though few and far between, were specially covered. Mantharā, it may be recalled, first came to know of the impending coronation of Rāma as the crown prince when she noticed unusual activities of the people and the decorations all around. She or Kaikeyī had no prior information about the king's decision as he decided everything within a short time. Kausalyā, it goes without saying, had her own people to keep watch on Kaikeyī's apartments particularly on the visits of the king. The pious Sumitrā having no duplicity, was devoted to Kausalyā and she used to get all information from her. Lakṣmaṇa who was a young man of action befitting a kṣatriya, apparently collected information on various developments through his trusted people. In view of Rāma's universal popularity, the people themselves of their own accord, informed him about the various developments in the kingdom. Prime Minister Sumantra and other senior royal functionaries with whom he had close personal relationship, also kept him informed about all important state matters. We have mentioned earlier about the possible precautionary measures taken by Daśaratha in the context of Rāma's installation as the crown prince apprehending some move on the part of Bharata. In the *Rāmāyaṇa* all these developments were not clearly mentioned. But in the then volatile situation at Ayodhyā marked by intrigues and conspiracies, we may conclude with reasonable certainty, the events took shape on the lines as depicted above. A spy network was sure to grow in such a fertile situation.

The reason why Daśaratha and others had no prior information about Kaikeyī's decision to ask for the boons, is not far to seek. The main reason was that there was no forethought in the plan. It was devised on the spur of the moment. Rāma's coronation was the immediate provocation. Had there been a time lag, the plan would have leaked out with Daśaratha taking counter-measures to scuttle it in consultation with his ministers and others. The situation in that case would have taken a different turn possibly causing greater predicament for Daśaratha with the evitable revelation of his promise given to Kaikeyī's father.

10

Rāma Settles in the Forest and Bharata's Efforts to Bring Him Back

As the main story goes, in the meantime Rāma with Sītā and Lakṣmaṇa after crossing the river stayed for the night at a suitable place in the forest. The next morning they reached the hermitage of Sage Bharadvāja who on learning their purpose, asked them to stay with him. Rāma pleaded his inability saying as this place was not far from Ayodhyā, the people would throng here to see him and Sītā causing unnecessary disturbances. He requested Sage Bharadvāja to select for them a place far in the interior where they could live peacefully. Accordingly on advice from the sage, they proceeded the next day along the forest path towards Citrakūṭa mountains and reached the hermitage of Sage Vālmīki. On hearing Rāma's story of banishment, Vālmīki selected a suitable site for their stay near his hermitage. In a small hut constructed by Lakṣmaṇa on the site, Rāma with Sītā and Lakṣmaṇa began to live happily forgetting all their sorrows of banishment.

At Ayodhyā, meanwhile, there developed a great uncertainty following the death of King Daśaratha. All the sons of the king were away from the capital. Bharata and Śatrughna were in far away Kekaya kingdom, while Rāma and Lakṣmaṇa were in the forest. As it would not be proper to cremate the king's body in the absence of his sons, the body was kept preserved in a large oil-filled vessel. Immediately on the advice of Sage Vasiṣṭha a messenger was sent to Kekaya kingdom to bring Bharata to Ayodhyā. The messenger and his companions were strictly warned not to disclose the king's death and other developments in the capital to Bharata. They were advised only to tell him, his presence was urgently required at Ayodhyā for some important royal functions. On receipt of the message, Bharata along with Śatrughna returned to Ayodhyā without any loss of time and was surprised to see sadness all around. With a disturbed mind he went straight to the king's apartments. Without finding him there, he came to his mother's apartments and saw Kaikeyī sitting on a golden couch.

Bharata paid obeisance to mother Kaikeyī by touching her feet, when he was dearly embraced by her. After replying to the inquiries about the well-being of his grandfather and others at Kekaya, Bharata asked Kaikeyī, "Mother, our father stays mostly in your apartments. But I am not seeing him here. Where is he?" As Kaikeyī gave him the news of the king's death, Bharata fell down on the ground lamenting in grief. Kaikeyī consoled him and said, "My son, it is you who will now be the king. It does not behove well for a saintly person like you to remain grief-stricken." Mother's words did have no impact on his mind. He wanted to know the whereabouts of Rāma and said, "Rāma, my devout eldest brother is like my father. I want to know everything father had said before his death." Kaikeyī said Rāma had departed to the forest wearing deer skin and tree bark. Bharata became perturbed to hear the news and wondered what could be the sinful act for the atonement of which Rāma had to go the forest. On being asked to tell him the reason, Kaikeyī narrating the entire story said, "Before Rāma's coronation as the crown prince, I asked for his banishment to the forest and your installation as the crown prince against the two boons promised earlier by the king. On my prayer being granted, Rāma along with Sītā and Lakṣmaṇa have departed to the forest. Due to pangs of separation from Rāma, the king has lost his life. All this I have done for your good. Give up your grief and have patience.

The trouble-free kingdom of Ayodhyā is now yours. Be crowned as the king after performing the last rites of your father."

The grief-stricken Bharata on hearing the story flew into a rage and denounced Kaikeyī in the harshest possible language holding her entirely responsible for the banishment of Rāma and the death of their father. Expressing his determination not to fulfil her desire, he announced, he would bring back Rāma from the forest and serve under him. Kaikeyī deeply hurt at the words of Bharata began to cry in a piteous tone.

Kausalyā on hearing loud altercations in Kaikeyī's apartments understood, Bharata had returned from Kekaya. She proceeded to meet him when Bharata with Śatrughna also came out of her mother's apartments to see her. On the way Kausalyā became unconscious on being embraced by Bharata and Śatrughna. After recovery, she told him, "Bharata, you wanted the kingdom; you have got it. You have gained the kingdom so early only because of your mother's treachery. Myself and Sumitrā have decided to proceed to the forest to meet Rāma soon after the last rites of your father. Make necessary arrangements for our departure. This large kingdom is now under your rule."

Bharata was pained to hear Kausalyā's words. He respectfully submitted, "O Gracious Aryan lady, I am innocent. I know nothing of Rāma's banishment. At the instigation of my mother, Rāma has been banished to the forest. I want her destruction." Kausalyā understood, Bharata was not in any way involved in this conspiracy and blessed him saying, "You shall ultimately depart to the abode of virtue."

The next day on the direction of Sage Vasiṣṭha, Bharata cremated the body of the king. At the end of the mourning period, the *śrāddha* ceremony was also duly performed. At one time Śatrughna out of anger proceeded to kill maid Mantharā. Bharata restrained him saying, "Women should not be killed. You forgive her. The virtuous Rāma will never approve of your action."

On the fourteenth day, Sage Vasiṣṭha and the royal ministers requested Bharata to be installed as the king as the kingdom had been bequeathed to him by the king before his death. Rejecting the proposal, Bharata said, "According to our family customs and traditions, the eldest son is the rightful claimant to the kingdom. Accordingly our eldest brother Rāma will be the king of Ayodhyā. I shall myself live in the forest for fourteen years. I shall bring back Rāma from the forest." Thereafter Bharata proceeded to the Daṇḍaka forest with a large army. A number of engineers of the royal public works department, soil experts, diggers, and other persons having knowledge about the conditions of the forest accompanied him. Happy at the news of Bharata's decision to bring back Rāma, Kausalyā, Sumitrā and Kaikeyī also followed Bharata in a separate chariot. On Bharata's wishes, Sage Vasiṣṭha, Prime Minister Sumantra and the other senior ministers joined the entourage.

Bharata while traversing many areas, established his first camp at the bank of the Ganges near Śṛṅgerapura (near modern Chunar or Chandalgarh in UP), capital of Guhaka, the hunter king. At the sight of such a large army from Ayodhyā, Guhaka, unaware of the real purpose of Bharata, became worried. He told his ministers and the near relatives, "It appears the evil-minded Bharata has come to either kill us or make us prisoners. On the orders of King Daśaratha, his eldest son Rāmacandra has been banished to the forest. Bharata, son of Kaikeyī, has certainly planned to kill Rāmacandra in the forest in order to peacefully enjoy the kingdom without any rival. Rāma is my friend and master. We must see, no harm comes to Rāma. Let our army be deployed on the two banks and also in the river on the boats to maintain strict vigil. We shall allow Bharata to cross the river with his army only on being satisfied he harbours no evil motive against Rāma." Accordingly on

Guhaka's orders, his army was deployed at all strategic places. It goes without saying his intelligence agents were also alerted to collect information on the movements and activities of Bharata's army.

Having thus deployed his armed forces and the intelligence agents, Guhaka proceeded towards the camp of Bharata carrying with him various items of foodstuff and gifts. On seeing Guhaka coming, Sumantra told Bharata, "Guhaka, the old king of the local hunters, possesses wide experience about the Daṇḍaka forest. He happens to be the friend of Rāma. He is certainly aware of the whereabouts of Rāma, Sītā and Lakṣmaṇa in the forest. He is coming to meet you. You may receive him with due courtesy." Guhaka with his companions on being received by Bharata, humbly told him, "We are not unknown to you. We are all your servants. We have brought some food items and drinks for your entertainment. This is our fervent request, you kindly leave this place tomorrow after being entertained by us today." In reply Bharata said, "O Hunter King, you are the friend of my preceptor Rāma. You have arranged food and drinks for my army for which I am extremely grateful. Your intention is indeed noble. I badly need your help in one matter. You have full knowledge about the difficult terrain of the forest. Kindly let me know the path leading to the hermitage of Sage Bharadvāja."

Guhaka said in reply, "You need not worry for this. My men who have the knowledge of the area will accompany you. I myself shall also be your companion. But I am honestly and frankly asking you one question. Are you going to Rāma with any evil motive? This large army of yours has raised such a fear in our mind." Expressing no ill-feeling for Guhaka's suspicion about his motive, Bharata explained in a sweet voice, "Rāma is our eldest brother. I respect him like my own father. I am going to bring him back from the forest. Believe my words as true. Guhaka, do not hold any adverse opinion against me."

Guhaka was convinced about the sincerity of Bharata. In a happy mind he said, "Bharata, you are really virtuous and blessed. You are giving up the kingdom which you have obtained without any efforts. This greatness of sacrifice will give you everlasting fame in the world." Thereafter Guhaka while narrating the events during Rāma's journey to the forest said, "Rāma and Sītā that night slept on the ground at this river bank." On hearing this, Bharata fainted. After he gained composure soon after at the nursing of Kausalyā and others, Guhaka said, "Rāma, Sītā and Lakṣmaṇa that night remained on fast by drinking only the Ganges water. They did not touch the food stuff which I brought for them. Lakṣmaṇa after massaging for some time the feet of Rāma, remained on guard for the whole night underneath a nearby tree armed with the bow and the arrows. Myself along with my relatives remained awake for the night with Lakṣmaṇa." Bharata heaved a sigh of pain on hearing Guhaka.

Guhaka though belonging to the so-called lowest śūdra class of the hunters, was a person of great wisdom with unquestionable loyalty to the monarchy at Ayodhyā. While deploying his forces in an effort to prevent Bharata's entry into the forest in search of Rāma, he himself went to Bharata and held direct talks with him in a gesture of conciliation to know his real motive. For the conflict resolution he, like a real statesman, refrained from taking resort to any rashness. His prudent decision, as we know, paid dividends and the otherwise inevitable armed conflict was avoided. Guhaka's deployment of his tiny forces against the formidable Ayodhyā army in the face of his inevitable defeat, reflects his determination to fight and die for Rāma, his friend and master. When Bharata's honesty of purpose was established beyond doubt, Guhaka and his men went all out to help him in search of Rāma in the forest. We cannot but feel a deep sense of regard for Guhaka for his simplicity, loyalty and devotion as also for his pragmatism and strength of character.

The next morning Bharata's army personnel with their equipment, foodstuff and other articles were transported to the other bank by the boats arranged by Guhaka. Bharata and others crossed the river by several large boats and proceeded towards the hermitage of Sage Bharadvāja along the path shown by Guhaka and his followers. On the way after ordering the army and all others to stay on, Bharata changed to new sacred clothes and arrived at the hermitage of Bharadavāja unarmed only accompanied by Sage Vasiṣṭha. As he paid his obeisance to the sage, he (Sage Bharadvāja) could recognize him to be the son of King Daśaratha and welcomed him to the hermitage. He knew after the death of Daśaratha, Bharata was now the new ruler of the kingdom. Sage Bharadvāja accordingly asked him, "Bharata, you are now supposed to remain busy at Ayodhyā with royal duties. What did prompt you to come here? Don't you have any evil motive against Rāma now living in the forest? Speak out your real motive."

Deeply hurt at the words of Sage Bharadvāja, Bharata with tears in his eyes said, "O Bhagavan, if even you suspect my motive, death is now preferable to me. I have absolutely no hand in the banishment of Rāma. During my absence as a result of my mother's evil counsel our father has banished Rāma to the forest giving the kingdom to me. But I am terribly unhappy with my mother's actions. I have not accepted the throne as wished by my mother. I have come to bring back Rāmacandra. He is the rightful king of Ayodhyā. Kindly have pity on me realizing my real motive. Now kindly tell me the whereabouts of Rāmacandra."

Expressing satisfaction at his words, Sage Bharadvāja said, "Bharata, you are born in the famous Raghu clan. This has been your correct decision. I know your mind. I suspected you only to strengthen your faith. Rāma, Sītā and Lakṣmaṇa are presently staying in the Citrakūṭa mountains. Today take rest here along with your ministers and others and leave for the Citrakūṭa mountains tomorrow morning. Sage Bharadvāja, thereafter performed a very strange deed. By dint of his divine powers, he in no time had a large beautiful palace with many ancillary houses and stables built-up at the hermitage where all the royal guests as also the army and the horses of the chariots were accommodated. That night all were lavishly entertained with various items of delicious food and drinks, while fodder and water were provided to the horses.

The next morning Bharata with his entourage left for the Citrakūṭa mountains along the path indicated by Sage Bharadvāja. Before his departure the sage told him, "Bharata, do not find fault with your mother. This banishment in future will prove beneficial to the *deva*s, the *gandharva*s, the *asura*s and the humans." After crossing a long distance along the forest path, Bharata halted at a suitable place and sent out some of his trusted scouts in different directions in search of Rāma and Lakṣmaṇa. They soon brought the information, they had seen from a distance the escape of smoke from a place in the forest. The scouts no doubt did a correct thing by not proceeding to the source of the smoke. The smoke actually was coming out of Rāma's hermitage. The scouts could not have escaped the notice of Lakṣmaṇa who was maintaining a strict vigil all around the hermitage. Their lives might have even been in danger had they been apprehended by Lakṣmaṇa on the suspicion they were Bharata's spies engaged to collect information out of some evil motive about their place of stay in the forest. Lakṣmaṇa, we know, firmly believed, Bharata was a party to Kaikeyī's conspiracy in the banishment of Rāma and he might even take extreme steps against Rāma to safeguard his kingdom.

In the meantime Rāma from his hermitage heard the clamour of Bharata's army at a distance. He also noticed, the deer and other animals of the forest running about in panic. On the direction of Rāma, Lakṣmaṇa climbed a tall *śāla* tree and saw the presence of a large army. From the top of the tree, he gave the information to Rāma and said, "O Great Aryan, immediately extinguish the smoke. Send Sītā inside the cave and remain prepared for war duly armed." On being asked about the identity of the army, Lakṣmaṇa said, "Certainly Bharata has come with this army to kill us in order to safeguard his newly acquired kingdom. From the staff and the flag it appears the army has come from Ayodhyā. I am taking the vow, today I shall kill Bharata along with his entire army."

Asking Lakṣmaṇa not to hold any adverse opinion against Bharata, Rāma said, "Bharata is affectionate towards his brothers. He is perhaps coming to take us back to Ayodhyā. If you have used such harsh words against Bharata only for the sake of our kingdom, I shall ask him to hand over the kingdom to you." Being ashamed at the words of Rāma, Lakṣmaṇa said perhaps King Daśaratha had come to see him. Agreeing with Lakṣmaṇa, Rāma said, "Our father has perhaps come to see all of us. But with the army I do not see the personal divine umbrella of our father. This has created some doubt in my mind. In any case, you may now come down from the tree and do as directed by me."

Meanwhile, on being briefed by the scouts, Bharata first deployed his army in different directions and then deputed Śatrughna and Guhaka along with the agents in search of Rāma and Lakṣmaṇa in all sides. The agents included a few youths of Guhaka having good knowledge of the forest. Bharata himself joined the search along with some royal officials and others. Gradually he entered deep into the forest and after climbing a *śāla* tree, saw smoke coming out of a place at some distance. He understood, this was the hermitage of Rāma. He got down from the tree and proceeded towards the hermitage accompanied by the mothers, Sage Vasiṣṭha and others. On approaching the hermitage he suddenly saw Rāma standing with matted hair and wearing deer skin and tree bark. Bharata felt a terrible pain to see Rāma who always lived in comfort, in that condition. Leaving others behind he rushed to Rāma and fell at his feet weeping. He could utter only the words "O Great Aryan."

Rāma affectionately lifted Bharata and after taking him on his lap, asked him many questions. He asked him the reason of his coming to his hermitage and observed it had not been proper on his part to undertake this journey to the forest when the father was living. (Rāma still then was not aware of their father's death. He thought Bharata had been installed as the crown prince following his banishment to the forest.)

After enquiring about the welfare of their father, the mothers and others at Ayodhyā, Rāma spoke to Bharata on *rājadharma* (royal duties) and various other subjects. He advised Bharata to pay proper respect to the learned people by appointing them in responsible royal positions. In order to ensure good governance, he asked Bharata to select for his cabinet only those persons who were well-versed in the Śāstras (scriptures), self-restrained and intelligent with good lineage. He explained, a king's success mainly depended on proper consultations. Consultations should be held only with those ministers who were conversant with the Śāstras. At the same time the consultations must always be kept secret so that no undesirable persons could get access to them. Any premature disclosure of the secrets, he warned, would cause great harm to the king. Consultations, Rāma pointed out, should never be held alone or with many. No purpose would be served if consultations were held with one person only as in that case the king would be deprived of the considered opinion of others. Again consultations with many were liable to be disclosed to others. The king, he warned, must remain extremely vigilant in such matters. Rāma asked Bharata to complete all good works without any delay whatsoever. He also advised him to strictly ensure, none of his rival kings got any idea about his plans of action against them. Bharata was warned not to unnecessarily provoke his subjects by harsh punishments. In no case, he said, any innocent people should be punished. He was advised to follow a middle path in his behaviour with others. Rāma, however, maintained, greedy warriors, evil-minded physicians and the persons known to be loyal but with proneness to speak ill of the king, must be destroyed without showing them any mercy.

Rāma advised Bharata to appoint as army commanders only those persons who were contented, physically strong, even-minded, virtuous, faithful, competent and of good lineage and to pay them proper respect. He asked him to timely disburse pay, allowances and other benefits to the army to ensure their allegiance. The payments to the servants should also be made regularly: otherwise they might be provoked to do harm to the king. He particularly advised Bharata to keep the people, specially the well-to-do sections, always satisfied. He explained, the allegiance of the people should be so deep that they would not hesitate to give up their lives for the good of the king. As messengers, he suggested appointment of only those persons who were experienced, simple-minded, intelligent, learned and skilled in the art of speaking. Emphasizing the importance of the secret agents, Rāma said information should always be verified through three mutually unknown agents before taking action on it. Otherwise the king would have to take the risk of acting on the unconfirmed information, which was undesirable.

Giving Bharata necessary instructions regarding his conduct in the battlefield, Rāma said retreating enemy soldiers should never be attacked. He asked Bharata not to keep any truck with the atheists or with those who were the followers of Sage Cārvāka, an exponent of materialism. Emphasizing the importance of agriculture and the cattle wealth, he advised Bharata to look after them properly. Regarding a king's duty, he said, it should be the constant endeavour of the king to ensure the welfare and the protection of the people in accordance with the tenets of religion. This, he explained, was the *rājadharma*. While advising Bharata to protect the women and to properly look after their welfare, he warned him not to share with them any royal decisions as they were indifferent in maintaining secrecy. He also warned Bharata to scrupulously avoid any attachment with the prostitutes and any unusual addiction to horse or elephant riding.

Rāma advised Bharata to shun atheism, falsehood, anger, carelessness, procrastination, avoidance of the company with the wise people, laziness, closeness to the ignorant people, indifference to keep secrets and other vices of the king. At the end, he asked him to establish himself as a great king by governing the kingdom with justice and fairness and ensuring the welfare and happiness of his people.

In the *Mahābhārata* we have heard similar pronouncements on the duties and responsibilities of the king from sage Nārada, grandfather Bhīṣma, Prime Minister Vidura and other wise men. To work for the welfare of the subjects is *rājadharma.* This *dharma* can only be performed when the king himself is free from all vices and his personal conduct remains beyond reproach. We shall see later how Rāma by strictly adhering to the principles of *rājadharma* was able to establish Rāmarājya in his kingdom where the protection of the good and the suppression of the bad were ensured and the people belonging to all classes by following their respective *dharma*s, lived in peace and happiness. From Rāma's elaboration of the principles of *rājadharma,* we find the secret agents those days, as of now, had a great role to play in ensuring the security and stability of the country. The kings and the rulers were then fully aware of the methodology of the recruitment, training and deployment of the secret agents. We can say without any contradiction, the principles of *rājadharma* as elaborated in the days of our great epics, are fully relevant today particularly in the context of the prevailing decadent social order due mainly to the unrighteous conduct of our leadership.

Bharata listened to Rāma's instructions in complete silence. On being again asked to state the reasons of his visit, he said, "O Great Aryan, our father has died of grief after sending you to the forest, without any fault of mine, at the conspiracy of mother Kaikeyī. Our widowed mothers and other venerable persons have all come along with me from Ayodhyā. I am your servant. It is our fervent request, you kindly get yourself crowned today itself as the king of Ayodhyā." Saying this, Bharata fell again at Rāma's feet."

Rāma lifted him and after embracing him said, "Brother, you are virtuous with an unblemished character. How can you take resort to dishonest means for the greed of the kingdom? I find no fault of yours in my banishment to the forest. Do not rebuke mother Kaikeyī out of anger. I have come to the forest on the wishes of our parents. I shall remain in the forest." Shocked at the news of their father's death, Rāma remained unconscious for some time. On recovery, he along with the brothers performed the last rites of the father at the nearby Mandākinī River. In the meantime the mothers, Sage Vasiṣṭha, Sage Jābāli and others joined Rāma, Sītā and Lakṣmaṇa. That night they all stayed in Rāma's hermitage.

The next morning Bharata again requested Rāma to take over the reins of the kingdom on return to Ayodhyā. But Rāma remained firm in his decision to stay in the forest. Bharata then said, "I admit, our father has given the kingdom to me. But I am now handing over the kingdom to you. You alone are capable of governing this vast kingdom. I have refused to be crowned as the king only because I want to hand over the kingdom to you. All sections of the people are eager to see you as their king."

Bharata's words had no impact on Rāma. At this time Sage Jābāli said, "O Kākutstha (descendant of King Kakutstha), you are an ascetic with a placid mind. It is not unknown to you, everything in this world including parents and wealth has temporary existence. No virtuous person feels any attachment to them. Your father King Daśaratha is dead. He has no existence whatsoever. Now judging the objective condition, you give up the hard forest life and get crowned as the king of Ayodhyā."

Denouncing Jābāli's observations as atheism, Rāma insulted him in harsh language. He even said the late king had not acted wisely by taking a person of such negative ideas like him in his council of ministers. He asserted, he would under no circumstance go against the wishes of his parents and accept the throne. At this moment Sage Vasiṣṭha told Rāma, Jābāli who was fully aware of the realities of human nature, had spoken all these things only to ensure the return of the kingdom to him. Narrating the history of the Ikṣvāku dynasty, he then said, "Rāma, you are the eldest son of the virtuous Daśaratha. In this dynasty only the eldest son ascends to the throne. It will not be proper for you to break this well-established tradition. Ascend to the throne of Ayodhyā like your illustrious father. I assure you your acceptance of my suggestion will in no way stand in the way of your salvation. You shall get enough opportunity to perform religious rites in course of your royal duties in the midst of the ministers, own relatives and the subordinate kings. Do not ignore the words of your virtuous mothers. Accept the prayer of Bharata." Still there was no change in the mind of Rāma. Bharata decided to remain on fast till Rāma agreed to accept the throne. Both Rāma and Bharata stood firm in their respective decisions. At one time on Rāma's request, Bharata broke the fast. He, however, resolved to stay on in the forest along with Rāma for fourteen years thus creating a deadlock without any one yielding to the other. At last Bharata placed in front of Rāma a pair of golden sandals he had brought from Ayodhyā and requested him to wear them. Rāma doing so, Bharata made obeisance to the sandals and said, "O Parantapa (most austere), this pair of sandals is the embodiment of happiness and wealth. I shall entrust the entire monarchy to the sandals and govern the kingdom on your behalf from a village away from Ayodhyā for fourteen years. I shall then wear deer skin and tree bark and live only on fruits and roots like you. If I don't meet you after fourteen years, I shall give up my life on the burning pyre." Gladly agreeing with his decision, Rāma embraced Bharata and Śatrughna and asked them not to harbour any anger against mother Kaikeyī. Bharata then went around Rāma and left with tears in his eyes for Ayodhyā with the pair of sandals placed on the best elephant, after taking leave of Rāma, Sītā and Lakṣmaṇa, along with the mothers, Sage Vasiṣṭha and others escorted by the army. The mothers' choked voice with tears made the farewell scene all the more pathetic. As the convoy went out of sight, Rāma, Sītā and Lakṣmaṇa silently entered their hut with tearful eyes.

Thus the virtuous Rāma kept his promise given to the parents with regard to his banishment to the forest. He unhesitatingly disregarded all efforts to make him the king. He considered the hard forest life insignificant compared to the fulfilment of his promise. Rāma is great indeed. Bharata's greatness is also unique. He refused the kingdom which was bequeathed to him by his father and left no stone unturned to get the eldest brother Rāma crowned as the king. Bharata's sacrifice together with his devotion and loyalty to the eldest brother is a rare event. This is an ideal example of a brother's love and loyalty for another brother. Rāma became great by willingly accepting the forest life on the wishes of the father. And Bharata became great by refusing to obey the father's wishes. This seems to be a competitive rivalry for greatness between the two virtuous brothers. In this honest competition, both the brothers came out equally victorious. The sacrifices gladly undertaken by the brothers emphasize the truth of the maxim, as explained in the scriptures, that happiness lies in renunciation. Following the example of Rāma, Bharata by showing an extreme sense of sacrifice on depriving himself of the royal comforts, governed the kingdom on Rāma's behalf with sandals as his representative from an ordinary village turned into a forest, wearing deer skin and tree bark and taking only fruits and the roots. This is virtually a kind of banishment of Bharata to the forest voluntarily undertaken. Unlike Rāma, Bharata is now saddled with the arduous task of governing the vast kingdom on the principles of *rājadharma* as laid down by him. On minute judgement, it would be evident, in greatness Bharata has even surpassed Rāma. During the period of banishment in the forest, Rāma has now no burden of the royal responsibilities.

We have seen how this saintly Bharata had to suffer the pangs of defame out of sheer bad luck. King Daśaratha, we know, looked upon him with suspicion on the issue of the succession. Rāma too was suspicious of him. The eldest mother Kausalyā denounced Bharata as a conspirator along with his mother Kaikeyī in the banishment of Rāma. Brother Lakṣmaṇa even took the vow of killing the "conspirator" Bharata over Rāma's banishment. The royal ministers and the general people harboured adverse opinion against Bharata. The hunter king Guhaka, a friend and devotee of Rāma, even mobilized his forces to prevent Bharata's entry with the army into the forest, as he thought, to "kill" Rāma. Bharata's presence in the forest with a large army according to even Sage Bharadvāja was motivated by some evil design against Rāma. Lakṣmaṇa asked Rāma to remain ready for war against Bharata at the sight of his army at the Citrakūṭa mountains. Following his conquest of Laṅkā, Rāma sent Hanumān, we shall see later, to first ascertain the intentions of Bharata. Rāma surprisingly even then could not shake off his suspicion against Bharata. Some suspicion still lingered in his mind whether Bharata would willingly hand over the kingdom to him as promised. We are aware, Bharata, truthful and virtuous as he was, was able to establish his honesty, integrity and innocence before all. He emerged as a really saintly person without any ill-motive against Rāma. True to his promise he gladly handed over the kingdom to Rāma on his return to Ayodhyā with the royal treasury increased tenfold as a result of his benevolent administration.

Of the four brothers, some faults are noticed in Lakṣmaṇa, Śatrughna and even in Rāma; but Bharata was spotless. This great character of Bharata deeply touches our mind and we feel hurt when a saintly person like him was misunderstood by everybody causing him deep mental anguish. Our head bows down in regard for this great prince. The depiction of such a great character like Bharata is indeed a wonderful creation of the *Rāmāyaṇa*'s poet.

On return, while the mothers, Sage Vasiṣṭha and others stayed at Ayodhyā, Bharata turned Nandīgrām, a nearby village into a forest and set to govern the kingdom from there as an ascetic, as promised, in the name of Rāma with the sandals placed on a decorated pedestal as the symbol of his authority.

11

Humiliation of Śūrpaṇakhā

MEANWHILE, Rāma after a few days left Citrakūṭa mountains as the memory of the visit of Bharata and the mothers there was unbearable to him, to establish his hermitage at a new place. Moreover, the sanctity of the area was marred by the excrements of the elephants and horses of Bharata's army. On the way Rāma met Sage Atri in his hermitage and narrated the story of his banishment to the forest. On his direction, Sītā separately met his wife Anasūyā and received from her instructions about wife's duties towards the husband. Anasūyā explained, "Sītā, my blessings are on you. You shall earn fame and virtue by following the faith of your husband. Always keep in mind, it is the husband who is the dearest friend of the wife." Sītā informed her, she had received similar advice from her mother on the eve of the marriage and narrated the story of her marriage with Rāma. She said, she had voluntarily accepted the banishment and was now devotedly serving her husband disregarding all discomforts of forest life. Greatly satisfied at the words of Sītā, Anasūyā presented to her divine garments and ornaments. That night Rāma spent the night at the hermitage of Sage Atri and left for his new destination the next morning. Before departure, Sage Atri while warning him about the terrorising *rākṣasa*s in the forest, asked him to destroy them at the earliest opportunity. We shall see later the ornaments presented by Anasūyā were thrown by Sītā to the ground from the chariot of Rāvaṇa after her abduction indicating the path of her travel and thereby facilitating her search by Rāma and Lakṣmaṇa.

On the way Rāma, Sītā and Lakṣmaṇa were suddenly attacked by a ferocious-looking *rākṣasa* by name Virodha. In the fierce battle that ensued, Virodha despite being seriously wounded, remained alive on the strength of the boon obtained from Lord Brahmā. He was a *gandharva* before by name Damburu. On the curse of Kubera (the God of Wealth) for the dereliction of duty, he had become a *rākṣasa*. On his prayer for salvation, Kubera predicted he (Damburu) would regain the appearance of *gandharva* and go to heaven when he would die at the hands of Rāma, the eldest son of King Daśaratha. After disclosing all these facts, he breathed his last. Before his death, he asked Rāma to proceed to the hermitage of Sage Śarabhaṅga who was staying only half a *yojana* away. Accordingly Rāma and Lakṣmaṇa after burying his dead body, appeared at his hermitage. At this time Sage Śarabhaṅga was preparing for his voluntary death. After casting a look at Rāma, he happily entered the burning pyre and departed to heaven on assuming a divine body as a young man. Following the death of Sage Śarabhaṅga, a number of local ascetics met Rāma with the request to destroy the terrorizing *rākṣasa*s so that they could peacefully pursue their religious activities. Spending a few days with them, Rāma came to the hermitage of Sage Agastya who was very happy to see him and gave him many divine weapons. The *rākṣasa*s were afraid of Sage Agastya for his spiritual powers and as such they did not dare to create any disturbances to his hermitage. The sage invited Rāma to stay with him in his hermitage. As his purpose of destroying the *rākṣasa*s would not be served if he stayed here, Rāma respectfully refused the invitation. On his direction Rāma with Sītā and Lakṣmaṇa then moved to the charming Pañcavaṭī forest (only 3 km away from modern Nasik in the state of Maharashtra) and established their hermitage there. On way to the Pañcavaṭī forest, Rāma met a huge vulture. This vulture who was a wise person narrated before Rāma the origin of the animal world. Later he disclosed his identity and said, "My name is Jaṭāyū. The name of my elder brother is Sampāti.

I happen to be the friend of your father. I shall protect Sītā during the absence of Lakṣmaṇa and you." Happy at his words, Rāma dearly embraced him.

At the Pañcavaṭī forest, Rāma, Sītā and Lakṣmaṇa were passing their days very happily. One day a ferocious-looking *rākṣasī* appeared at the hermitage and was immediately attracted towards Rāma on seeing his handsome appearance. Having a strong yearning to get Rāma as her husband, she said, "Rāma, I am a love-sick *rākṣasī*. My name is Śūrpaṇakhā. Rāvaṇa, the conqueror of the three worlds is my brother. You forsake your ugly-looking Sītā and accept me as your wife. I shall immediately kill Sītā and Lakṣmaṇa and feed on their flesh. I am in possession of *māyā* power. I shall happily move in the Daṇḍaka forest with you enjoying its beautiful sights." Rāma was greatly amused at the words of Śūrpaṇakhā. With a little smile, he said, "I am married. My brother Lakṣmaṇa is still unmarried. He is a handsome young man. He is fit to be your husband." Śūrpaṇakhā immediately appeared before Lakṣmaṇa who was standing nearby and asked him to accept her as his wife. Lakṣmaṇa laughed at the words of Śūrpaṇakhā and said, "I am subservient to my eldest brother Rāma. You shall have to spend your life like an ordinary slave woman if you marry me. You are spotlessly beautiful. You better be happy as the second wife of Rāma. It may be, Rāma will then forsake the ugly-looking Sītā and live only with you."

Śūrpaṇakhā could not understand the jokes of Rāma and Lakṣmaṇa. She believed their words and thought Rāma was not accepting her as his wife because of his deep attachment to Sītā. Considering Sītā to be the main impediment to their marriage, Śūrpaṇakhā rushed to kill her. Asking Lakṣmaṇa to protect Sītā from the hands of Śūrpaṇakhā, Rāma observed it had not been proper for them to engage in jokes with an evil-minded non-Aryan and directed Lakṣmaṇa to disfigure the lustful Śūrpaṇakhā. Accordingly Lakṣmaṇa with his sword severed Śūrpaṇakhā's nose and the ears. Thus rejected and wounded, Śūrpaṇakhā besmeared with blood ran to the forest raising a loud roar and reported the incident to her step-brother Khara who had camped in the Daṇḍaka forest with a large *rākṣasa* army.

Furious at the distress of Śūrpaṇakhā, Khara despatched a contingent of *rākṣasa* army to kill Rāma, Lakṣmaṇa and Sītā; but they all lost their lives at the arrows of Rāma. Śūrpaṇakhā who watched the destruction of the *rākṣasa*s from a distance, immediately informed Khara, who then proceeded to Rāma's hermitage with his two powerful generals by name Dūṣaṇa and Triśira and a large *rākṣasa* army. In the fierce battle Rāma destroyed both Dūṣaṇa and Triśira and a large number of *rākṣasa*s. The rest fled away out of panic. Though fear gripped his mind at the rout of the *rākṣasa* army, Khara fighting with all courage and determination and using his *māyā* power, harassed Rāma for quite some time. At the end Khara pierced by Rāma's arrows, fell down dead on the ground. At the death of Khara, the gods and minstrels sounded war-drums and showered flowers on Rāma out of joy. The sages congratulated Rāma for establishing peace in the Daṇḍaka forest by successfully destroying the *rākṣasa*s. As the battle ended, Sītā and Lakṣmaṇa came out of their hiding in the cave. Sītā was relieved, Rāma had remained unhurt, while Lakṣmaṇa embraced him for his wonderful victory over the *rākṣasa* army.

Meanwhile, a *rākṣasa* by name Akampana on fleeing from the battle, reached Laṅkā and reported the whole incident including the severing of the nose and the ears of Śūrpaṇakhā to Rāvaṇa. He said because of the valour of Rāma and Lakṣmaṇa, the entire *rākṣasa* army had been driven out of the Janasthāna (Daṇḍaka forest). On hearing the terrible news, Rāvaṇa flew into a rage with bloodshot eyes and declared, he would immediately proceed to the Janasthāna and destroy Rāma and Lakṣmaṇa. Akampana then said, "I have the fear, even the *deva*s, the *gandharva*s and the *rākṣasa*s together will not be able to defeat them. But there is still a means to kill Rāma. He has got a beautiful wife by name Sītā who is staying with him. You may go to the Janasthāna and abduct her by taking recourse to some deception. I am certain, Rāma will not live long in the absence of Sītā."

Akampana's suggestion was found acceptable to Rāvaṇa, who without any loss of time, appeared at the hermitage of Mārīca by his flying chariot and asked for his help in the matter. He believed, it was possible only for Mārīca to help him in the abduction of Sītā as he was capable of assuming different forms by his *māyā* power. We know, Rāma without killing Mārīca threw him to the sea out of compassion when he (Mārīca) attacked him in the forest. Since then there was a change of heart in Mārīca and he engaged himself in religious austerities by constructing a small hermitage in the forest. Gradually he became free from his old *rākṣasa*-like evil ways of life. Rāvaṇa's decision to abduct Sītā created an adverse reaction in his mind. In clear terms he told Rāvaṇa, "Mahārāja, the person who has encouraged you in this act, is your greatest enemy. Do not invite destruction of the *rākṣasa* clan by abducting Sītā. Rāma's power and strength is beyond your comprehension. Though a human, he is a veritable lion. This lion is now asleep. Do not rouse him. Give up your evil design against Sītā. Kindly return to Laṅkā and remain happy with your own wives." Rāvaṇa thought over the just words of Mārīca and returned to Laṅkā.

12

Śūrpaṇakhā's Exposition of Spy-Policy and Rājadharma before Rāvaṇa

In the Daṇḍaka forest, meanwhile, Śūrpaṇakhā remained dumbfounded and fear-stricken at the destruction of the *rākṣasa* army. She realized Rāma was second to none. What he had done, could not be done by any other person. Finding the Daṇḍaka forest unsafe for her she returned to Laṅkā. Rāvaṇa seated on the throne was then holding consultations with his council of ministers in the royal court. Śūrpaṇakhā with severed nose and the ears rushed to the court and angrily charged him saying, "Rāvaṇa, you are licentious, autocrat and greedy. You do not care to keep any information about the happenings in your kingdom. Such an indifferent king loses in no time all respect before his subjects. The king who disregards his duties soon gets destroyed with his kingdom. The king who is engaged only in sensual pleasures and luxury, does not keep any information of his kingdom through spies and remains cut-off from the outside world, is soon forsaken by his own people. You have forgotten the truth, no king can expect to add to his wealth and prosperity if he remains indifferent to the task of regaining his lost territory. Rāvaṇa, you are by nature fickle-minded. You have under you a number of trained agents for collection of intelligence; but you have not properly utilized their services. You have utterly neglected the security of the kingdom having failed to take advantage of the training and knowledge of your secret agents. If you carry on like this, how would you preserve your throne in the face of the enemy *deva*s, *gandharvas* and the *asuras*? You are actually behaving like a boy without having any intelligence. You are completely oblivious of your royal duties and responsibilities. The king who does not keep the royal treasury and the secret agents under his control and does not perform the *rājadharma,* is just an ordinary person. The king sees all future events through his secret agents. A worthy king is always far-sighted.

"Rāvaṇa, there is no deployment of secret agents in your kingdom. This is why you are in the dark about all important developments. The ministers are all your sycophants. They are all men of ordinary intelligence. For this the Janasthāna has been lost to you with the destruction of the *rākṣasa* army as also your near relatives. Even this very terrible information is not known to you. Rāma is a person of indomitable courage and perseverance. He has purified the Janasthāna and assured all protection to the sages. The Janasthāna is now safe for them. But Rāvaṇa, you are greedy and power-hungry with no capacity of independent judgement. You are virtually a prisoner of your incompetent and worthless ministers. In times of danger the people unhesitatingly forsake the king who is greedy, proud and wicked. Even his own kinsmen treat him as their enemy. Always remember, the king who is alert, experienced, self-restrained and virtuous, is only capable of protecting his kingdom. The king who governs his kingdom with justice, earns everybody's esteem. But Rāvaṇa, you are devoid of all the qualities of a king. You are a great tormentor of others. Besides, you are incapable of making any distinction between the right and the wrong. There is no doubt you shall soon be destroyed with your kingdom."

Rāvaṇa silently heard Śūrpaṇakhā and remained thoughtful for some time. Later, on his enquiries about the particulars of Rāma, Śūrpaṇakhā while describing the handsome appearance as also the power and strength of Rāma and brother Lakṣmaṇa and the charm and beauty of wife

Sītā, observed, "Such an exquisitely beautiful and well-mannered woman is only suitable to be your wife. You may make every effort to demoralize and weaken Rāma and Lakṣmaṇa by some deception and obtain Sītā as your wife." This abominable advice of Śūrpaṇakhā to abduct a married woman by deceitful means is indicative of the destructive character of the *rākṣasas* and stands in sharp contrast to her narration of the lofty ideas before Rāvaṇa about the just conduct of the king. This mutually contradictory characteristic disposition is indeed the distinguishing feature of the *rākṣasas*.

Our surprise, however, knows no bounds when we hear from the lips of Śūrpaṇakhā, a ferocious-looking *rākṣasī* the wonderful enunciation of the principles of *rājadharma,* security and intelligence collection to ensure the stability and the integrity of the kingdom. We are also surprised at her courage to rebuke the mighty Rāvaṇa, the conqueror of the three worlds, in the open court in the presence of his ministers, for his failure to keep information about the happenings of his kingdom. There was, of course, no exaggeration of her accusations against Rāvaṇa. There was in fact no effort on his part to obtain any prior information about the power and strength of Rāma and Lakṣmaṇa. This indifference perhaps stemmed from the fact he did not expect any danger from the weak humans when he had conquered the *devas*, the *gandharvas* and the others as covered by the boons obtained from Lord Brahmā. Surrounded by a group of sycophant ministers, Rāvaṇa actually remained immersed in worldly pleasures completely neglecting his royal duties. Rāvaṇa was not aware of the background of the birth of Rāma as human incarnation of Supreme God Viṣṇu for the sole purpose of destroying Rāvaṇa and the *rākṣasas* to end his reign of terror. Rāma, we know, got divine weapons from sage Viśvāmitra and others with all the characteristic details about the *rākṣasas* including their physical prowess and the dangerous *māyā* power. Rāvaṇa, on the other hand, remained always callous in this regard and did not care to take any lesson from the earlier destruction of Tāḍakā Rākṣasī and Rākṣasa Subāhu at the hands of Rāma. Though the destruction of the *rākṣasas* and of Rāvaṇa was a divine inevitability as depicted by the poet, the massacre of the huge *rākṣasa* army under Khara in the Daṇḍaka forest, would not have been so easy had Rāvaṇa, himself a very powerful person with the boons of Lord Brahmā having all resources under his command, taken steps to obtain prior information about the particulars of Rāma and his power and strength and prepared for the battle accordingly. Here Rāvaṇa failed miserably as a king. Śūrpaṇakhā's statement indicates, the secret service was an important tool in those days as at present in the hands of the king and any king who will ignore it must invite his own peril. This actually happened to Rāvaṇa.

Rāvaṇa in his mind accepted the suggestion of Śūrpaṇakhā and decided to act accordingly. He was, however, afraid of his wife Mandodarī who, he knew, would never approve of such an immoral act of abducting Sītā by deceitful means. He thus kept his plan secret from everybody in the palace and stealthily came to the royal chariot-garage. Without any loss of time he flew with the charioteer in his *puṣpaka vimāna* (aerial chariot formerly belonging to Kubera) to the hermitage of Mārīca. On being asked by Mārīca about the reasons of his coming back so soon, Rāvaṇa told him, "Mārīca, listen carefully to what I say. In the Janasthāna Rāma has destroyed my brothers Khara and Dūṣaṇa with the entire *rākṣasa* army. On his direction, his brother Lakṣmaṇa without any reason has severed the nose and the ears of our sister Śūrpaṇakhā and insulted our race. Rāma is a worthless prince and has been banished by his father to the forest certainly for some serious crime. Though dressed as an ascetic, he is perverted, cruel and greedy. His purpose is only to cause harm to others. I am determined to take revenge on him for his misdeeds. I need your help urgently. You are capable of assuming various beautiful forms with your *māyā* power. You shall have to assume the form of a golden deer with silver spots and move about in front of the hermitage of Rāma. Sītā on seeing you in that form will certainly request Rāma and Lakṣmaṇa to capture you for her. As the two brothers will leave the hermitage for you leaving Sītā alone, I shall then carry her off easily. Rāma in the absence of Sītā will be demoralized losing all his manly spirits. It will then be easy for me to kill him. I shall kill you immediately if you refuse to obey my orders."

13

Abduction of Sītā by Rāvaṇa

RĀVAṆA thus coerced Mārīca by threat to accompany him in his chariot. As the chariot landed some distance away from Rāma's hermitage, Mārīca, as ordered by Rāvaṇa, assumed the form of a wonderful deer and began to roam about in front of the hermitage. Lakṣmaṇa on spotting such a strange deer, told Rāma apprehensively, "This deer is certainly the wizard Mārīca. In the past Mārīca in the form of such an illusory deer, had allured and killed many kings while on hunting in the forest." Sītā enamoured of the beauty of the deer, however, requested Rāma to capture the deer for her. Rāma himself was also charmed to see the deer. Disregarding Lakṣmaṇa's warning, he asked him to protect Sītā and went out to capture the deer. But the deer by jumping in different directions went out of sight and again reappeared and gradually entered deep into the forest. Having failed to capture the deer, Rāma became angry and pierced its heart with his arrow. The deer before its death reassumed the former self and loudly shouted in Rāma's voice "O Sītā. O Lakṣmaṇa" as directed by Rāvaṇa. Rāma remembering Lakṣmaṇa's warning realized, the deer was actually the wizard Mārīca.

Meanwhile, in the hermitage, Sītā on hearing the shouts thought Rāma was in danger and asked Lakṣmaṇa to proceed to his help immediately. Lakṣmaṇa expressed his unwillingness to leave the hermitage keeping Sītā unprotected. On this Sītā became furious and rebuked Lakṣmaṇa in the harshest possible language. She said, "Lakṣmaṇa, I find you are actually Rāma's enemy while posing as his friend. You have remained unconcerned even after knowing Rāma's danger. I realize you have taken this decision only to gain me." Saying this, Sītā continued to hurl strong invectives on Lakṣmaṇa while weeping profusely. Lakṣmaṇa while consoling Sītā said, "O Devī, the *devas*, *gandhavas*, *asuras*, *nāgas*, and the *rākṣasas* even unitedly would not be able to cause any harm to Rāma. Rāma is invincible in the war. You are unnecessarily getting worried for Rāma. In this terrible forest I cannot leave the hermitage leaving you alone." At these words of Lakṣmaṇa, Sītā grew terribly furious and inflicted more severe abuses on him casting aside all decencies. Addressing him with utter disrespect she said, "You are a person of vile character and this I have fully understood. It is only with the purpose of gaining me you have accompanied Rāma to the forest. Perhaps you are a spy of Bharata. Remember, your wishes will not be fulfilled. Without Rāma I shall give up my life in your very presence." Even after this, Lakṣmaṇa tried to console Sītā in the most persuasive language; but she remained adamant. Deeply hurt at the ugly inflictions of Sītā, Lakṣmaṇa with extreme reluctance left the hermitage leaving her alone.

As soon as Lakṣmaṇa left the hermitage, Rāvaṇa in the guise of a calm and dignified looking ascetic, appeared at the hermitage and humbly enquired of Sītā, while praising her beauty and gracefulness, why she was living alone in this dangerous forest. Elated at the good words of the ascetic about her beauty and gracefulness, Sītā without suspecting anything, made arrangements for his entertainment. On being asked about her antecedents, Sītā while giving all details including the reasons for the banishment of her husband Rāma to the forest, said that her husband and his brother Lakṣmaṇa would be returning soon from the adjoining forest where they had gone to collect fruits and roots. She requested the ascetic to take rest at the hermitage for some time. She did not disclose the developments centring round the golden deer.

Then suddenly Rāvaṇa assuming his real form proudly gave out his identity and called upon Sītā to become his wife. He assured her, she would be living very happily in the midst of pomp and grandeur in his gilded capital of Laṅkā. On hearing this despicable proposal of Rāvaṇa, Sītā flew into a rage and reproved him in the harshest language. Denouncing him as villainous, lustful and rude, she warned, Rāvaṇa with his entire kingdom would be destroyed if he dared to cause any harm to her. She said, "It is possible to remain alive even after abducting the wife of Indra, but it is impossible to remain alive after abducting the wife of Rāma." Without paying any attention to Sītā's words, Rāvaṇa said, "O Beautiful Lady, accept me as your husband if you want to become the wife of a great king who is well known in the three worlds. I myself happen to be the only person who is suitable to be your husband. Rāma is dispossessed of his kingdom, unfortunate and weak. He has given up him kingdom at the words of a mere woman and is now living in this forest in a wretched condition. There is no justification for you to remain faithful to such a dull-witted foolish person."

Saying this, Rāvaṇa held the tuft of Sītā's hair by the left hand and the two thighs by the right hand, and forcibly took her to his chariot parked some distance away. Sītā then began to cry loudly calling upon Rāma and Lakṣmaṇa to come to her rescue. In utter despair, she also prayed to the trees of the forest, forest deity, birds and animals and the river Godāvarī to immediately inform Rāma about her abduction by the sinful Rāvaṇa. Then suddenly she came to notice Jaṭāyū, the king of vultures sitting on the branch of a tree and implored upon him to immediately inform Rāma and Lakṣmaṇa about her abduction. He told Jaṭāyū, it would not be possible for him to resist Rāvaṇa alone as he was strong, boastful and armed.

Jaṭāyū then looked at the sky and saw Sītā in Rāvaṇa's flying chariot. From the branch of the tree itself he told Rāvaṇa, "O Brother Daśānana (one having ten heads), I am an old pious person firmly true to my promise. My name is Jaṭāyū. I am the powerful king of the birds. Rāmacandra who is the king of all people, is wedded to the welfare of the entire mankind. The woman whom you have abducted, is his lawfully married wife. It is illegal on the part of a pious king to touch the body of another person's wife. You immediately desist from this heinous act. As a king your duty is to protect the wives of the other people as you protect your own wife. But you seem to have forgotten your duty completely. You are indeed a sinful person with a fickle mind. The wealth and kingdom of a despotic king like you will never be permanent. Your destruction is inevitable. Rāma and Lakṣmaṇa are now far away. It is not possible to inform them about this terrible news. Despite my old age I would try my best to resist your misdeed."

Saying this Jaṭāyū flew to the sky and ferociously attacked Rāvaṇa in the chariot. The ensuing battle with Rāvaṇa continued for quite some time. Jaṭāyū with his sharp claws caused severe wounds in several parts of Rāvaṇa's body. Rāvaṇa's shower of arrows was destroyed with the violent flutter of his powerful wings. Even Rāvaṇa's hair was blown away with the flutter. Eventually Rāvaṇa's bow and arrows were destroyed. His charioteer was killed and the chariot severely damaged. Thus tormented, Rāvaṇa mustering all his strength, drew out his sword and severed Jaṭāyū's two wings, the feet and the two sides of his body. Jaṭāyū was severely wounded and he fell down on the ground. At this moment Rāvaṇa with Sītā firmly held in his hands also landed there. On seeing Jaṭāyū in his dying condition, Sītā began to lament pitifully while calling Rāma and Lakṣmaṇa. Relieved at the imminent death of Jaṭāyū, Rāvaṇa without further loss of time, held Sītā by the hair and flew through the sky towards Laṅkā by using his *māyā* power.

At one time, in the continuing confusion, Sītā's anklet, necklace and some other ornaments fell down from the flying chariot. Sītā continued to chastise Rāvaṇa for his misdeed in harsh language. Suddenly she noticed a group of five monkeys sitting together on a mountain-peak below and dropped down, unnoticed by Rāvaṇa, her scarf and some items of her ornaments. Thereafter Rāvaṇa without encountering any further trouble reached Laṅkā safely. At Laṅkā Rāvaṇa kept Sītā confined in one of the apartments of the palace and deployed a few fierce-looking *rākṣasī*s to guard her. He directed them to provide her all comforts and warned not to allow any other men or women to meet her. He further warned, the *rākṣasī*s would meet instant death if his orders were violated in any way.

Meanwhile, Rāvaṇa on coming out of the inner apartments began to think over his next step. Realizing the urgency of collecting information about Rāma's movements and activities in the forest he deputed a group of reliable *rākṣasa*s to Janasthāna. He directed them to kill Rāma if there was an opportunity. Apparently Śūrpaṇakhā's criticism of Rāvaṇa's indifference to the developments in Janasthāna was still fresh in his memory. It appears the *rākṣasa*s deputed by Rāvaṇa to Janasthāna were experts both in the collection of intelligence and also in the art of warfare. There was, however, no feed-back information about the results of their enquiries. Perhaps Rāvaṇa could not pay any attention to this matter because of his preoccupation with other works. This was, however, a costly omission.

The attack on Rāvaṇa by Jaṭāyū brings forth several issues which deserve proper elaboration. First, the attack which mauled Rāvaṇa severely, indicates Rāma who is living in the forest virtually forlorn, is not without any friends. Rāvaṇa actually got a taste of the resistance he would encounter for his heinous crime, in the coming days. It was evident to Rāvaṇa, Rāma would leave no stone unturned to search out Sītā and punish the offender. This fear actually prompted him to send *rākṣasa* emissaries to Janasthāna to ascertain his movements and activities. Secondly, the attack indicates Jaṭāyū's deep loyalty and devotion to Rāma. He, despite his infirmity of old age, did not hesitate even for a moment to resist Rāvaṇa at the cost of his life, as he was promise-bound to protect Sītā during the absence of Rāma and Lakṣmaṇa from their hermitage. Our head bows down in respect for Jaṭāyū for his supreme sacrifice in upholding *dharma*. Thirdly, the attack, as we shall see later when Rāma and Lakṣmaṇa met dying Jaṭāyū, helped disclose the identity of Rāvaṇa and the route he followed in reaching Laṅkā. The find of Sītā's scarf, ornaments, etc. on the ground also conclusively proved her identity thereby confirming it was Rāvaṇa who carried her to Laṅkā. Lastly, it may be mentioned Sītā even when she was firmly held by Rāvaṇa and was in extreme distress, maintained her composure and without losing her mental equanimity, managed to drop down her ornaments, etc. unnoticed by Rāvaṇa, in order to indicate his flight route with a view to facilitating her rescue. All this together with the details obtained from dying Jaṭāyū as also subsequently from Sugrīva and Hanumān, helped Rāma and Lakṣmaṇa to prepare their offensive with the help of Sugrīva's *vānara senā* against Rāvaṇa in Laṅkā. The attack thus proved to be the first turning point in the matter of search and rescue of Sītā from Rāvaṇa's captivity and the eventual destruction of Rāvaṇa at the hands of Rāma. Sītā's dogged defiance and strength of character shown from the day of her abduction persisted throughout her period of captivity in the Aśoka Vāṭikā in Laṅkā and she remained unscathed and was rescued by victorious Rāma.

There are many versions of *Rāmāyaṇa*. In some of the versions it has been mentioned, the Sītā abducted by Rāvaṇa was not the real Sītā; she was actually the *māyā*-Sītā (Sītā created by illusion). It seems, on the thought that the devout people would be deeply hurt if Sītā who is actually the Goddess Lakṣmī, consort of Lord Viṣṇu of whom Rāma is the incarnation, is molested by sinful Rāvaṇa, this introduction of *māyā*-Sītā has been conceptualized. According to this story Agni, the Fire God on the eve of Sītā's abduction, took her away and kept the *māyā*-Sītā in her place. Rāvaṇa mistook this *māyā*-Sītā as real Sītā and forcibly carried her away when she was alone in the hermitage. After the conquest of Laṅkā when Sītā entered into the funeral fire to prove her purity, the Fire God came out of the burning fire with real Sītā and handed her over to Rāma. In the *Vālmīki Rāmāyaṇa* also there is the mention of *māyā*-Sītā, but it was in a different context when Laṅkā was under seige by the *vānara senā* under the command of Rāma. Rāvaṇa by dint of illusion created this *māyā*-Sītā in order to cause confusion in the enemy ranks though Rāvaṇa's efforts proved unsuccessful (details later). As narrated by poet Vālmīki in his *Rāmāyaṇa*, it was the real Sītā who was abducted by Rāvaṇa and the same Sītā was brought out of the burning fire in Laṅkā by the Fire God. In yet another version of *Rāmāyaṇa*, Rāma on the eve of Sītā's abduction, brought Śabarī (Sage Mataṅga's maid, a woman belonging to the hunting tribe — details later) who reportedly resembled Sītā, to his hermitage in complete secrecy even without the knowledge of Lakṣmaṇa, and sent Sītā to a hiding place. This Śabarī mistaken as Sītā was abducted by Rāvaṇa. According to this story Śabarī was destroyed in the burning fire in Laṅkā, while the real Sītā was brought out from behind by Vibhīṣaṇa. Everybody thought, Sītā had come out of the burning fire on establishing her purity.

Meanwhile, Rāvaṇa felt somewhat satisfied at the successful abduction of Sītā and the deputation of *rākṣasa* emissaries to Janasthāna to enquire about Rāma. As he thought over Sītā, he became intoxicated with lust. He came to the apartments of Sītā and found her weeping in terrible mental agony guarded by the *rākṣasīs*. Rāvaṇa forcibly took Sītā outside and began to show her beautiful buildings and other pleasant sceneries to impress her. In order to change her mind towards him, he told Sītā, "In the three worlds none is equal to me. Rāma is short-lived and weak. Moreover, he has been deposed from his kingdom. He is now living in the forest as an ascetic. You please forsake him and accept me as your husband. It is impossible for a person like him without any resources, to rescue you from this impregnable Laṅkā. There is also none in the three worlds who can forcibly rescue you from here. You shall enjoy all the resources of the entire kingdom of Laṅkā if you agree to become my wife. We all shall remain subservient to you. All your sufferings of the forest life have now ended. You may now enjoy the fruits of your good deeds here. All objects of enjoyment are available in plenty in the palace. Enjoy everything with me. O beautiful lady, I have forcibly captured the *puṣpaka vimāna* of Kubera, my step-brother. This chariot is huge, pleasant and can move at the speed of the mind. Let us have a pleasure-trip in this chariot. Give up your sorrow. Let your beautiful face be resplendent again with brightness."

Sītā despite being overwhelmed with grief, ignored with contempt, the pleadings and platitudes of Rāvaṇa. She with no fear in her mind, placed a piece of grass in between Rāvaṇa and herself indicating a warning to Rāvaṇa not to advance towards her any further and said, "O! *rākṣasa*, in this world the great Rāma is known as a truthful person always firm in his vow. Rāma, a person of great courage and strength along with Lakṣmaṇa, will soon arrive here and destroy you.

"Gods and demons may not be able to kill you; but you shall not escape death from the hands of Rāma by acting against him as his enemy. Your strength, pride and arrogance will all be vanquished by Rāma. Along with you your entire *rākṣasa* clan will also be destroyed. You cannot touch my person. My body is now without any consciousness. I am unconcerned as to what you may do with it. I shall rather give up my life; but I shall not allow any dishonour to besmirch my life."

Rāvaṇa remained silent for some time on hearing the harsh words of Sītā. Later he angrily directed the *rākṣasī*s to humble her pride by resorting to threats and gesticulations. Immediately the fierce-looking *rākṣasīs* in a menacing posture surrounded Sītā. Afterwards on Rāvaṇa's orders Sītā was removed to Aśoka Vāṭikā where the *rākṣasīs* tried to win her over both with threats and shouts as also with sweet words. Sītā in the midst of this mental torture fainted while remembering Rāma and Lakṣmaṇa.

Meanwhile, in the Daṇḍaka forest Rāma after killing Mārīca hurriedly proceeded towards his hermitage. On the way he witnessed bad omens and became worried over some possible mishap befalling Sītā. Soon he met Lakṣmaṇa. He rebuked Lakṣmaṇa for leaving the hermitage keeping Sītā alone and said, "The golden deer was Mārīca himself and he had enticed me deep into the forest. His real identity was disclosed after he was killed by me. I apprehend some serious danger to Sītā." Lakṣmaṇa realized how deeply Rāma had been hurt and sought to explain the circumstances which compelled him to leave the hermitage. In a sorrowful mind he said, "O Aryan, I have not willingly left Sītā alone at the hermitage. At the harsh words of Sītā, I have been compelled to leave her alone On repeatedly hearing from the forest in your voice the words, "O! Lakṣmaṇa, help me," Sītā thought some danger had befallen you. She accordingly asked me to immediately leave the hermitage for your help. I sought to explain to Sītā, this voice was not yours: it has been imitated by some frightened *rākṣasa* as a deceptive trick. I further explained, you are invincible in the world. Not even the gods, not to speak of the *rākṣasas*, would be able to cause any harm to you. I asked Sītā not to get worried at all; but she did not listen. While weeping profusely she started chastizing me in the harshest possible language. She even insinuated, I harbour sinister motive against her and this was why I am refusing to leave the hermitage for your help even when your life is in imminent danger. She threatened to commit suicide if I did not immediately go out for your help. In these circumstances

I have been compelled to reluctantly leave the hermitage in violation of your instructions."

Rāma listened to Lakṣmaṇa patiently and said with a heavy hurt, "Brother, it has been a serious mistake on your part to leave the hermitage at the words of an angry woman. I am unhappy with you for your decision to leave Sītā alone in the hermitage in the midst of this dangerous forest. It has also been wrong on the part of Sītā to speak such harsh words against you."

Behind the abduction of Sītā lies the meticulously planned intelligence operation of Rāvaṇa. From the destruction of the huge *rākṣasa* army with their valiant commanders Khara and Dūṣaṇa by Rāma in Janasthāna, Rāvaṇa understood it would be difficult to defeat Rāma in any frontal attack. The inputs obtained from Akampana, Śūrpaṇakhā and Mārīca provided further confirmation to this idea. Akampana and Śūrpaṇakhā instigated Rāvaṇa to abduct Sītā by adopting some trickery. They argued, Rāma would lose heart and become weak if his beloved wife Sītā was abducted and it would then be easy for Rāvaṇa to kill him. Rāvaṇa decided to follow this course of action. He was aware, Mārīca who was capable of assuming various forms was the only person whose help would be necessary for the success of his design. He, accordingly, as we know, approached Mārīca, and sought his help explaining his plan of action to abduct Sītā. On his refusal, Rāvaṇa threatened Mārīca with dire consequence. Mārīca understood his death was inevitable at the hands of Rāvaṇa if he did not obey his command. On the other hand, he realized, he would meet sure death at the hands of Rāma in course of the execution of the plan. He preferred death at the hands of virtuous Rāma to those of wicked Rāvaṇa and as such agreed to assume the form of a golden deer to entice away Rāma and Lakṣmaṇa from their hermitage to facilitate Sītā's abduction. We are aware, the events happened exactly in the same pattern and

Mārīca was killed by Rāma while Sītā staying alone in the hermitage was successfully abducted by Rāvaṇa.

Without going into the question of morality, we cannot but praise Rāvaṇa for his well-conceived plan and its successful execution. He acted very intelligently when he appeared before Sītā in the guise of a pious ascetic. He praised her beauty and gracefulness and thus won over her confidence. He knew very well nothing is more pleasing to the ears of a woman than the praise of her beauty. Without suspecting anything, Sītā invited the ascetic inside and arranged for his entertainments. The ascetic softly and sympathetically talked with Sītā and thus created a congenial situation for her abduction. All this went on in a clock-wise precision. There was no faltering or innocuous uttering on the part of Rāvaṇa which might cause any suspicion in Sītā's mind.

We are aware, in the *Mahābhārata*, the Pāṇḍavas on many occasions killed Kaurava warriors by resorting to fraud and deceit on the advice of Kṛṣṇa throwing to the winds all principles of justice and morality. Kṛṣṇa unambiguously explained, without his *māyā* power, fraud and deceit the Pāṇḍavas could not come out victorious against the Kauravas. Even the gods, he pointed out, resorted to falsehood in subjugating the demons. In those days, as at present, use of unfair means in warfare was an accepted principle. In the so-called *dharmayuddha* (war for the cause of justice) of *Mahābhārata*, fraud, deceit and *māyā* power were virtually the principal weapons of the Pāṇḍavas. Rāvaṇa resorted to the same weapons of fraud and trickery to abduct Sītā though ultimate victory eluded him unlike the Pāṇḍavas who came out victorious. Rāvaṇa, the sinful tormentor of the three worlds was vanquished by righteous and valiant Rāma. Perhaps success of any method depends on place, time and circumstances. The same method may succeed at one time and fail in another.

The abduction of Sītā is the principal event in the *Rāmāyaṇa*. Rāvaṇa's sin being completed with his heinous act of abduction, his end came at the hands of Rāma and Sītā was rescued. Later under Rāma's benevolent rule peace and prosperity was established in his kingdom and the people were happy. The good ultimately triumphed over the bad. The abduction of Sītā so meticulously planned and executed by Rāvaṇa ultimately proved to be a boomerang against him.

14

Search for Sītā in the Forest

MEANWHILE, Rāma on entering the hermitage along with Lakṣmaṇa became bewildered without finding Sītā. On search of the adjoining areas also Sītā was not found. In the absence of Sītā, Rāma began to lament and at one time he became unconscious. After regaining his composure, he asked Lakṣmaṇa to return to Ayodhyā. In a state of lamentation he said, in the forest itself he would give up his life as he was unable to remain alive without Sītā. He continued to lament and again lost his consciousness.

Consoling Rāma, Lakṣmaṇa said, "O Aryan, kindly give up your grief. Have patience. Let us engage ourselves in search of Sītā with renewed vigour. No enterprising person does get afflicted with grief in any danger." Without paying any heed to Lakṣmaṇa, Rāma in a piteous voice pleaded with the trees, animals and birds, mountains and rivers of the forest to disclose the whereabouts of Sītā. Without hearing any answer from anyone, Rāma assumed a fierce-looking appearance and in a menacing cry warned, he would destroy the entire world if Sītā was not produced immediately before him.

On seeing Rāma in such a violent mood, Lakṣmaṇa with folded hands said, "In the past you were soft-natured and restrained and devoted to the welfare of all people. I have never seen you in such an angry mood. Do not give up your gentle nature. It is improper to destroy everybody for the fault of one. Some distance away I am seeing some broken parts of a chariot and some clothes. It appears a battle has been fought recently in this area. I am unable to find out why such a battle has been fought here in this forest. We shall have to find out what actually happened. Brother, we shall search ocean, rivers, mountains, forest, and even the lands of the gods and the *gandharvas* to find out the abductors of Sītā. Initially we shall try to find out Sītā following the principles of cordiality, peace, modesty and fair-play. If our efforts fail, we shall then take proper steps in applying force."

Lakṣmaṇa's words had no impact on Rāma, who continued to lament as before. Lakṣmaṇa then addressing Rāma narrated the glorious history of the royal dynasty of Ayodhyā and said, "Our father has obtained you as his son after performing various sacrificial rites. For your sake he has given up his life in grief. You are fully conversant with the principles of religion. You are endowed with all the virtues. If a person of your stature cannot bear the present distress, who else can do it? Be calm. Misfortune may befall any person. Even Indra and the gods could not avoid misfortune. It appears none can escape the inevitability of fate. Do not grieve. Death or abduction — whatever has befallen Sītā — it does not look proper for you to grieve like ordinary people. The wise men remain unmoved even in great danger. O great warrior, in the past you told me about these lofty principles many times. What advice can I give you? Even Bṛhaspati, the preceptor of the gods is incapable of giving any advice to you. O the great embodiment of wisdom, even the gods are unable to fathom your wisdom. At present your wisdom and intelligence are lying dormant at the absence of Sītā. I am only trying to revive the same. You possess both divine and worldly powers. Kindly rekindle those powers and proceed to destroy the enemy."

Rāma's grief subsided at the reasonable statement of Lakṣmaṇa. He immediately held his bow and the arrows and asked Lakṣmaṇa to devise ways for the rescue of Sītā. Lakṣmaṇa stated in reply, "Our first duty would be to search Janasthāna thoroughly to find out Sītā. This Janasthāna is covered with innumerable trees and creepers. Besides, there are many mountains, stone boulders, caves and deer. Many ferocious *rākṣasa*s live here. The habitations of *gandharva*s and the *kinnara*s are also visible. Let us search all these places. We must not lose our patience out of panic."

On hearing Lakṣmaṇa, Rāma in an angry mood joined a very powerful arrow to his bow and went out in the forest along with Lakṣmaṇa in their search operation. At one place they saw Jaṭāyū lying smeared with blood. Without recognizing Jaṭāyū, Rāma thought him to be a *rākṣasa* in the guise of vulture and raised his bow to kill him. Seeing Rāma in this menacing mood, Jaṭāyū in a piteous voice said, "Sītā Devī whom you are searching for and also my life have been carried away by Rāvaṇa." Saying this he narrated the story of abduction of Sītā, his battle with Rāvaṇa and the circumstances of his getting seriously injured at the hands of Rāvaṇa. He stated, "Rāvaṇa's broken bow, arrows and the parts of his chariot are lying here. Rāvaṇa's charioteer has also been killed by me. I fell down on the ground helplessly when Rāvaṇa severed my two wings with his sword. During this opportunity Rāvaṇa flew away with Sītā by the aerial path. Now you shall not gain anything by killing me."

Rāma and Lakṣmaṇa recognizing Jaṭāyū threw away their bows and embraced him while wailing. Later, on being asked by Rāma about the whereabouts of Sītā, Jaṭāyū in great pain said, "The sinful Rāvaṇa happens to be the king of the *rākṣasa*s. He has abducted Sītā by using his *māyā* power and escaped towards south. Under the influence of his *māyā* power all sides were covered with storm. I myself felt exhausted. But the moment of abduction was auspicious. If anything is lost or stolen at this moment, the owner is sure to get it back. You need not worry at all for Sītā. After destroying Rāvaṇa in war you shall certainly get her back early." Jaṭāyū was then in his last moments. Rāma wanted to know further details about Rāvaṇa. Jaṭāyū could only say Rāvaṇa was the son of Sage Viśravā and the brother of Kubera. Saying this Jaṭāyū breathed his last.

At the death of Jaṭāyū, Rāma in a sorrowful mind told Lakṣmaṇa, "Brother, Jaṭāyū was born many years ago. He was a true friend of us. He has given his life while trying to rescue Sītā from the hands of the sinful Rāvaṇa. The influence of time is inviolable. It is a different story in respect of the wise men. But even among the birds and animals there is no dearth of righteous elements. Jaṭāyū has died while doing good to me. My sorrow for Jaṭāyū is now deeper than that for Sītā's abduction. He is as venerable as our illustrious father." Thereafter, Rāma and Lakṣmaṇa cremated the body of Jaṭāyū on the bank of the Godāvarī and performed religious rites for the peace of his departed soul.

After performing the last rites of Jaṭāyū, Rāma and Lakṣmaṇa entered deep into the forest in search of Sītā. On the way they came across a fierce-looking deformed *rākṣasī*. She embraced Lakṣmaṇa and said he was her beloved husband. Lakṣmaṇa became enraged and severed with his sword her nose, ears and breasts. Crying loudly the *rākṣasī* hurriedly left the place.

Proceeding further Rāma and Lakṣmaṇa came to notice a huge *rākṣasa* on the way. The *rākṣasa* was a *kabandha* (headless). He had a large chest without any head and his mouth was embedded in the belly. He had one eye which was burning like the bright sun. The *rākṣasa* was then devouring the animals and birds of the forest by attracting them with his hands stretched out. As Rāma and Lakṣmaṇa came near, they were also attracted to him and firmly held. Rāma, however, was not perturbed. Lakṣmaṇa, on the other hand, became benumbed and asked Rāma to leave the place immediately. Assuring Lakṣmaṇa, Rāma without any loss of time severed the right hand of the *rākṣasa*. On this Lakṣmaṇa took courage and severed his left hand. The *rākṣasa*, without the hands, after getting the identity of Rāma and Lakṣmaṇa, narrated the story of his life. He said, "I am Danu, the son of Aditi (mother of the gods). Previously I was handsome and powerful. But I used to disturb the sages disregarding my reputation. On the curse of Sage Sthūlaśira I have lost my handsome appearance. On my prayer the sage told me I would regain my former appearance when Rāma, the son of Daśaratha would sever my hands. Thereafter on satisfying Lord Brahmā with my austerities, I got the boon of long life. But again I got deranged and went in war against Indra, who then broke my thighs with his *vajra* (thunder-bolt missile). When I begged for my life, Indra without killing me, had thrust my mouth together with the sharp teeth into the belly and had given me the power to attract animals and birds by stretching my hands to a long distance, to feed upon. Since then I am staying here feeding on the animals and birds. Indra told me I would die and depart to heaven when Rāma and Lakṣmaṇa would sever my two arms. Rāma, my death is imminent. I am now liberated only for you. Burn my body in a pit of fire. I shall then give you some good advice as a friend."

Rāma then told Kabandha, "If you know the person who has carried away Sītā and the place where she has been kept confined, then immediately disclose all details." Kabandha said in reply, "I am now bereft of divine vision. I am accordingly unable to remember the place of stay of Sītā at this moment. First you burn my body in fire. I shall get back my previous appearance only after my body is burnt and then only I shall be able to disclose all details about Sītā."

As Rāma and Lakṣmaṇa burned Kabandha's body, he regained his former handsome appearance and after wearing divine clothes and garlands, began to fly towards the heaven in a divine chariot sent from there. While flying along the aerial path, Kabandha said, "O Son of Raghu, I am telling you the means to rescue Sītā. In this world six methods like reconciliation, war, etc. are prescribed for the achievement of the objectives. You shall have to follow these methods to serve your purpose. It is the duty of every person in distress to establish proper relationship with another person who has also similarly fallen into distress. I am not finding any other means by which you can achieve your objectives. Rāma, I am also telling you how you shall be able to establish friendship with the desired person. Sugrīva is a monkey of great valour. He happens to be the son of the wife of Ṛṣyarāja with union with the Sun God. Vālī, the king of Kiṣkindhā (in the Bellary area of present Andhra Pradesh) who is the son of Indra, happens to be his elder brother. On being driven away from the kingdom by brother Vālī, Sugrīva is at present living, along with his four *vānara* companions, on the Ṛṣyamūka mountains on the bank of the river Pampā. He is patient, wise, radiant, generous, competent and very clever. This Sugrīva is your friend and he will come to your help in search of Sītā. Do not belittle him as the chief of the *vānara*s. Please immediately meet Sugrīva and enter into friendship with him by keeping the burning fire as witness. Vālī is his arch enemy. Out of his fear, Sugrīva is living on Ṛṣyamūka mountains. No place in this world is unknown to him. Sugrīva will search out Sītā from wherever — be it Rāvaṇa's palace or any other secret place — she is kept confined, and hand her over to you."

Kabandha thereafter explained the location of Ṛṣyamūka mountains and the route to follow to reach there. He said, "Lord Brahmā had built these mountains long back. The garden at the plateau of the mountains is known as 'Mataṅga forest'." Previously Sage Mataṅga used to live here with his disciples. Now they are no more. Only the maid by name Śabarī is living here. She is a pious woman engaged in religious austerities. Rāma, she is waiting for you in great eagerness. On seeing you she will depart to the heaven. There is a beautiful lake in the Ṛṣyamūka mountains. The noble Sugrīva along with his *vānara* companions lives on the bank of this lake. Sometimes he also lives on the peak of the mountains. Please meet him without any fear. Your purpose will be served." Saying this, Kabandha departed to the heaven.

Following the route indicated by Kabandha, Rāma and

Lakṣmaṇa reached the old hermitage of Sage Mataṅga. On entering inside they met Śabarī, who recognizing them, touched their feet and paid obeisance with great devotion. On being asked by Rāma whether she had conquered anger and desire by performing austerities, Śabarī said, "Rāma, on seeing you all my austerities have now been successful. Today my body is completely pure. Even the heaven is now under my control. I have collected flowers and other articles from the forest for your worship. Kindly accept and oblige." After accepting the offer, Rāma said, "I have already come to know about the austere lives of you and of your preceptor. I now want to see everything of this holy hermitage."

Accordingly Śabarī went round the hermitage with Rāma and Lakṣmaṇa and showed them all its important places, while narrating the glorious activities of the past sages. At the end with the permission of Rāma, Śabarī entered into the burning pyre and gave up her life. Thus ended the long waiting of Śabarī on her attaining salvation after seeing Rāma.

Rāma and Lakṣmaṇa, thereafter, proceeded towards the Mataṅga forest. On the way Rāma was again overwhelmed with grief remembering Sītā's distress in captivity as he saw pleasing sceneries of the forest and of the Pampā River flowing along with multi-coloured fishes playing in merriment. He thought, Sītā would have been very happy to see these beautiful sights. At one time he became benumbed and asked Lakṣmaṇa to return to Ayodhyā. He said without Sītā, it would not be possible for him to remain alive. Consoling Rāma, Lakṣmaṇa said, "O Aryan, hold your patience. Give up your grief. Lost things cannot be regained without efforts. In the world fortitude is strength. With this fortitude we shall rescue Sītā. Your soul is great and pure. Why are you forgetting that?" At the consoling words of Lakṣmaṇa, Rāma came to his senses. He silently proceeded along enjoying the beautiful sights all around. Ultimately Rāma and Lakṣmaṇa reached the foot of the Ṛṣyamūka mountain.

15

Alliance of Rāma with Sugrīva

SUGRĪVA saw Rāma and Lakṣmaṇa from the mountain top and told his *vānara* companions in a frightened mood, "These two armed persons were certainly Vālī's spies, who had come in disguise under the garb of tree barks to search for us in this forest." The *vānara*s looking below saw the two strangers and immediately took Sugrīva to a hiding place where they remained surrounding him. Later Hanumān who happened to be the principal advisor of Sugrīva told him, "O Lord of the *vānara*s, I am not finding Vālī among them. I think you should have no fear from Vālī. You are a wise person. With your wisdom you please judge the situation and take an appropriate decision." In reply Sugrīva said, "I am frightened thinking these two persons were Vālī's spies. The lives of even the well-intentioned people get endangered if the enemy in disguise is trusted without proper verification. First, we are to ascertain the intention of these two persons by deputing some agents in disguise." Saying this he asked Hanumān to himself find out, in the guise of an ordinary person, the real purpose of their visit here by talking to them.

Hanumān, accordingly, in the guise of a brāhmaṇa, appeared before Rāma and Lakṣmaṇa and said in a sweet voice, "O Great Saints, I find golden radiation coming out of your bodies. Both of you are strong and exquisitely handsome in appearance. You both are also armed with various weapons. Kindly disclose the purpose of your visit here in this deep forest." Finding Rāma and Lakṣmaṇa without any response, Hanumān again said, "I am telling you for your information, one pious *vānara* chief by name Sugrīva lives in these mountains. He has travelled round the world out of fear on being driven out of his kingdom by his elder brother Vālī. On his direction I have appeared before you. I happen to be his minister. I am the son of the Wind God — *vānara* by caste. I am capable of moving everywhere. I can also assume many forms. In order to perform some good works for Sugrīva I have come to you in the guise of a brāhmaṇa. I am telling you humbly, the great-souled Sugrīva is eager to establish friendship with you."

Hanumān was skilled in speech, virtuous and versed in Sanskrit. He was actually endowed with all the virtues. Later we shall come across accomplishment of many wonderful deeds of Hanumān. Rāma was very much pleased with the words of Hanumān. He whispered to Lakṣmaṇa, "Brother, Hanumān has come with the message of the same great *vānara* chief Sugrīva whom we are searching for. His art of speaking is faultless. There was no grammatical mistake whatsoever. Choice of words was flawless. It is possible only for a person versed in the Vedas to express his mind so methodically. I have not noticed any sign of suspicion in his eyes and the face or in his body language. His words are pleasing and beneficial. You exchange words with him in a sweet voice."

As directed by Rāma, Lakṣmaṇa disclosed their identity to Hanumān and after narrating the circumstances of their banishment to the forest, the abduction of Sītā, their meeting with Danu, son of Diti and the latter's instruction to seek help from Sugrīva for the rescue of Sītā, said, "O Hanumān, today the illustrious Rāma, the eldest son of King Daśaratha, has come here to seek the help of Sugrīva. I would request the *vānara* chief Sugrīva to come to the help of Rāma in his terrible calamity along with his followers." Assuring Lakṣmaṇa of all help, Hanumān said, "Sugrīva, the son of the Sun God will help Rāma in all respects in the rescue of Sītā." On his request Rāma and Lakṣmaṇa agreed to meet Sugrīva and accordingly Hanumān, assuming his original form, took them on his back and came to Ṛṣyamūka mountains.

Thereafter Hanumān went to the hiding place of Sugrīva and while informing him of the arrival of Rāma and Lakṣmaṇa, narrated the glory of their family, the circumstances of their banishment to the forest, abduction of Sītā and Rāma's request for his help in her rescue as also all other details of his talks with Lakṣmaṇa. He requested Sugrīva to cordially welcome them saying they were highly venerable persons.

Sugrīva on being briefed by Hanumān came out of the hiding on assuming a graceful appearance and told Rāma in a pleasing voice, "I have heard from Hanumān about your various qualities. I am a monkey. It is indeed a great honour to me that you are eager to establish friendship with me. If you really want to have friendship with me then kindly accept my extended hand." Rāma with a happy mind readily shook hands with Sugrīva and embraced him. Thereafter Rāma and Sugrīva went round the fire ignited by Hanumān and formally entered into friendship.

After the ceremony, Sugrīva said, "O Rāma, from today you are a friend of mine. From now on there remains no distinction between our happiness and misery." Sugrīva then pulled down a branch of the tree and after taking his seat on it along with Rāma and Lakṣmaṇa said, "Friend, I have serious enmity with my elder bother Vālī. He has driven me out of my kingdom. He has even taken away my wife. Out of fear of Vālī, I have taken shelter in this mountain-fort. You please remove all my fear from the mind." Assuring Sugrīva, Rāma said, "You remain certain, I shall kill Vālī who has carried away your wife." Delightedly Sugrīva said, "I have heard from Hanumān the entire story of abduction of your wife by the *rākṣasa*s. I promise, I would rescue your wife and hand her over to you. One day I along with my *vānara* companions saw a cruel *rākṣasa* carrying away one woman by the aerial path. She was then loudly crying uttering the words 'O Rāma, O Lakṣmaṇa. Seeing us below, she dropped a scarf and some gold ornaments on the mountains. We have preserved these articles in the cave. You may identify the articles if you see them.'" Sugrīva soon produced the articles before Rāma and Lakṣmaṇa. Rāma recognizing the articles to be those of Sītā, fell down on the ground losing his composure. Rāma told Lakṣmaṇa, certainly Sītā had thrown these articles below when she was being carried away. Lakṣmaṇa said, "As I was daily paying obeisance to Sītā's feet, I could recognize only the two anklets of her feet. Other articles I am unable to recognize."

Stricken with sorrow as Rāma wanted to know the location of Rāvaṇa, Sugrīva said, "I do not know his family history, his location or his power and strength. Yet I promise, I would rescue Sītā and hand her over to you. O friend, have patience giving up all grief. It is unbecoming of a person of your stature to show such signs of weakness. Being an insignificant monkey myself I am not showing any sign of grief even after losing my own wife. You are a great soul, patient and self-restrained. What shall I say about you? With patience control all your grief. In danger, financial stringency or deadly crisis he who holds his patience by dint of wisdom, is never overtaken by grief. Take resort to your inherent strength. Do never give indulgence to grief. He who is overtaken by grief, loses all peace. He also loses his strength. Kindly act as I said as a friend. I am not giving you any advice; I am only telling you some good words."

At the consoling words of Sugrīva, Rāma regained his normal senses. Embracing him, he said, "Friend, you have done your duty as a well-wishing sympathetic friend. It is a rare fortune to get a friend like you in such a danger. My only request to you is that there must not be any delay is rescuing Sītā. O Lord of the *vānaras*, please know it for certain, my promise given to you will be fully implemented. Vālī will certainly be killed by me" Sugrīva was happy with the assurance of Rāma.

The next day in course of discussions, Rāma wanted to know more about Sugrīva's sorrows and sufferings including the background of his enmity with Vālī. In reply Sugrīva said, "My eldest brother Vālī is an extremely powerful person. He subdued and conquered many enemies. Our father used to love him very much. I myself also looked upon him with great devotion. On the death of our father Vālī was unanimously crowned as the king of the *vānara* kingdom, while I was installed as the crown prince. In the beginning everything was proceeding smoothly under Vālī's strong administration. Earlier there was a powerful *dānava* (demon) by name Dundubhi. One day he attacked and destroyed the main gate of Vālī's palace when a battle ensued between the two. In the battle Dundubhi was severely wounded and his body was thrown away by Vālī to a distance one *yojana* (about 12 km) in the centre of the hermitage of Sage Mataṅga (details later). Dundubhi's son Māyāvī was also equally strong like his father. Moreover, he was in possession of *māyā* power. Over a woman there was a dispute between Vālī and Māyāvī. One night Māyāvī appeared in front of the gate of Kiṣkindhā and with a loud roar challenged Vālī for a fight. Disregarding the advice of others not to venture out in the night, Vālī left the palace in a great rage to kill Māyāvī. Out of love I also accompanied him. On seeing us two brothers, Māyāvī, out of fear, fled in a hurry and entered into an impassable mountain cave. We also reached the mouth of the cave after some time. Asking me to stay outside, Vālī alone entered inside. Even after one year, Vālī did not come out of the cave. I also waited for him patiently. One day on seeing blood coming out of the cave, I thought, Vālī had been killed at the hands of Māyāvī. With a sorrowful mind I returned to Kiṣkindhā. Vālī's ministers then installed me as the king of the *vānara* kingdom. One day Vālī suddenly returned to Kiṣkindhā and became furious on seeing me occupying the throne. I sought to explain the circumstances leading to my departure from the mouth of the cave. I also wanted to return the kingdom to him. But he did not listen to any of my pleas. He imprisoned my trusted ministers and banished me from the kingdom. He also took away my wife.

Being exiled with only one piece of apparel, I am now moving from place to place, out of fear of Vālī, along with some of my companions. Rāma, I am extremely stricken with fear of Vālī. Kill Vālī and remove my fear."

On hearing Sugrīva, Rāma said "I fully realize the depth of your grief in the context of my own distress. I shall remove all your distress and grief by killing Vālī."

Though somewhat relieved at the promise of Rāma, Sugrīva was not fully sure whether he (Rāma) would be able to kill Vālī. He thus very intelligently tried to gauge the power and strength of Rāma. Describing the power and strength of Vālī, he referred to the death of valiant *dānava* Dundubhi at his hands and his body being thrown away by him to the far away hermitage of Sage Mataṅga. Continuing he said, "Sage Mataṅga on seeing the blood-smeared body of Dundubhi in his hermitage, flew into a rage and cursed that the fool who had defiled the hermitage and destroyed the trees and other articles, would meet sure death if he ventured to come within one *yojana* of his hermitage. His followers would also meet the same fate. Vālī's followers who were living in these mountains, immediately left the place and reported the matter to Vālī. Following this curse, Vālī and his followers stopped visiting R̥ṣyamūka mountains. On learning that these mountains were out of bounds for Vālī and his followers, I have come down here with my companions and am living without any fear of Vālī. Rāma, there is no end of Vālī's power and strength. You are seeing seven palm trees in front of you. Vālī is capable of making the trees bare of leaves by shaking them by dint of his physical strength. Please try to realize how you shall kill Vālī in any battle."

On hearing Sugrīva, Lakṣmaṇa said with a smile, " Sugrīva, what work you want Rāma to perform so that he can create confidence in you about his capability of killing Vālī?" Sugrīva said in reply, "Rāma's capability to kill Vālī would be proved without doubt if he can sever at least one of these palm trees by only one of his arrows and if he can throw by his feet the heap of bones of dead Dundubhi to a distance of 12 hundred *dhanus* (one *dhanu* = 4 cubits)." Sugrīva then turned to Rāma and said, "Friend, I am aware of the power and strength of my brother Vālī. I also have confidence in your heroism. But I have no personal experience of your valour. It is not my purpose to belittle you or to put any fear in your mind. I am very much worried at the terrible activities of Vālī. Your words are enough proof, you are capable of killing Vālī."

Rāma then with a little smile said, "I am immediately giving you credible proof of my might." Saying this, he effortlessly lifted with his toes the heap of bones of Dundubhi and threw them away to a distance of 10 *yojanas*. On seeing Rāma's work, Sugrīva again said, "Dundubhi's body being left in the open for a long time has dried up and become light like grass. This is why it has been easy for you to throw the bones to such a distance. But when Vālī threw the body, it was wet and had flesh and as such its weight was very heavy. From your work I could not decide with certainty who is more powerful between you and Vālī. I shall get an idea of your power if you can sever by your arrow the palm tree standing in front of us."

Rāma immediately struck the tree with his arrow. The arrow not only severed one tree, but it passed through as many as seven other trees, and after piercing the mountains reached the *pātāla* (underworld). In no time the arrow again returned to the quiver of Rāma. On witnessing this wonderful work of Rāma, Sugrīva was struck with utter surprise. He immediately touched the feet of Rāma and with folded hands said, "You are the supreme hero. You are superior to all others versed in the use of arms. You are capable of defeating even Indra and the gods, not to speak of Vālī. I am now free from all grief on getting a friend like you. Rāma, kindly kill my greatest enemy Vālī today itself."

16

Death of Vālī

THEREAFTER Rāma, Lakṣmaṇa and Sugrīva along with Hanumān and others went to Kiṣkindhā. While Rāma and Lakṣmaṇa remained hidden behind a tree with their bows and arrows, Sugrīva proceeded to the main gate of the palace raising a loud roar like a tiger. On hearing the roar, Vālī came out when a battle ensued between the two. Rāma could not recognize who between the two brothers was Vālī as they looked alike and as such he refrained from shooting any arrow. Meanwhile, Sugrīva on being defeated in the battle fled towards the Ṛṣyamūka mountains for fear of life without meeting Rāma and Lakṣmaṇa. Vālī pursued Sugrīva up to the foot of the mountains and returned to Kiṣkindhā out of fear of the curse of Sage Mataṅga. Thus Sugrīva escaped sure death. Soon after when Rāma and Lakṣmaṇa met Sugrīva along with Hanumān, he said with great regret, "Rāma, you boasted about your valour, you would kill Vālī; but you did not shoot any arrow on him. What is this behaviour of yours? Had I known that you would not kill Vālī, I would have remained here without going to Kiṣkindhā. For you only I had to suffer so badly today at the hands of Vālī."

Expressing regret Rāma said, "Friend, your and Vālī's voice, look, words, dress, etc. being alike, I could not recognize who was Vālī. Accordingly I refrained from using my arrow lest it should kill you. Friend, in this dense forest you are my only refuge. Can I do any harm to you? Without any fear you again immediately engage yourself in battle with Vālī. This time you shall put on some distinguishing marks so that I can easily recognize you." Turning to Lakṣmaṇa Rāma said, "In this forest I find in plenty beautiful *gajapuṣpī* (a kind of creeper flowers). Lakṣmaṇa, you prepare a garland of these flowers and put it around the neck of Sugrīva." After Lakṣmaṇa put the garland around Sugrīva's neck, they all again proceeded to Kiṣkindhā.

As directed by Rāma, Sugrīva on reaching Kiṣkindhā that night itself, challenged Vālī for battle with a loud roar. Rāma and Lakṣmaṇa, as before, remained in hiding behind a tree. On hearing the roar, Vālī came out of the palace for the purpose of attacking Sugrīva. At this moment Tārā, Vālī's wife warned him saying, "O Great Hero, give up your anger. I do not think it proper for you to go for battle with Sugrīva this night itself. You may go for the fight tomorrow morning if you are determined for a fight. Sugrīva on being defeated and oppressed by you has again returned for a fight. This has caused apprehension in my mind. His arrogant call for fight with a loud roar, indicates he has been assured of help by someone else. I am also giving you another beneficial information. The other day our son Aṅgada while moving in the forest, had come to know from the spies that the two forest-dwelling sons of Daśaratha, king of Ayodhyā, named Rāma and Lakṣmaṇa, had reached Ṛṣyamūka mountains to do some good works for Sugrīva. Of the two brothers, Rāma is reported to be a great hero and invincible in war. He is also said to be repository of many noble qualities and a friend of all who are in distress. It would not be proper for you to antagonise Rāma. I am also giving you another piece of good advice. Kindly listen and accept it. Settle all disputes with Sugrīva and install him as the crown prince. Always remember, Sugrīva is your best friend and well-wisher. At the same time establish friendship with Rāma."

Sharply rebuking Tārā, Vālī said, "My arch enemy Sugrīva is roaring outside for a fight. I am unable to withstand his arrogance any more. You are worried for me apprehending danger from Rāma. My trust is that the virtuous Rāma will not be involved in any sinful act. I have no enmity with him. You return to the palace without fear. I am returning after defeating Sugrīva just now."

As Vālī proceeded further, a fierce battle ensued between the two brothers. In course of the battle which continued for long, Sugrīva became physically exhausted. He began to look around for Rāma's help. Rāma then recognizing Sugrīva with the garland around his neck, shot Vālī from behind the tree piercing his chest. Falling down on the ground on being severely wounded, Vālī saw Rāma and Lakṣmaṇa and told Rāma in a harsh tone, "Rāma, you have killed me unjustly though you are said to be a virtuous person. I was fighting with another person. I have not attacked you. You possess all the royal qualities. Because of all these qualities of yours and of your noble lineage, I was certain no harm would come to me from you and accordingly I, disregarding all warnings of Tārā, got engaged in battle with Sugrīva. And you hiding behind a tree, unjustly shot me with arrow. Now I understand my assessment was wrong. You are actually a great villain. Under the garb of a pious man you are really sinful. I am born in the monkey clan. We move in the forest and live on the forest fruits and roots. You stay in village and live on rice. There is no justification for you to kill me. War generally breaks out for grabbing land and property. You have certainly no desire to obtain our fruits and roots. You are despotic, mean-minded and restless. You have no greatness befitting a king. Like a serpent striking a sleeping person, you have killed me remaining unseen. I understand, for the good of Sugrīva, you have killed me. If I was told about the rescue of Sītā, I could have done it in only one day. I would have brought Rāvaṇa here binding his neck with a rope. All living creatures are certain to die. I have no sorrow for my death. Rāma, try to understand what you would gain from my death."

Saying all this, Vālī's mouth dried up. Simultaneously the pain in the body caused by the strike of the arrow, became unbearable. Vālī remained silent.

Rāma, while defending his action, said, "O king of the *vānaras*! you are completely ignorant of virtue and vice, and of the worldly customs and behaviour. Due to this ignorance and because of restlessness befitting a monkey, you are unnecessarily speaking against me. You may know this entire world is under the control of the kings of the Ikṣvāku dynasty. Presently the great truthful Bharata is governing this world. Under his orders we who are also virtuous, are punishing those who have deviated from the righteous path. You are lustful and have committed contemptible deeds disregarding the duties of a king. All virtuous people treat their younger brothers and their own virtuous disciples, as their own sons. But you, on renouncing the basic tenets of *sanātana dharma* (eternal religion), have carried away Rumā, the wife of your younger brother Sugrīva who is like your own daughter-in-law. Death is the just punishment for a person like you who is licentious and has deviated from the righteous path. There is another reason for your death. From behind the trees and without coming into the open I have killed you stealthily. This act may be considered improper by you; but I have no mental remorse or grief for my act. In the hunting of the wild animals and birds of the forest, the people openly or secretly use nets or snares and other deceitful means. The question of the conduct of these wild animals and birds or their fleeing for fear of life, is here completely immaterial. The meat-eating people do kill them for their own living. The virtuous kings have been hunting them in the same way from time immemorial. There is nothing wrong in it. I have killed you treating you as a *śākhāmṛga* (a kind of monkey). For this grief or sorrow is meaningless."

Realizing the truth of Rāma's words Vālī said, "O Great Soul, your statement is true no doubt. You are fully conversant with the tenets of religion. I belong to the low monkey clan. I am unable to give any reply to your words. Mistakenly I spoke harsh words against you. Kindly forgive me for this. I am in the forefront of those who have deviated from the path of *dharma*. Deliver me by teaching religious tenets. Rāma, I have only one request to you. Protect my son Aṅgada. He is a mere boy — as dear as my own life. Treat Sugrīva and Aṅgada equally. And also ensure, Tārā, my virtuous wife is not humiliated by Sugrīva in any way. She forbade me not to go for any duel with Sugrīva. As ordained by fate I got killed by you disregarding her just advice."

Realizing Vālī had attained enlightenment, Rāma by way of assurance told him, "O Lord of the *vānara*s, do not think I did commit anything wrong by killing you secretly. And you also forget, you are guilty of misdeed by going against religious tenets. I do possess wide experience in religious matters. Listen carefully. He who punishes a person deserving punishment and the person who unhesitatingly accepts the punishment — both of them — enjoy complete bliss for their respective duties. You are now free from all sins by getting this punishment. Give up all your grief, mental delusion and fear. None can transgress the consequences of the actions of his previous life. You may rest assured, no harm would touch your son Aṅgada. He will grow in the midst of love and affection of Sugrīva and myself." Being pleased with the just words of Rāma, Vālī said, "Rāma, forgive me for my words spoken against you out of ignorance."

On the death of Vālī, his wife Tārā, overwhelmed with grief, began to lament narrating his various qualities. Seeing her pitiable condition, Sugrīva felt a terrible remorse at the unjust killing of his brother. He told Rāma, "O king, your promise to give the kingdom to me has been fulfilled. Previously I was angry with my brother for insulting me and wanted his death. But he, I must admit, did never try to kill me; he only wanted me to leave the kingdom. Now on his death I am deeply mortified. I am actually a hated destroyer of my own clan and stand deprived of all respect from my fellow countrymen. Aṅgada, my brother's beloved son will now die in a state of terrible grief. Tārā too will not live long without her husband and the son. In the situation I have decided to give up my own life in the burning fire. In my absence the *vānaras* on your order will help you in the search of Sītā. Rāma, kindly allow me to enter into the fire."

Rāma on hearing the piteous words of Sugrīva, became utterly bewildered and on looking around with tears in his eyes saw Tārā, stricken with grief, lying on the ground embracing her dead husband. The ministers then lifted Tārā and were escorting her to the palace. On the way Tārā saw Rāma and told him, "O Hero, you are blessed with all the virtues. None is capable of knowing you easily. Kill me with the same arrow with which you have killed Vālī. Without me his soul will never rest in peace. As you are in grief without Sītā, Vālī too is in grief without me even after departing to the heaven. I am Vālī's soul. On my death Vālī's death will be fulfilled. I assure you, no sin will accrue to you for killing a woman. O king of the kings, I shall not be able to live long without my husband."

Consoling grieving Sugrīva, Tārā and Aṅgada, Rāma said, "It is of no use to mourn for the dead. Try to understand, destiny or luck is at the root of all events. None can transgress it. The pious men are aware, all joys and sorrows are the results of one's own actions according to the laws of time. Vālī enjoyed royal wealth and happiness being endowed with all virtues of reconciliation and generosity. Now by dint of his noble deeds, he has on his death acquired the right of enjoying the heavenly bliss. For this it is not proper for you to grieve. Immediately arrange for his funeral." Thereafter Aṅgada under the supervision of Sugrīva cremated the body of Vālī with the help of the *vānaras*. Rāma in a sorrowful mind offered oblation of water for the peace of the departed soul of Vālī.

On completion of the last rites of Vālī, Hanumān appeared before Rāma along with the *vānara* leaders and told him, "O great Rāma, because of your grace, Sugrīva has gained this large ancestral kingdom of Kiṣkindhā. Now kindly permit him to be installed on the throne after entering the palace with his friends. You also kindly enter this beautiful palace and increase the delight of others by your gracious presence on this solemn occasion."

Rāma said in reply, "O Hanumān, I am honour-bound by the orders of our father. I would live in the forest for fourteen years and not in any village or town. You all enter the palace and install Sugrīva as the king." Turning to Sugrīva, Rāma said, "Sugrīva, you install Aṅgada as the crown prince. He is the eldest son of your brother Vālī and equal to his father Indra in power and strength. He is the fittest person to be the crown prince. Now monsoons are expected soon. During these four months of rains, long journey is not suitable. You enter the palace, while I am returning to Ṛṣyamūka mountains along with Lakṣmaṇa. After the rains in the month of *Kārttika* (seventh month of the year) you may take steps for the search and rescue of Sītā." Sugrīva promised to do the needful and on entering the palace installed himself as the king. In compliance with Rāma's direction, Aṅgada was made the crown prince. Rāma then moved to Ṛṣyamūka mountains along with Lakṣmaṇa and waited patiently for the rainy season to end.

Rāma's friendship with Sugrīva and the latter's installation as the King of Kiṣkindhā on Vālī's death which paved the way for the rescue of Sītā, are the two important incidents requiring proper elaboration. We are aware, on the direction of Kabandha, Rāma and Lakṣmaṇa arrived at the Ṛṣyamūka mountains to seek Sugrīva's help in the search and rescue of Sītā. Though Rāma was assured, he would get all help from Sugrīva, he was not certain how far he (Sugrīva) would be of real help to him in such an extremely difficult task. We know, Sugrīva and his *vānara* companions first suspected unknown Rāma and Lakṣmaṇa to be Vālī's spies with intent to cause harm to them and shifted to a safe hide-out out of fear. Sugrīva who was intelligent with a deep common sense, did not, however, take recourse to any reckless action on the spur of the moment. He instead in consultation with his companions decided to ascertain the intention of the two foreigners. We have seen how Hanumān, Sugrīva's minister, on his direction appeared before Rāma and Lakṣmaṇa in the guise of an ascetic and spoke to them completely winning over their confidence. We are wonder-struck to see how intelligently and meticulously Hanumān conducted himself during the talks. As Hanumān talked with Lakṣmaṇa, Rāma standing nearby carefully noticed his demeanour, body language, expression of his eyes and the face and his use of flawless Sanskrit and was convinced about his sincerity of purpose. Rāma also realized Hanumān was not an ordinary person. He was actually a learned person with many qualities and could be fully relied upon. Rāma readily agreed to meet Sugrīva who was said to be eager to seek Rāma's help to regain his own wife and the kingdom from Vālī. When Sugrīva met Rāma, he in course of talks immediately understood, Rāma was the right person who was capable of helping him in realizing his objectives. Rāma similarly understood, Sugrīva would help him in the search and rescue of Sītā with his *vānara senā* once he was installed on the throne of Kiṣkindhā on Vālī's death. On Rāma assuring Sugrīva he would kill Vālī, friendship was established between them. Establishment of friendship between the two unknown persons in such a short time underlining their deep understanding of human nature, was indeed rare and novel. This also indicated, both Rāma and Sugrīva possessed great presence of mind and shrewdness befitting experienced intelligence operators. We in the intelligence had occasions to establish friendship with unknown strangers using similar methods.

We shall now analyse the incident of death of Vālī at the hands of Rāma. In this regard we have heard the explanation of Rāma and the eventual acceptance of the same by Vālī who even asked for forgiveness of Rāma for using harsh words against him. We, however, are unable to accept Rāma's role in the death of Vālī from the core of our heart. In the society he stands condemned for his unethical action. In the Mahābhārata war, for the death of venerable Guru Droṇācarya due to the false statement of Yudhiṣṭhira, Arjuna cursed him (Yudhiṣṭhira) saying he would remain ever condemned for his falsehood as Rāma was condemned for killing Vālī by treachery. Yudhiṣṭhira till his death repented for his action. Rāma principally killed Vālī for three reasons. First, Rāma maintioned, Vālī had committed a great offence in carrying away Sugrīva's wife Rumā. Second, Vālī's death was in fulfilment of Rāma's promise solemnly given to Sugrīva. The third reason was somewhat laughable. Rāma claimed to have killed Vālī by deceit treating him as an ordinary forest animal just like a hunter. According to Rāma there was nothing wrong in it.

It is no doubt utterly wrong on the part of Vālī to take Sugrīva's wife as his concubine on his banishment from the kingdom. It may, however, be mentioned here the customs of the *vānara* society are different from those of human society. In the *vānara* society it is a normal custom for the victorious king to treat the wives and the women of the vanquished king as his concubines and as such Vālī as the king took Sugrīva's wife as his concubine on his defeat and banishment. It may be pointed out (details later) Sugrīva after the death of Vālī on regaining the kingdom, had no qualms in taking Tārā, Vālī's wife as his concubine. Rāma, however, completely ignored this wrong action of Sugrīva and took no steps against him. Aṅgada, Vālī's son however, all along harboured a deep sorrow in his mind. It is surprising despite Rāma's strong denunciation of Vālī's action in taking Sugrīva's wife as his concubine, Sugrīva did not hesitate to commit the same act in taking Tārā as his concubine. It is no doubt stated in the *Rāmāyaṇa,* Tārā willingly accepted this position. This rather indicates the prevailing custom in the *vānara* society to take as concubines the wives and the women of the vanquished kings.

Now the controversial death of Vālī at the hands of Rāma. We know, Rāma assured Sugrīva, he would kill Vālī. In the death of Vālī, Rāma's promise given to Sugrīva was fulfilled. It was incumbent on his part as a kṣatriya king to keep his promise in all circumstances. But Rāma had no enmity with Vālī. Why should he decide to make such a serious promise of killing Vālī only on the basis of Sugrīva's charges against him and on Sugrīva's assurance of help in rescuing Sītā, without fully judging its implications? It seems to be an instance of instant payment against a post-dated cheque. Apparently Rāma in utter distress at the abduction of Sītā was eager to grab any offer of help in the rescue of Sītā as a drowning man catches at a straw. Rāma's decision to kill Vālī apparently stemmed from this consideration. We are aware when Vālī and Sugrīva were engaged in fighting, Rāma hiding himself behind a tree shot dead Vālī without coming into the open. It was an established convention in those days, no third person would intervene in a fight between two warriors. This was particularly mentioned in the *Mahābhārata.* This convention was certainly in vogue in the *Rāmāyaṇa* days also though there was no specific mention about it. It was expected of the virtuous Rāma, he would scrupulously follow this principle of war. But he did not. He instead killed Vālī stealthily without engaging himself in any frontal combat — a despicable act indeed deserving condemnation. The people and the society have never supported Rāma's action for which he has remained ever condemned.

Vālī, as told by Sugrīva, was a very powerful person. His possessed immense physical strength. Besides, he was a skilled wrestler. On the other hand Rāma, though strong physically, had no expertise in wrestling. He was versed in the art and science of archery. His aim was infallible. Leaving aside his divine powers, in wrestling Rāma was no match to Vālī. Had he engaged himself with Vālī in wrestling, the result might have been disastrous for him. When Rāma's aim was to kill Vālī, he had no other alternative than to strike him with his arrow. From this standpoint Rāma was perfectly justified in his action.

We may now discuss certain other issues in the context of Vālī's physical strength. Once Rāvaṇa in course of his military campaign arrived at Kiṣkindhā to have a fight with Vālī who was then the king with Sugrīva as the crown prince. On Rāvaṇa's arrival, Sugrīva and the other *vānara* leaders told him, for him (Rāvaṇa) there was no suitable rival present now at Kiṣkindhā; Vālī, his actual rival, had gone to the four seas to perform his usual evening worship and would soon return. While requesting Rāvaṇa to wait, they warned him, he would meet sure death if he (Rāvaṇa) dared to have a fight with Vālī. Rāvaṇa was also informed, at this time Vālī would be available at the bank of the south sea. Rāvaṇa after sharply rebuking the *vānara* leaders for their derogatory words, immediately left for the south sea by his *puṣpaka vimāna*. On arrival Rāvaṇa after alighting from the *vimāna* saw Vālī in meditation some distance away and stealthily proceeded towards him to catch him. Vālī then suddenly noticed Rāvaṇa and realizing his evil design, remained motionless feigning to be engrossed in deep meditation. As Rāvaṇa came near, Vālī swiftly held him in his armpit and rose to the sky. Taken completely aback, Rāvaṇa despite his efforts to belabour him with his sharp nails, failed to come out of Vālī's clutches. Rāvaṇa's followers in the *vimāna* also unsuccessfully tried to rescue him. In this way Vālī holding Rāvaṇa firmly in his armpit performed his worship also on the banks of the other three seas. Thereafter Vālī returned to his hermitage near Kiṣkindhā and released Rāvaṇa there.

On being released, Rāvaṇa, the conqueror of the three worlds lavishly praised Vālī for his power and strength. He said, "O great king of the *vānaras*, you are as great as Indra, the king of the gods. I am the king of the *rākṣasas*, I came to have a fight with you. Now I have got a taste of the fight. I myself got confined in your armpit. You held me as if I was an animal and showed me around the four seas. At this I felt no fatigue at all. It is not possible for anyone else except you to carry me in this way. I have seen with my own eyes your wonderful power and strength. With fire as the witness I am fervently seeking your friendship. From today my kingdom and wealth will remain under the joint control of both of us." Vālī readily agreed with Rāvaṇa's proposal. Then a fire was lit and keeping it as the witness, the two great kings — Rāvaṇa, the King of the *rākṣasas* of Laṅkā and Vālī, the King of the *vānaras* of Kiṣkindhā — were united as brothers. After the ceremony, Vālī brought Rāvaṇa to Kiṣkindhā where Rāvaṇa stayed for one month enjoying his hospitality. Thereafter, Rāvaṇa's ministers, with the approval of Vālī, brought him to Laṅkā.

It may be recalled, Vālī on being wounded by Rāma's arrow said had he known about Sītā's abduction by Rāvaṇa earlier, he would have easily ensured her rescue in no time by bringing Rāvaṇa here with his neck tied with a rope. This was not a mere boastful claim. Vālī had actually that power. But due to the twist of circumstances, Rāma had to seek the help of Sugrīva for the rescue of Sītā. We think, the promise to kill Vālī was a hasty decision on the part of Rāma. He as a person of self-composed nature, was expected to proceed in the matter after deeper deliberation. It appears, had Rāma known about Rāvaṇa's defeat at the hands of Vālī and his subsequent friendship with him before, he would not have perhaps taken the decision to kill Vālī. Surprisingly Sugrīva completely suppressed from Rāma this fact of Rāvaṇa's friendship with Vālī after his defeat. Vālī was a pious simple-hearted warrior. He had great devotion for Rāma. He was sure, Rāma would never take recourse to any unethical means to kill him. This was why Vālī came out of the palace in the night itself to fight with Sugrīva disregarding wife Tārā's warning. Besides, Vālī was a benevolent ruler. The people were safe and happy under his rule. He had no support to the nefarious activities of Rāvaṇa. We feel, Rāma, a person of great wisdom and knowledge, could have easily brought about a rapprochement between the two brothers, which also was the wish of Tārā, a woman of great foresight. In that case with the combined efforts of Vālī and Sugrīva, Sītā's rescue would have been quickened and she would not have to languish in captivity in great distress at Laṅkā for almost a year. Rāma's mental agony at the absence of Sītā would also have ended soon. On deeper consideration, it appears it is Rāma who gained nothing from the death of Vālī — that too by unethical means. Sugrīva was in fact the actual gainer. He got Vālī killed by Rāma and in the process gained the kingdom of Kiṣkindhā, which, otherwise, was an impossible task for him. The forecast of Vālī that Rāma would not gain anything from his death, came to be true. Rāma truly for his act of unethical killing of Vālī, has remained ever contemptible in the society.

We are aware, Sugrīva ascended to the throne of Kiṣkindhā at the request of the ministers and other *vānara* leaders when he returned to the capital thinking Vālī had been killed by Māyāvī inside the cave. Sugrīva should have understood, a person of superhuman power like Vālī could not be killed by an ordinary demon. He should have waited further at the mouth of the cave for the return of Vālī from inside the cave as ordered by him. On return to the capital after killing the demon, Vālī finding Sugrīva occupying the throne, became enraged and banished him from the kingdom. The question may arise how far it was justified for Sugrīva to occupy the throne without fully ascertaining the truth or otherwise of Vālī's death. He only acted on the presumption that Vālī had lost his life at the hands of Māyāvī inside the cave only after seeing blood stream coming out. Why did he not initiate exhaustive investigation inside the cave with the help of the *vānara* army? Till the truth was found out, he could have ruled the kingdom as Vālī's representative without formally occupying the throne, following the example of Bharata who governed the Ayodhyā kingdom as Rāma's representative without being installed as the king ignoring everybody's request to the contrary. It would be reasonable to suspect, Sugrīva all along cherished a desire to occupy the throne and he grabbed the first opportunity provided by the temporary absence of Sugrīva. His subsequent conduct seems to confirm our suspicion. Only after Vālī death, Sugrīva understood his folly and expressed his desire to give up his life in the burning pyre. This lends further confirmation to his wrong doings against his own brother. Evidently his conduct as a brother is in sharp contrast to that of Bharata. In whatever way we may interpret Sugrīva's controversial role, there is, however, no gainsaying the fact, he was a man of many virtues. He remained ever loyal and faithful to Rāma. After initial dithering, he, as promised, deputed Hanumān and other *vānara* leaders and the *vānara* army to different directions in search of Sītā. He and his *vānara* army particularly Hanumān immensely contributed to the destruction of the formidable *rākṣasa* army, which helped Rāma and Lakṣmaṇa to destroy Rāvaṇa and other *rākṣasa* warriors leading to the eventual rescue of Sītā from captivity.

Rāma's third justification for killing Vālī as forest animal like a hunter was palpably untenable. We are aware of many noble qualities of Vālī as also of his power and strength. He defeated Rāvaṇa, the conqueror of the three worlds. On account of various divine reasons he and his followers got this physical form of monkey. He could, however, assume human form any time. It would be wrong to treat him as an ordinary forest animal. It appears, had he got the slightest indication of Rāma's presence before he was shot, Vālī could have easily held him in his armpit pre-empting any action on his part as he did in the case of Rāvaṇa. Rāma could save himself from this predicament as Vālī failed to notice him, hidden as he was behind a tree, and also because he was deeply engrossed in the fight with Sugrīva.

Over the death of Vālī, Rāma had also his share of grief. Praying for the peace of his soul, he offered oblation of water. In an effort to assuage the grief of Tārā and the other *vānara* leaders, Rāma took steps to install Aṅgada as the crown prince. He assured Tārā, Aṅgada would grow under the loving care of Sugrīva and himself and there was nothing to fear for his safety. All this appears to be an admission of his guilt in killing Vālī by deceitful means. Vālī's acceptance of Rāma's justification of his action against him on the eve of his death, was in fact a proof of his own greatness and reiteration of his devotion to Rāma. It appears, the gravely injured Vālī was overwhelmed by the words of Rāma, a person of superior personality and knowledge This has in no case enhanced Rāma's prestige and stature which remained mired in his unethical act. Rāma's explanation to the dying Vālī on the tenets of religion sounded hollow and irrelevant in the prevailing mournful atmosphere.

We are aware, Vālī's agents were able to collect timely information about the arrival of Rāma and Lakṣmaṇa at Ṛṣyamūka mountains as also Rāma's virtues and his power and strength and his friendship with Sugrīva. They passed on the information to Aṅgada. This was indeed a marvellous intelligence operation in an area which was out of bounds for Vālī and his followers on the curse of Sage Mātaṅga. It appears, the agents were deployed around the prohibited area to maintain visual watch on the developments in the mountains. On the basis of this information obtained from Aṅgada, we know, Tārā unsuccessfully tried to prevent Vālī from going out for a fight with Sugrīva. Vālī could not conceive Rāma's friendship with Sugrīva would take precedence over his sense of justice and fair-play. His death, unfortunate as it was, was not due to any lack of information about his impending danger, but to circumstances beyond his control. In any case we cannot but praise Vālī's intelligence service for its ability to collect information even in the extremely difficult situation.

Now we shall revert to the main story. Sugrīva on gaining the prosperous Kiṣkindhā kingdom, was soon fascinated by the company of the palace women. He fell prey to evil conduct and became indifferent to his responsibilities as the king. He showed no interest in the collection of revenue. All the royal duties were now in the hands of the ministers. Alarmed at the moral degradation of Sugrīva, the virtuous Hanumān at the end of the monsoons appeared before him and reminded him about his promise to Rāma. He said, "O King, he who treats wealth, punishment, friendship and the soul equally, is only capable of enjoying his kingdom. And the person who does not endeavour to perform the good work of his friend with dignity and enthusiasm, is sure to encounter many dangers. The monsoons are over. You immediately proceed for the search of Sītā, the beloved wife of Rāma. Earlier Rāma has done good to you. Now it is your turn to do good to him. Remember, Vālī committed no harm to Rāma. Even then, for the sake of friendship with you, he for your good did not hesitate to kill Vālī with the full knowledge of its impropriety, by resorting to deceitful means. You are capable of moving anywhere without restraint. You have under you countless unconquerable monkeys. You depute them to different directions in search of Sītā after determining their respective duties."

On listening to the correct advice of Hanumān, Sugrīva directed *vānara* commander Nīla to mobilize the entire *vānara* army at Kiṣkindhā with their local commanders. After issuing the order, Sugrīva immediately entered the inner apartments of the palace.

17

Rāma Deputes Lakṣmaṇa to Kiṣkindhā to Remind Sugrīva to Start Search for Sītā

MEANWHILE, at Ṛṣyamūka mountains Rāma one day in an extremely disturbed mind began to lament the absence of Sītā. At this time Lakṣmaṇa was in the nearby forest for the collection of fruits and roots. Finding Rāma on return in that condition, Lakṣmaṇa in a sorrowful mind said, "O Aryan, being subdued by passion, you are unnecessarily harming your manliness. Give up you passion and concentrate your mind on *karma-yoga* (self-dedication to the work of one's life). Grief originates in passion and it destroys peace of mind. By ensuring your mental delight, strengthen your manliness by taking recourse to *karma-yoga*. Seek assistance of friends and material resources. Your wife Sītā cannot be gained so easily by anybody else. The destruction of the abductors of Sītā is inevitable."

"Listening to the just words of Lakṣmaṇa, Rāma said, "Brother, your words are fully in conformity with the principles of politics and religion. For the search of Sītā we shall have to proceed on the course charted by you." Saying this Rāma again became morose and after describing the beautiful sights outside stated with regret, "Lakṣmaṇa, today I have no kingdom, have lost my beloved wife and stand banished in the forest. I am really a wretched person. I do not notice any efforts by Sugrīva for the rescue of Sītā as promised though monsoons are now over. He has thought, I am without any kingdom, helpless, insulted by Rāvaṇa, poor, inhabitant of a distant land and a seeker of his protection. This is why this wicked king of the *vānaras* has the audacity to ignore me like this. Lakṣmaṇa, you immediately proceed to Kiṣkindhā and warn Sugrīva, I shall kill him along with all his relatives if he does not proceed to act in compliance with his promise given to me."

Lakṣmaṇa in a flame of anger against Sugrīva at once got up armed with his bow and arrows. Seeing his menacing mood, Rāma thought, Lakṣmaṇa was proceeding to Kiṣkindhā to kill Sugrīva. In order to pacify him, Rāma said, "O son of Sumitrā, it would not be proper for a hero like you to commit any sinful act swayed by rashness. He who can control his anger, is the real hero. Give up your determination to kill Sugrīva who is a friend of us and try to preserve friendly relations with him. Without being harsh, remind him in pleasing words about his promise to rescue Sītā." Rāma's advice to Lakṣmaṇa was correct in all respects. In the present situation Sugrīva was their only hope in the matter of Sītā's rescue. It would be suicidal to antagonize him unnecessarily whatever might be his fault.

At the just words of Rāma, Lakṣmaṇa's anger subsided. With only one arrow in his quiver, he appeared at Kiṣkindhā. Again he was overtaken by anger. Seeing Lakṣmaṇa's angry appearance, the *vānara* army men deployed in front of the palace fled away in panic. The commander informed Sugrīva about Lakṣmaṇa's arrival as also his menacing mood. But Sugrīva turned a deaf ear to his words. He was then engrossed in amoral enjoyment with Tārā. On the orders of the ministers, the *vānara* army was again deployed around the palace. At this time, as Aṅgada came out, Lakṣmaṇa, with eyes burning with rage, told him to remind Sugrīva of his promise of help in the search and rescue of Sītā.

The lustful Sugrīva was then asleep out of exhaustion. He could not hear any word of Aṅgada. Suddenly at the hue and cry of the *vānaras* outside, Sugrīva was roused from sleep when

Aṅgada again conveyed Lakṣmaṇa's message to him. At this time two ministers by name Yakṣa and Prava entered inside and said, "O king, kindly meet Lakṣmaṇa immediately and pacify his rage. Also kindly take urgent steps for the rescue of Sītā as promised by you."

Understanding the gravity of the situation, Sugrīva asked the ministers to ascertain the reasons of Lakṣmaṇa's anger. He said, "I had no fear from Rāma or Lakṣmaṇa. But if the mind is enraged, it may cause unnecessary alarm. It is easy to establish friendship; but it is difficult to maintain that friendship. Even at the slightest provocation friendly relations can be snapped. I am apprehensive, thinking, I could not do anything in return for the good done to me by the great Rāma."

Hanumān who was present there said, "O King, it speaks of your greatness that you have not forgotten Rāma's benefaction. Rāma discarding all fear has installed you as the king of Kiṣkindhā by killing the great hero Vālī. Rāma is your genuine friend. It appears, out of affection he has become angry with you. Because of your involvement in merriment, you have forgotten your duty towards him. In the matter of rescue of Sītā you are still indifferent. You are guilty before Rāma. Kindly appear before Lakṣmaṇa with folded hands and try to bring cheerfulness in his mind. If Rāma is angry, he with his bow and the arrows can subdue the entire world along with the gods, demons and the *gandharvas*."

Thereafter, on being directed by Sugrīva, Aṅgada brought Lakṣmaṇa inside the palace. On seeing the palace, Lakṣmaṇa realized it was as gorgeous as Amarāvatī of Kubera full of innumerable priceless materials. At that time there was a programme of dance and music in the inner apartments. Lakṣmaṇa came to notice many beautiful well-dressed young women moving around. At one place he suddenly stopped on hearing the rustling sound of the wearing apparel of the women and in an angry mood created a terrible sound with the twang of his bow refusing to enter into Sugrīva's apartments.

On hearing the twang of the bow, Sugrīva understood Lakṣmaṇa's arrival. Deeply terrified, he told Tārā, "O dear, please meet Lakṣmaṇa and pacify him with pleasing words. Tell him I shall meet him later." Then Tārā overwhelmed under the influence of liquor appeared before Lakṣmaṇa walking in unsteady steps in dishevelled dress and asked him in a consoling tone, "O Prince, What is the reason of your anger? Who has violated your orders?"

Lakṣmaṇa understood, Vālī's wife Tārā was now Sugrīva's concubine. Controlling his anger he told her in a pleasing tone, "Your husband Sugrīva has forgotten the tenets of religion being guided by sheer passion for sensuous pleasure. He is now enjoying a lustful life in the company of women. But we are immersed in terrible grief. He is not taking any steps in mobilizing his army for the promised search for Sītā. Truth, devotion to religion and eagerness for the accomplishment of the promised duty — these are qualities of a genuine friend. Sugrīva has forsaken everything. You are not unaware of the principles of ethics. Please determine the course of action for the fulfilment of our objective."

Assuring Lakṣmaṇa, Tārā said, "O Prince, Sugrīva is fully conscious about his duty towards Rāma. Please forgive him if there is any mistake on his part. I am aware, Sugrīva intoxicated with lust, is in the company of women. You are not unaware, time and space or virtue and vice have no meaning for persons blinded with lust. Presently Sugrīva intoxicated with passion, is enamoured of me. I am not ashamed of this. We know, even the great sages endowed with spiritual power, have fallen prey to passion under the spell of illusion. And Sugrīva is an ordinary monkey. Moreover, he is now the king of such a prosperous kingdom. It is no surprise, Sugrīva has now been overwhelmed with lust. O Great Hero, you are pure and virtuous. Kindly enter inside."

On entering inside, Lakṣmaṇa found Sugrīva seated on a golden throne deeply embracing wife Rumā surrounded by many women. Finding him in such a state, Lakṣmaṇa angrily said, "The king who is strong, illustrious, grateful, kind and truthful, is worshiped by the people. But the king who is irreligious and indifferent to act on his promise given to his friend, is ungrateful. An ungrateful person is always fit to be killed. Without keeping your promise regarding rescue of Sītā, you are engrossed in lustful enjoyment. If you are unwilling to act according to your promise, you shall be killed like Vālī."

Sugrīva remained silent without giving any reply to Lakṣmaṇa's words. Tārā in reply said, "Lakṣmaṇa, it has not been proper for you to use such harsh words towards Sugrīva. Sugrīva has never forgotten Rāma's good work for him. After a long time he has come to see good days and on being overwhelmed with lust, has failed to perform his duty losing his sense of judgement. The great Sage Viśvāmitra in the same way being attracted to *apsarā* Gṛtāci, had lost his sense of judgement. Rāma certainly will pardon Sugrīva who is born of an ordinary *vānara* clan, for this deviation. For your information I am telling you, Sugrīva has already directed the *vānara* chiefs to assemble at Kiṣkindhā with their *vānara* army. Sugrīva is now awaiting their arrival. As soon as the *vānara* army will arrive here, the work for the rescue of Sītā will start in full swing. The *vānara* army is expected to arrive any time."

At the assuring words of Tārā, Lakṣmaṇa was pleased and his anger subsided. At this Sugrīva said, "O son of Sumitrā, by the grace of Rāma I have regained this *vānara* kingdom. Who is there who can show disregard to the great Rāma? He will certainly rescue Sītā with my help and kill Rāvaṇa. I am the slave of a slave of Rāma. Please pardon me if I have done any thing wrong."

Being pleased at the words of Sugrīva, Lakṣmaṇa said, "Sugrīva, you are really virtuous, grateful and not averse to fighting. Who is the learned person who can speak like this except Rāma and you? You are equal to Rāma in power and bravery. Fate has made Rāma and you mutually dependent. You immediately proceed to Rāma and console him. In the absence of Sītā he is passing his days in extreme sorrow. Please pardon me for using harsh words to you."

18

Sugrīva's Vānara Soldiers Begin the Search

MEANWHILE, countless *vānara* soldiers under their commanders arrived at Kiṣkindhā from the different parts of the country. Sugrīva on Lakṣmaṇa's direction came to Ṛṣyamūka mountains along with many *vānara* followers and bowed his head at the feet of Rāma. Raising him affectionately, Rāma embraced him saying, "O the greatest *vānara*, the king who remains engaged in the destruction of the enemy and in the cultivation of friendship, is blessed with virtue, wealth and fulfilment of desire — the three highly aspired human pursuits. He is also assured of divine justice. Now is the time for the rescue of Sītā. You may take necessary steps in this regard in consultation with your ministers."

Sugrīva said, "O mighty King, the hundreds of most eminent *vānara* chiefs you are seeing here, have brought all the most powerful *vānara*s of the world. They are all legitimate descendants of gods and the *gandharva*s. They are fierce-looking great warriors having deep experience about the impassable paths of the forest and the forest fortresses. They are now waiting surrounded by countless *vānara* soldiers. Crores of additional *vānara* soldiers will soon arrive from Sumeru and Vindhya mountains. This great *vānara* army will rescue Sītā after killing Rāvaṇa." Rāma expressed satisfaction at the huge endeavour and preparations of Sugrīva.

Thereafter, Sugrīva deputed the *vānara* chiefs to the four directions after briefing them about their duties and responsibilities. *Vānara* hero Vitnata was sent to the east, Nīla, Hanumān, Jāmbavān and other chiefs under the leadership of Aṅgada to the south, Tārā's father Suśīna to the west and chief Śatavala to the north. Strong contingents of *vānara* soldiers were attached in each group. Sugrīva instructed the group leaders to minutely search all the mountains, hills, rivers, mountains-peaks, human habitations, etc. in their respective areas after indicating their exact locations and the method of search. He sternly warned against any perfunctory search. He asked the group leaders to complete the search within one month and then return to Kiṣkindhā. He warned, any deviation from his orders would invite instant death.

Amongst the *vānara* chiefs Hanumān was considered to be most dependable by Sugrīva. Turning to him he said, "O son of the Wind God, you have unrestricted movement everywhere. Nothing is unknown to you. You possess strength, wisdom and prowess. You are also versed in moral philosophy. I am specially dependent on you in the search of Sītā."

At the words of Sugrīva, Rāma understood, the rescue of Sītā would be accomplished only by Hanumān. In a happy mind he handed over to Hanumān his ring engraved with his name and said, "O *vānara* chief, Sītā on seeing this ring will understand, it is I who have sent you to her. The ring will also help you to gain complete trust and confidence of Sītā." Hanumān after accepting the ring engraved with Rāma's name reverently placed it on his head and paid homage to Rāma by bowing to the ground.

After the departure of the *vānara* leaders for their respective destinations, Rāma wanted to know from Sugrīva how he had come to know the locations of all the places in the world. Sugrīva then again narrated the background of his differences with his brother Vālī, his banishment from the kingdom of Kiṣkindhā, his movement from one place to another out of fear of Vālī and his ultimate sojourn in

Ṛṣyamūka mountains on its being out of bounds for Vālī and his followers due to the curse of Sage Mataṅga and said in this way he had been able to collect all these details. On hearing Sugrīva, Rāma and Lakṣmaṇa became simultaneously surprised and happy. They were also deeply impressed at the adroitness shown by Sugrīva in briefing the *vānara* leaders on their duties and responsibilities in the matter of search of Sītā.

Within one month the *vānara* leaders who were deputed to the north, west and the east returned to Kiṣkindhā and reported to Sugrīva that they did not find Sītā anywhere despite their thorough search in all the areas as directed. Hanumān and other *vānara* leaders deputed to the south under the leadership of Aṅgada did not return even after the expiry of the stipulated period of one month. Sugrīva assured Rāma, Hanumān would certainly be able to ascertain Sītā's whereabouts as he had proceeded along the exact route of her abduction.

Meanwhile, the *vānara* leaders and their monkey soldiers under Aṅgada did not find Sītā anywhere despite their thorough search of the entire southern region and became exhausted and tired. Suddenly they came to notice a ray of light coming from inside a mountain cave and after proceeding in the direction of the light entered into the cave where a row of buildings of silver and gold unfolded before them. In one of the buildings they saw one woman ascetic who disclosed, on being asked by Hanumān, that this *māyā* forest and the buildings had been built by architect Maya Dānava, who obtained the boon of knowledge of fine art from Lord Brahmā after observing severe austerities for a thousand years. Later Maya Dānava was killed by Indra for his crime of falling in love with an *apsaras* by name Hemā. The woman ascetic gave her name as Svarṇaprabhā, who happened to be the intimate friend of Hemā. On her request Svarṇaprabhā had been looking after this great forest and the buildings. Afterwards, Svarṇaprabhā quenched the hunger and thirst of the *vānara*s by entertainments and showed them the path of exit from there. The *vānara*s exited through this path and reached the shore of the sea.

The scheduled time of return as determined by Sugrīva was already over. The work on the search of Sītā was still incomplete. In this situation the *vānara* soldiers became frightened on the thought, their death was inevitable at the hands of Sugrīva if they decided to return to Kiṣkindhā now. Aṅgada opined it would be preferable to die by fasting to getting killed at the hands of Sugrīva. The other *vānara* leaders expressed the view, they should better give up their lives here if they did not get any definite information about Sītā. At this time *vānara* commander Tara suggested, they all could take shelter in mountain caves in safety without any fear from Rāma or Sugrīva and live on the forest fruits and roots. The suggestions of Aṅgada and Tara were not liked by wise Hanumān and some other *vānara* leaders. Hanumān found in the suggestions an indication of retreat from the ordered task of search of Sītā. He in an eloquent speech by carefully applying the principles of *sāma, dāma, daṇḍa* and *bheda* was able to create dissensions amongst the *vānara* soldiers. In an attempt to dispel all fears from the mind of Aṅgada, he said, "O Crown Prince, you are more skilful than your father in warfare. In the administration of the kingdom you are equally competent. Give up your fear and hesitation. Disregard the words of the fickle-minded *vānara*s. They shall not remain loyal to you for long on being detached from their own people. Jāmavanta (Jāṁbavān), Nīla, Suhūrta and myself would under no circumstances remain separated from Sugrīva. Remember, the strong can live by antagonizing the weak. But this is not possible for the weak. You cannot be safe even by taking shelter in the caves. Lakṣmaṇa's sharp arrows will kill you by piercing the mountain caves. I know Sugrīva very well. He is firmly true to his promise and happens to be your well-wisher He cannot hurt your mother by doing any harm to you. You proceed to Kiṣkindhā along with us. We have been unsuccessful in finding Sītā even after thorough search in all the places as ordered by Sugrīva. We shall frankly submit before Sugrīva all details of our search. We shall also explain the reasons for the delay. I fully trust, he will do no harm to us."

Aṅgada said in reply, "You have mentioned about many virtues of Sugrīva; but I do not think he really possesses all those virtues. The person who can enjoy the wife of his eldest brother even when he is living, certainly deserves utter condemnation. Disregarding the orders of his eldest brother Vālī, he without remaining on guard at the cave, closed its mouth with a stone and seized the throne on returning to Kiṣkindhā. Without taking any steps for the search of Sītā, as promised, he was passing his days enjoining the company of women. He came to his senses only at the threat of Lakṣmaṇa. Actually Sugrīva is sinful, ungrateful, irreligious and fickle-minded. He is wicked, cruel and atrocious. Now if we return to Kiṣkindhā without being successful in our search for Sītā, we are sure to die at the hands of Sugrīva."

Saying this Aṅgada asked the *vānara* soldiers to return to Kiṣkindhā and himself made preparation to die by fasting along with some old *vānaras*. At this time some *vānara* soldiers brought Sampāti, brother of Jaṭāyu before Aṅgada thinking him to be their enemy. Sampāti was living in the nearby mountains on being wounded. He disclosed, after the death of Vitrāsura, he along with his youngest brother Jaṭāyu rose to the sky on way to *svargarājya* to kill Indra. As he came close to the sun, Jaṭāyu became unconscious because of its terrible heat, when Sampāti covered him by spreading his two wings. But Sampāti's two wings got burnt by the sun's heat and he fell down on the ground. Since then he had no information about Jaṭāyu. It may be recalled Jaṭāyu also fell down on the ground at Janasthāna on being burned by the heat of the sun.

Giving the information of Jaṭāyu's death at the hands of Rāvaṇa, Aṅgada told Sampāti, they had come here in search of Sītā, Rāma's wife on the basis of information furnished by Jaṭāyu before his death and wanted to know the whereabouts of Rāvaṇa. In reply Sampāti said, "One day I noticed from these mountains, the sinful Rāvaṇa had been flying through the aerial path with a beautiful woman. Now I understand this woman was no other than Sītā. Rāvaṇa is the son of Sage Viśravā and the brother of Kubera. He lives in Laṅkā, surrounded by sea. Amongst the clan of the birds, we only can reach the end of the sky. We possess divine eyes. With this power I am seeing from here itself both Sītā and Rāvaṇa. O *vānaras*, now try to devise a plan to cross the sea. If this is done, you may meet Sītā and rescue her."

Later, Sampāti with the help of the *vānara*s went to the sea and offered oblations of water for the peace of the soul of Jaṭāyu. On return to the shore, Sampāti narrated further details of his stay in these mountains. He said, "One day I happened to meet Sage Niśākara here. He was a great sage and knew the past, present and future. He was aware of all the details regarding the abduction of Sītā. That you shall be coming here on the orders of Sugrīva for the search of Sītā, was also known to him. On his direction I gave you this information about Sītā." As he was talking with the *vānara*s, Sampāti suddenly got back his two wings in the presence of everybody. This, he said, was due to the good wishes of Sage Niśākara.

19

Hanumān Crosses the Sea and Meets with Sītā in Laṅkā

ARMED with the information furnished by Sampāti, the *vānara* leaders held consultations about the problem of crossing the sea, but could not arrive at any decision. The *vānara* soldiers became depressed. Hanumān remained seated in a lonely place in silence. In this gloomy atmosphere *vānara* leader Jāmavanta (Jāṁbavān) addressing Hanumān said, "O *vānara* hero, in power and strength you are equal to Sugrīva and even with Rāma and Lakṣmaṇa. Why are so dispirited in the matter of crossing the sea?"

Saying this, Jāmavanta (Jāṁbavān) narrated the history of Hanumān's birth. He said, "Previously, there was an exquisitely beautiful *apsaras* by name Puñjikasthalā. After her marriage with Kesarī, the king of the *vānara*s, she came to be known as Añjanā. One day she was moving on the mountain-peak during rains when Pavana Deva (Wind God) being enamoured of her beauty, sexually united with her. From this union you were born. After your birth, Añjanā went to the forest for the collection of fruits leaving you alone. Without finding your mother, you began to cry. At this time seeing the rising sun in the sky, you in a terrible speed moved towards the sun to catch him thinking him to be a big fruit. The Sun God felt amused seeing a tiny monkey approaching him. The Wind God turning cold like snow moved behind you in order to protect you from the heat of the sun. The god Rāhu complained to Indra that a monkey was trying to devour the sun though he (sun) has been ordained by him as his food. At this Indra got enraged and pierced your left *hanu* (cheek) with his *vajra* (thunder-bolt-like missile) and you accordingly were named Hanumān. As a result you fell down dead. Your father Vāyu (Wind God) then went to a cave holding you in his arms. He became angry with Indra and as a revenge stunned the flow of air causing terrible distress to all the living creatures making them almost breathless. There arose a loud lamentation all around. The gods finding the situation critical went to Lord Brahmā and prayed for suitable steps to pacify the Wind God. Lord Brahmā then went to the Wind God in the cave with Indra and other gods and pacified him by bringing you back to life. Brahmā on being pleased gave the boon that his Brahmā power and his Brahmāstra (weapon) would have no effect on you. Indra bestowed on you the boon that his weapon (*vajra*) will cause you no harm. He also gave you the boon of voluntary death. The Sun God bestowed on you the one-hundredth part of his prowess and promised to teach you Sanskrit and all the Śāstras (scriptures) so as to make you an eloquent speaker. On your coming of age he taught you all the subjects. The other gods including Yama also bestowed on you the boon of immunity from their respective weapons."

Narrating the wonderful story of Hanumān's birth, Jāmavanta (Jāṁbavān) said, "O Hero, being the son of the Wind God, you are as powerful as your father. You are also blessed with the boons of all the gods. Give up your sadness and mustering all the courage, cross this great sea."

On knowing his birth history from Jāmavanta (Jāṁbavān), Hanumān in a happy mood assumed his own form much to the delight of the *vānara* soldiers. He then climbed the nearby Mahendra hill and swelled his body manifold. Thereafter he jumped to the sky in tremendous speed and after crossing the sea landed at the foot of the Trikūṭa hill. On this Trikūṭa hill is located the capital city of Laṅkā. Hanumān felt no fatigue in covering this long journey. While enjoying the beautiful sights all around, he soon reached close to the city boundary and found a deep trench all around. He also noticed armed *rākṣasa*s stationed everywhere. Gradually Hanumān appeared in front of the north gate. He understood, it would not be easy to enter into the well-protected city. In this situation he found no opportunity to apply any of the principles of *sāma, dāma, daṇḍa* and *bheda* to achieve his purpose. He remained careful lest his purpose of the rescue of Sītā should get foiled due to any wrong step.

In the meantime darkness descended with the setting of the sun. At the opportune moment, Hanumān shrunk his body and entered into the city after assuming the form of a small cat. From the ramparts he found it was a city of immense wealth and prosperity like the city of Amarāvatī of Kubera. He was struck with awe to see the rows of buildings with beautiful architecture having ornamental gates and doors of gold and jewels, well-maintained flower gardens, pleasant forests, lakes, etc. He stealthily proceeded further inside enjoying the beautiful sights when suddenly he was stopped and slapped by the presiding deity of Laṅkā — a *rākṣasī*. Hanumān immediately in a counterattack laid her on the ground with a terrible blow. The *rākṣasī* then told Hanumān, "O Hero, be gracious and protect me. I am telling you a truth. At the time of bestowing his boon on me, Lord Brahmā predicted, great fear would befall the *rākṣasa*s when a monkey would defeat me. On seeing you I understand, the *rākṣasa*s are now in great danger. Only for the sake of Sītā, the sinful Rāvaṇa and his *rākṣasa* clan are now on way to destruction. You may freely move and search for Sītā."

As instructed, Hanumān in the guise of the cat, began to move from building to building in search of Sītā. The *rākṣasa* guards did not notice his movements. Sounds of sweet music and dance, deep recitations of hymns as also of loud and horrible shoutings were heard from some of the buildings. In some other buildings Hanumān found a group of *rākṣasa*s busy reading the Vedas and singing in praise of Rāvaṇa. In one building he noticed a gathering of *rākṣasa* spies. They were all dressed in disguise. Some of them were covered with cow-hide while some had matted hair. Some had their heads shaven. Some of them were not very bulky, some not very thin, some not very tall, while some were dwarfish. Some of the spies were ugly-looking while some had various shapes. Some of them were good-looking. All were strong-built and armed with various weapons. A few of the spies had only one eye, one ear and one nipple. They were all cruel and deformed. Hanumān understood, Rāvaṇa used to collect information with the help of these spies.

Meanwhile, in the moonlight the city turned wonderfully beautiful. Hanumān saw many beautiful women in the different apartments. But nowhere he did find Sītā. Proceeding further he entered into the magnificent apartments of Rāvaṇa and saw him lying in his golden bedstead. In another bedstead he saw Mandodarī, the beautiful wife of Rāvaṇa and thought her to be Sītā. But immediately he understood his mistake and left the place. He then searched for Sītā in Rāvaṇa's wine bar, museum, the building for nocturnal pleasant walk and many other places. But nowhere Sītā was found. At one time Hanumān lost his enthusiasm. He thought, it would be better for him to give up his life by fasting than returning without being successful. Immediately thereafter he started his search forsaking his depression. Gradually he entered into Rāvaṇa's beautiful Aśoka Vāṭikā and found one beautiful woman in a sorrowful mind sitting on its steps surrounded by many *rākṣasī*s. He understood, she was no other than Rāma's wife. As he saw Sītā, tears rolled down from Hanumān's eyes. He in his mind paid obeisance to the feet of Rāma.

That night Rāvaṇa, blinded with lust, appeared before Sītā in the Aśoka Vāṭikā accompanied by many women. Seeing Rāvaṇa coming, Sītā got frightened and began to weep after covering her breasts with the two thighs and the palms. In an effort to allure her, Rāvaṇa by gestures and in sweet words, while expressing his desire, said, "O Beautiful Woman, do not be afraid of me. I am constantly desiring you. Be devoted to me. It is the religion of the *rākṣasa* clan to forcibly abduct the wives of others and to have union by force with others' women. Even then I am determined, I would not touch your body unless you agree to accept me willingly. Obtain all your desirable things by adoring me. Give up your delusion. I have got many beautiful wives. Remain gracefully present amongst them as the chief queen. In prowess and military tactics, I am unrivalled. None has the power to defeat me. What would you do with matted and poor Rāma forsaking my immense wealth? There is absolutely no chance of his coming victorious. He is now performing austerities as a penniless forest-dweller. The bare ground is his bed. Moreover, it is doubtful whether he is at all alive."

Scornfully disregarding Rāvaṇa's evil proposal, Sītā after placing a shred of grass in between them said, "O King of the *rākṣasa*s, remain satisfied in the company of your own wives. Remember, you shall never be able to obtain me. I am born in a great illustrious clan. I am the daughter-in-law of the pious Sūrya (sun) dynasty. I am faithfully devoted to one husband." Saying this, Sītā showing her back to Rāvaṇa again said, "I am the faithful wife of another person not fit to be enjoyed by you. Follow the religion of pious men. You should protect others' wives as you do in respect of your own wives. You shall suffer agony if your wife Mandodarī falls victim to the lust of others. The others shall also similarly suffer in the same situation. O King of the *rākṣasa*s, are there no wise men in this great city of Laṅkā who can give you honest advice? Perhaps such wise men are certainly there in the city. But you yourself are undisciplined and licentious. This is why you do not act according to their advice. You are inviting destruction of the entire *rākṣasa* clan by disregarding the advice of the wise men.

Remember, the king who is guided by the bad people and disregards the principles of truth and justice, is certain to lose in no time his kingdom and wealth. This beautiful golden city of Laṅkā is now on way to destruction due to the misdeeds of an inconsiderate person like you. Rāvaṇa, if you want to protect this great city, then return me to Rāmacandra and seek his forgiveness. Rāma always forgives those who surrender to him and seek his protection. He will also protect you. Otherwise, at the shower of arrows of Rāma and Lakṣmaṇa, this city will be totally destroyed and I shall also be free from this captivity. You shall not be able to save your life from the arrows of the all-powerful Rāma even by fleeing to a distant land."

Rāvaṇa in reply said, "O Sītā, I am terribly angry at your harsh words; but because of my love for you, I am controlling it and accordingly I have refrained from awarding you capital punishment. I am giving you two months' time to make up your mind. On the expiry of this period you must be prepared to be my bed-fellow. If you refuse, you shall be cut into pieces for the breakfast of the *rākṣasa*s."

Without being perturbed at the threat of Rāvaṇa, Sītā said, "O *rākṣasa,* it appears you have no well-wisher in this city. You shall not be able to save yourself even by fleeing away. With the force of my chastity I am capable of destroying you alive. But there is no approval from Rāma and moreover I am now engaged in religious austerities. This is why I have refrained from destroying you. I am the wife of Rāma. It was never possible for you to abduct me. At the dispensation of fate you were able to abduct me as you are destined to die at the hands of Rāma. You have abducted me like a coward when I was alone after deceitfully enticing away Rāma. Fie on you."

Flying into a rage, Rāvaṇa took the vow he would kill Sītā the same day. Relenting somewhat he later asked the *rākṣasī* guards to win over Sītā with sweet words and by other means and left the Aśoka Vāṭikā. Then the *rākṣasī*s started threatening

Sītā in the harshest language. Sītā, however, remained firm. She with a heavy heart began to blame her own fate for her present sufferings and prayed for the early arrival of Rāma and Lakṣmaṇa.

At this time one old *rākṣasī* by name Trijaṭā told Sītā, "I last night had a dream that the entire *rākṣasa* clan had been destroyed and that you had been rescued by Rāma and Lakṣmaṇa." Naturally Sītā was happy to hear Trijaṭā's predictions.

From behind the tree, Hanumān was attentively listening to the narration of Trijaṭā's dream, Sītā's lamentations and the shouting and scolding of the *rākṣasī*s and began to think about his course of action. He later softly spoke to Sītā's hearing in a low voice about the details of her abduction and disclosed, he had arrived here on Rāma's direction to search for her. Sītā was surprised to hear Hanumān's words and looked at him. He saw, Hanumān was also looking at her and was coming towards her. Sītā grew suspicious. She thought, perhaps Rāvaṇa himself had sent Hanumān in disguise for the fulfilment of his evil design. She became extremely frightened. Immediately after, she thought, "Let the words of Hanumān come true."

Hanumān appeared before Sītā and after paying obeisance to her feet unseen by others asked her in a sweet voice, "O Kamalākṣī (lotus-eyed), who are you? Why are you shedding tears in such dirty clothes? You appear to be a princess and a queen. Are you that Sītā whom Rāvaṇa has abducted from distant Janasthāna? You appear to be the wife of Rāma."

On hearing the name of Rāma, Sītā became pleased and revealed her identity. On this Hanumān in consoling words said, "O Devī, I am the emissary of Rāma. On his orders I have come to you. Both Rāma and Lakṣmaṇa are well." On hearing his words, Sītā again thought, Hanumān was certainly *māyāvī* (he who can create illusion) Rāvaṇa himself and accordingly remained silent without giving any reply. Understanding Sītā's mind, Hanumān said, "O Janakanandinī (daughter of King Janaka), I am the minister of Sugrīva, the King of Kiṣkindhā. My name is Hanumān. I am not *māyāvī* Rāvaṇa. Give up your fear and trust me."

Sītā then calmed down somewhat and on realizing the truth of Hanumān's words, asked him to describe the physical appearances of Rāma and Lakṣmaṇa. After furnishing the details, Hanumān narrated the plan for Sītā's rescue, his own birth history and other related matters. Hanumān, thereafter, handed over to Sītā the ring engraved with Rāma's name given to him by Rāma, on the eve of their departure, in order to gain her confidence. On being satisfied, Sītā while praising Hanumān for his power and strength, said, "O hero, you may tell Rāma on return, Rāvaṇa has given me only two month's time to make up my mind. After this period if I still refuse to share bed with him, he will kill me. For this Rāma will have to rescue me from here without delay. Rāvaṇa's brother Vibhīṣaṇa requested Rāvaṇa to return me to him; but he had refused. I got this information from Vibhīṣaṇa's daughter Kalā. One learned, virtuous, old *rākṣasa* by name Abindhya has warned Rāvaṇa, the destruction of the *rākṣasa* clan was inevitable if I am not freed from captivity. But Rāvaṇa has disregarded his advice also. We are aware of Rāma's power and strength. It is my firm belief, Rāma will soon rescue me from here."

Assuring Sītā, Hanumān said in reply, "On getting information from me Rāma will soon arrive here with a huge *vānara* and *valluka* (bear) army. Alternatively I would request you to mount on my back and I shall take you to Rāma by the aerial path. In this task do not consider me incapable. I can assume any form at will." Saying this Hanumān in order to gain Sītā's confidence, swelled his body many times and requested her to mount on his back. Sītā said, "O great *vānara*, I am aware of your prowess, wisdom, force and speed like the wind. Even then I think, your proposal is not practical. I may fall down from your back when you shall be flying at the speed of the wind. Moreover, the *rākṣasas* will try to intercept you with all their might. As you shall be busy in fighting with the *rākṣasas*, it will not be possible for me to keep my balance and I shall inevitably fall down. There is another matter which should be considered. If you yourself rescue me after killing the *rākṣasas*, Rāma's good name and reputation will be lost. In war there is always an uncertainty about victory and defeat. If the *rākṣasas* confine me in a secret hide-out after defeating you, then none will be able to find me out. It will be all the best if Rāma arrives here along with you and rescues me. O great hero, there is yet another most serious matter which you should try to understand. I am against touching another person's body willingly. It is true, Rāvaṇa touched my body on the day of my abduction; but I had then no control over my body. The best thing would be if Rāma rescues me after destroying Rāvaṇa along with the *rākṣasas*." Hanumān understood the significance of Sītā's arguments and prayed for an identifying token from her so that Rāma could be convinced about the truth of this meeting with her.

Sītā then said, "O wise *vānara*, I am telling you about an incident. This incident itself is the best token of my identity. During our stay at Citrakūṭa mountains, Rāma one day became tired while walking with me for a long time in the plains below and lied on my lap for rest with his body sweating all over. At that time one crow suddenly came there and struck me on the breast with his beak. I scared him away by throwing stones. But he came again and after piercing my breast, remained hidden at that place itself. As I tried to tighten my brassiere, my garments got loose. At my predicament Rāma started cutting jokes. Feeling ashamed I got up and scared the crow away. Being tired I lied on Rāma's lap. In the meantime the crow appeared again and bruised my breast once again with his beak. As my hot blood fell on his body, Rāma stood up and seeing my wound, he looked at the crow. This crow was no other than Indra's son Jayanta. On seeing Rāma, Jayanta out of fear tried to enter into the *pātāla*. Rāma then raised a shred of grass from the ground and after sanctifying it with incantations, joined it with his *brahmāstra* (one of the infallible missiles) to kill the crow. As a ball of fire appeared before him, Rāma threw it towards the crow. Jayanta in the guise of the crow after traversing many places appeared before his father Indra for protection. But Indra did not entertain him. The sages whom he approached did not also give him any protection. At last Jayanta finding no other alternative to save himself appeared before Rāma and begged for his forgiveness. Rāma protected him though he was fit to be killed. He told Jayanta his *brahmāstra* was infallible. Once released he had also no power to retrieve it. He asked Jayanta what he expected of him to do now. Jayanta prayed for his life and wanted his right eye to be destroyed by the *bramhāstra*. Accordingly the *bramhāstra* destroyed Jayanta's right eye. In this way Jayanta after losing his right eye left the place taking leave of Rāma."

On finishing the narration, Sītā told Hanumān, this incident was known to only Rāma and me and if he told the incident to him, Rāma would understand he (Hanumān) had actually met her. Later Hanumān discussed the plans of Sītā's rescue with her. At the end Sītā brought out from inside her garments a beautiful gem-studded ornament of her head and gave it to Hanumān with instructions to hand it over to Rāma. She said, "This token of my identity is specially known to Rāma. On seeing this ornament, Rāma will remember King Daśaratha, mother Kausalyā and me simultaneously."

20

Valiant Deeds of Hanumān in Laṅkā and Collection of Vital Intelligence about Rākṣasa Army

AFTER taking leave of Sītā, Hanumān thought, his main work had been completed on his meeting with Sītā. Now it was the time to test the power and strength of the *rākṣasa*s. He realized, this work could not be accomplished by applying the principles of *sāma, dāma, daṇḍa* and *bheda*. In the present situation only the third principle of *daṇḍa* (punishment) would be necessary. The simple and the sincere people could only be won over by applying the principle of *sāma*. These *rākṣasa*s were hard-hearted; this principle would be of no use here. In *dāma* only the poor people were subdued. The *rākṣasa*s had no dearth of wealth. And it would be impossible either to create dissensions amongst them. Therefore, Hanumān thought, the only path left now to test the power and strength of the *rākṣasa*s was the application of the principle of *daṇḍa* by showing his own power and strength. Hanumān further thought, on the death of the principal *rākṣasa* warriors, the *rākṣasa* army would be weakened. Another thought also came to his mind. During application of his own prowess, it would be possible to get an idea of the depth of the power and strength of the *rākṣasa*s. This would also help him in understanding the war strategies and tactics of the *rākṣasa* army.

As decided, Hanumān in the first instance destroyed the Aśoka Vāṭikā without, however, causing any damage to the place of stay of Sītā. He then climbed to the main gate of the garden and assumed a huge form by swelling his body in order to frighten the *rākṣasīs* guarding Sītā. Getting information from the *rākṣasīs* about the strange activities of Hanumān, Rāvaṇa despatched a strong contingent of *rākṣasa* army known as *kiṅkara* against him. In the fierce battle that ensued the entire *rākṣasa* army was destroyed at the hands of Hanumān. Thereafter Hanumān destroyed the beautiful *caitya* palace of Rāvaṇa (the temple where the deity of the royal family is worshipped) and firmly declared, he would accomplish his duty by destroying the entire Laṅkā city in presence of the *rākṣasas*. Then on Rāvaṇa's orders, *rākṣasa* hero Jambumāli, and other *rākṣasa* warriors proceeded against Hanumān; but they all lost their lives with their army in the battle. Rāvaṇa was worried and he this time deputed his valiant son Indrajit against Hanumān. In the battle Indrajit's various thunder-bolt-like missiles proved of no avail against Hanumān as he rose to the sky at the speed of the wind and remained outside the range of the missiles. Indrajit realized, this monkey could not be killed by any weapons. He then searched for *brahmāstra*; but immediately realized, this monkey could not be killed even with *brahmāstra*. He accordingly used the *brahmāstra* only to bind him. Hanumān thus bound became unconscious and he fell down on the ground. He, however, felt no pain in the body because of the boon bestowed upon him by Lord Brahmā. He understood, he would soon be able to free himself from this bondage. He feigned to be unconscious and remained motionless on the ground. The *rākṣasa* soldiers then tied Hanumān with a rope made of hemp and tree bark. Indrajit knew, any binding with another material would destroy the effect of the binding with *brahmāstra*. And this actually happened. Hanumān became free from the bondage of *brahmāstra*; but he did not show any sign of that openly. He remained motionless being tied with rope.

In this condition Hanumān was produced before Rāvaṇa. On Rāvaṇa's direction, the ministers asked Hanumān to disclose his identity. Hanumān said in reply, he was the emissary of Rāma and had come to this city on the orders of King Sugrīva of Kiṣkindhā. On being asked by minister Prahasta about the reasons for his destruction of the Aśoka Vāṭikā and for oppressing the *rākṣasa*s, Hanumān after narrating all the events regarding Rāma's exile to the forest, abduction of Sītā, Rāma's friendship with Sugrīva, killing of Vālī, Sugrīva's ascendancy to the throne of Kiṣkindhā, etc. said, "O King of the *rākṣasa*s, Sugrīva true to his promise has sent the *vānara* leaders to different directions in search of Sītā. Under their leadership countless *vānara* soldiers are now engaged in the search at all the places of the world including even the *pātāla*. There is no limit to the *vānara*s' power and strength. I am the son of the Wind God. After crossing the sea, I have reached here to see you. I have already met Sītā. You are a learned person. The tenets of religion are known to you. It has not been correct on your part to keep in confinement another person's wife. O King, none can live in peace in this world by doing any unpleasant work against Rāma. Please return Sītā to the hands of Rāma remembering the rules and laws of religion. Remember, none will be able to obtain Sītā by force. You have gained a long life under the influence of religion after undergoing immense physical sufferings because of your long and arduous religious austerities. This miraculous power acquired through religious austerities is your real force. Do not destroy this force by doing anything against the religion. Please try to understand the real significance of the incidents like Rāma's destruction of the *rākṣasa* army at Janasthāna, killing of the valiant Vālī and the alliance between Rāma and Sugrīva. Also think about your own welfare. Rāma is promise-bound to destroy all those responsible for Sītā's afflictions. There is none to resist Rāma."

At his plain-speaking, Rāvaṇa flew into a rage and ordered Hanumān's immediate execution. Intervening, brother Vibhīṣaṇa said, "O King, please give up your anger and listen to me. This monkey has come to you as an emissary. It will not be proper to kill him." Rāvaṇa said in reply, "This monkey has committed sinful acts. Death is his correct punishment." Vibhīṣaṇa, however, did not relent. He said, "The wise men do never approve of the death sentence on any emissary. There are many prescribed punishments for an emissary. Disfiguring of the limbs, shaving of the head, caning, marking of the body with distinguishing signs — these are some of the punishments applicable to an emissary. If at all death sentence has to be awarded, you better impose it on those who have sent him here. They are the real culprits. You may send your invincible army and bring here Rāma and Lakṣmaṇa as captives. It will be proper to show your prowess against those who are your real enemies."

At the suggestion of Vibhīṣaṇa, Rāvaṇa commuted the death sentence on Hanumān and directed the *rākṣasa*s to set fire to his tail. The *rākṣasa*s immediately wrapped the tail of Hanumān with cloth and set it on fire after smearing it with oil. On this Hanumān became angry and struck the *rākṣasa*s with his burning tail. Hanumān was then tied again with rope. The *rākṣasa*s, thereafter, took him round the city. At many places the citizens jeered at Hanumān denouncing him as an enemy spy. On getting this information Sītā in a grief-stricken heart engaged herself in the worship of the Fire God for the welfare of Hanumān. She prayed to the Fire God to keep his body cool without burning it. Hanumān actually felt no discomfort to his body though his tail was burning. He rather felt as if there was dewfall on his tail. He understood, he was not getting burnt by fire only because of the mercy of Sītā, divine influence of Rāma and the blessings of his father Wind God.

While walking along the street, Hanumān suddenly rose to the sky with a loud roar after unfastening himself and sat on a gateway. His body had then swollen like a mountain. Soon after he assumed a diminutive form and became free from the bondage. The *rākṣasa*s failed to rope him again.

Hanumān then began to move from one place to another with his burning tail and destroyed the palaces, buildings, forests, etc. of the city by setting them ablaze. A large number of *rākṣasas* also perished in the fire. Suddenly Hanumān thought, Sītā might have also been burnt in this devastating fire. At this time he understood from the conversation of the *cāraṇas* and *yakṣas* in the sky, Sītā had remained unhurt though the entire city had been destroyed. Hanumān immediately rushed to the Aśoka Vāṭikā and felt relieved to see Sītā remaining unhurt. After narrating the events in short, he took leave of Sītā and arrived at Mahendra hill on crossing the sea.

The *vānara* leaders were elated to hear Hanumān's meeting with Sītā as also the other incidents in Laṅkā. They all without any loss of time arrived before Rāma at Kiṣkindhā. Aṅgada walking ahead came to Rāma and after paying obeisance to him announced, Sītā was well. As Rāma wanted to know the place of stay of Sītā and her attitude towards him, the *vānaras* sent Hanumān before Rāma. Hanumān accordingly went to Rāma and after paying obeisance to him first handed over to him the gem-studded ornament which Sītā had given to him as a token of her identification saying he had met with Sītā in the Aśoka Vāṭikā in the city of Laṅkā and narrated all the incidents in Laṅkā. Later he spoke about the incident of the crow striking Sītā's breasts as told by her. He also mentioned how joyful Sītā was in receiving the ring engraved with Rāma's name. On completion of his narration, Hanumān requested Rāma to immediately devise the means to cross the sea. Rāma, Lakṣmaṇa and Sugrīva on getting Sītā's information were comforted and happy.

Profusely praising Hanumān for his work, Rāma said, "Hanumān, you have indeed accomplished a great work. It is impossible to perform such a work for any one else in the world. Laṅkā which is protected by the all-powerful Rāvaṇa is unconquerable even for the *devas*, *dānavas*, *yakṣas* and *gandharvas*. It is unthinkable for anyone else who is not equal to you in power and strength to enter Laṅkā. Hanumān, you have performed Sugrīva's other works also as his faithful servant. The wise men consider such servants as the greatest persons. Besides, you have not shown any meanness in the enemy's house. For your accomplishments Sugrīva no doubt is highly pleased. You have returned after seeing the Janakanandinī. By your work you have not only made us happy, you have also saved the entire Raghu clan. My only regret is that I have not yet been able to do any good work for my dearest messenger." Saying this, Rāma happily embraced Hanumān.

Immediately thereafter, Rāma was afflicted with the thought of crossing the insuperable sea. Understanding Rāma's mental distress, Sugrīva said, "O hero, give up all your worries. We know all the information about the enemy. As such you have nothing to worry. My *vānara* army is skilled in warfare and valiant. They shall not hesitate even to enter into fire for the sake of performing any good work for you. They are determined to rescue Sītā. It is indispensable to build a bridge across the sea to reach Laṅkā. Please devise some means to build a bridge over the sea. As soon as the bridge is built, you may be assured, our army have reached Laṅkā and defeated the enemy. Nothing is insurmountable for our army. Have patience giving up all mental inertia. It is the time for displaying our force. Power is man's pride."

Understanding the truth of Sugrīva's words, Rāma addressing Hanumān said, "O hero, with the force acquired by religious austerities, I can build a bridge or absorb the water to cross the sea. But you first tell me the defences of the city of Laṅkā."

Hanumān said, "O King, fierce-looking *rākṣasa*s are deployed to defend the city. Countless ferocious elephants, chariots, horses, etc. are moving in the streets. Assured with the defences, the people are carrying on their activities happily with complete freedom from care and worry. Because of the flawless defences it is impossible for the enemy to enter the city. There are four strong gateways to enter Laṅkā. All are encircled by deep protective trenches. With the help of special mechanical devices at the gateways, attacking enemy troops are intercepted outside by arrows and stone boulders. The *rākṣasa* troops armed with various sharp weapons are fully alert. The sides of the long ramparts around Laṅkā are made of gold and studded with various jewels. The capital city is surrounded by deep trenches with cold water. Fish, alligators and other dangerous aquatic animals are moving in the water of these trenches. For this the trenches are as dangerous as they are beautiful. To cross the trenches there are wide cause-ways at every gateway. Many large buildings are also located near the gateways. As the enemy troops arrive, draw-bridges are withdrawn with the help of the mechanical contrivances and they get drowned in the trenches. Of the four gateways mentioned earlier the northern gateway is unusually large and very strongly built. Made of gold this gateway is exquisitely beautiful and built on many pillars and platforms. Rāvaṇa climbs this gateway to observe the enemy troops.

"O Raghuvara (Lord of the line of Raghu), Laṅkā is protected by water-forts, hill-forts, tree-forts and many other artificial forts; for this even the gods do not dare to attack Laṅkā. In front of Laṅkā is the impassable great sea. Apart from the sea, other water-forts are also impassable as no boats ply there. For this no information about Laṅkā ever reaches the outside world. The Laṅkā-fort is located on the hill-top. Countless elephants and horses have been kept there. In power, prosperity and wealth, Laṅkā like Kubera's capital Amarāvatī, is unconquerable."

"O Raghunātha, at the eastern gateway unconquerable *rākṣasa* troops are stationed as guards with sharp weapons. These *rākṣasa*s are also proficient in sword warfare. In addition troops mounted on horses, elephants, chariots and on foot are located there. They all are holding swords and shields and are experts in using every type of weapon. The strength of the troops at the northern gateway is ten crores. They all are of good lineage and honoured by Rāvaṇa. Amongst them the strength of the troops on chariots and on horses is higher. At the centre there are countless troops. But I have been able to cause considerable damage to the *rākṣasa* army. I have destroyed the bridges, burned Laṅkā with fire and have filled the trenches with debris after breaking the strong-built ramparts. It is my belief, in some way or the other we shall be able to cross the sea. Kindly remain firm. Laṅkā is now in ruins. You need not require to send any other troops to Laṅkā. Only Aṅgada, Dvibidha, Mainda, Jāmavanta (Jāṁbavān), Pānasa, Nala, commander Nīla and myself shall be able to destroy the hills, forests, gateways, etc. of Laṅkā after crossing the sea. On your orders we may immediately start our military expedition."

21

Rāma's Laṅkā Campaign

ON getting details of Laṅkā's defences from Hanumān, Rāma immediately decided to launch the military campaign against Laṅkā. He told Hanumān, "However dangerous Rāvaṇa might be, I shall destroy Laṅkā at the earliest. Today is an auspicious day. We shall start our campaign today itself. The entire *vānara* army will accompany us." Later he issued some important directives. He directed, commander Nīla would proceed as the guide for the army moving in front of the advancing column. He told Nīla, "You should lead the column along the route where sufficient water as also fruits and roots are available. Always remain alert about the *rākṣasa*s. They may poison the water and the fruits and the roots. For this these will have to be protected. Along the route the *rākṣasa*s may also ambush our army. For this *vānara*s will have to climb the trees occasionally to watch the surroundings for any suspicious movements." Afterwards, Rāma directed the *vānara* leaders to form into separate groups and proceed with their respective troops. He asked them to leave behind at Kiṣkindhā all those *vānara*s who are physically weak and warned, the war for the conquest of Laṅkā would be extremely terrible.

After the briefing, Rāma and Lakṣmaṇa mounted respectively on the back of Hanumān and Aṅgada and proceeded towards south accompanied by a huge *vānara* army. After traversing many areas, the *vānara* army under Rāma's command reached in due course the northern bank of the sea. The *vānara* leaders made suitable arrangements for their stay and protection.

We shall now discuss the activities of Hanumān. We are aware, on the orders of Sugrīva, Hanumān, as Rāma's emissary, reached Laṅkā in search of Sītā after crossing the sea by the aerial path. We have seen, how Hanumān by dint of his divine powers defeated the presiding deity of Laṅkā — a *rākṣasī* — and meticulously searched for Sītā in all places and the buildings after entering the city in the form of a cat to avoid detection. He all along remained extremely careful in his movements. Though he did not find Sītā in any of these places, he nevertheless was able to collect useful information regarding Rāvaṇa's internal security arrangements. Hanumān's actions in the enemy's den disregarding his personal safety underline his sincerity of purpose as a loyal servant of Sugrīva as also his deep regard and devotion to Rāma. His single-handed conduct of the searches in such minute details is indeed rare even for any well-trained surveillance team of the modern-day intelligence organization.

Hanumān's deep sense of observation proved rewarding when he instantly recognized as Sītā the woman in dirty clothes sitting on the steps of the building in Rāvaṇa's Aśoka Vāṭikā. We have seen how Hanumān successfully hiding himself behind a tree managed to initiate talks with Sītā and ultimately won over her complete confidence with his persuasive and sweet words. With his credentials being proved without any doubt after the presentation of Rāma's ring to her, disclosure of his true identity and the purpose of visit, they talked freely on various subjects including plans of Sītā's rescue much to the relief of her distress. Hanumān true to his character remained concerned for the welfare of Sītā during the burning of Laṅkā and was relieved when he found her unhurt. Hanumān's meeting with Sītā in an extremely difficult situation is no doubt an unprecedented success. In ability, courage, precaution and cleverness Hanumān seemed to appear here as an experienced intelligence operator. We are surprised when we find, he accomplished everything alone without taking any other's help. Apparently the boons bestowed on him by Lord Brahmā and the other gods as also his education and training under the Sun God were behind this success. Hanumān was always conscious about the need to collect information about Laṅkā's defences. He accordingly fully utilized his temporary stay in Laṅkā in collecting every vital information in this regard. This information proved extremely useful to Rāma in formulating his strategy and tactics in the campaign against Laṅkā. We shall come across many such achievements of Hanumān as the events unfold.

22

Rāvaṇa Reviews War Situation and his Differences with Vibhīṣaṇa and Kumbhakarṇa

MEANWHILE, Rāvaṇa became worried on getting information though his spies about the mobilization of a huge *vānara* army under Rāma's command at the other side of the sea. He told his army commanders, "One ordinary monkey had returned unscathed after meeting with Sītā and devastating the city of Laṅkā. Rāma will soon arrive here with his army. In the situation give me your considered opinion about our duties." The *rākṣasa* army commanders after consultations amongst them said, "O Emperor, you are the conqueror of the three worlds; you have under you a huge well-trained and well-armed *rākṣasa* army. You have absolutely nothing to worry. On your orders your valiant son Indrajit will be able to destroy Rāma with his entire *vānara* army."

During the discussions *rākṣasa* commander Prahasta said, "O great King, on your orders I alone can destroy the entire *vānara* clan." Another commander by name Durmukha said, "One ordinary monkey has returned after insulting us. This is absolutely intolerable. Kindly issue orders to me. I shall alone destroy the *vānara* army." Thereafter *rākṣasa* commander Vajradaṁṣṭra said, "On your orders I can cross the sea and destroy Rāma, Lakṣmaṇa and Sugrīva. But I have a suggestion. Kindly listen carefully. Let a few *rākṣasa*s assuming human form appear before Rāma and tell him they have been sent by his younger brother Bharata to help him. Rāma then will certainly forsake the *vānara* army and join our army. At this opportunity we shall destroy the entire *vānara* army. Being cheated in this way Rāma and Lakṣmaṇa will be easily killed by us." Some other *rākṣasa* commanders also boastfully declared, they would also be able to destroy the *vānara* army alone.

Vibhīṣaṇa, the god-fearing younger brother of Rāvaṇa asked the boastful commanders to stop and submitted with folded hands, "O valiant commanders, please remember, work is not always accomplished by bravery. When the work cannot be accomplished by applying the principles of *sāma, dāma* and *bheda,* then only the fourth principle *daṇḍa* has to be applied as enjoined in the *Nītiśāstra* (the science of politics). Rāma is not an ordinary enemy. Rāma is always alert. He is proud of victory and possesses divine powers. He is free from anger and invincible. It is not possible to defeat him by force alone. You have witnessed the havoc created by a single monkey. Rāma has got under him countless valiant *vānaras*. Therefore it is utter foolishness to show disregard to the enemy."

Addressing Rāvaṇa, Vibhīṣaṇa then said, "O Lord of the *rākṣasas*, Sītā has been carried away to avenge the destruction of Khara and Dūṣaṇa along with *rākṣasa* army. But we have been plunged into great fear because of this action. We shall be free from fear if Sītā is released. O great King, give up your anger. Anger is impediment to happiness and religion. Follow that path which is conducive to devotion to God and righteous pursuits. Live happily with friends and relatives after handing over Sītā to Rāma."

Rāvaṇa heard Vibhīṣaṇa patiently without uttering a single word. He later dismissed the meeting and departed to his apartments.

The next morning Vibhīṣaṇa met Rāvaṇa alone and again requested him to return Sītā to Rāma, He explained, "From the very day Sītā has arrived at Laṅkā, various inauspicious omens have been noticed all around. These inauspicious omens will bring disaster to the entire *rākṣasa* clan. No minister out of fear could muster courage to bring this information to your knowledge. It is my bounden duty to bring to your knowledge what I have seen and heard. Now you may decide what you think best according to your intelligence and comprehension."

Rāvaṇa was then severely stricken in the fire of lust. Rejecting the just suggestion of Vibhīṣaṇa, he angrily said, "Nowhere I am seeing any signs of fear. Rāma will never get back Sītā. Rāma's defeat is inevitable even if he appears in the war along with Indra and the other gods." Saying this he dismissed Vibhīṣaṇa.

Pining for the love of Sītā, Rāvaṇa became addicted to heavy drinking and gradually became emaciated. He developed signs of mental confusion with regard to intelligence and judgement. Deciding war as the right path in the situation, he ordered mobilization of a huge number of *rākṣasa* troops for the defence of the city. Later in an assembly of the citizens, he explained the impending attack on Laṅkā of the *vānara* army led by Rāma and sought their cooperation and assistance in his war preparations. He said, "I have abducted Sītā, wife of Rāma from Janasthāna. Sītā's beauty has no comparison. On seeing Sītā I have been infatuated with love for her. Afflicted with passion I am now awfully tired. Rāma has reached the other side of the sea with a huge *vānara* army with the purpose of mounting an attack on Laṅkā. Though it is extremely difficult to cross this vast sea, even then I do not feel free from anxiety. You are all aware of our humiliation at the hands of an ordinary monkey. In the situation you may give me your considered opinion about our course of action. Now find out the means to destroy Rāma and Lakṣmaṇa." Kumbhakarṇa, brother of Rāvaṇa was present in this assembly. He became angry at the words of Rāvaṇa and said, "O King, you have abducted Sītā without consulting us. Now you shall gain nothing in having consultations with us. You have done an unjust act by deceitfully abducting Sītā. O king, the king who justly conducts the affairs of his kingdom on honest advice, does never suffer from any repentance subsequently. O king, it is not proper to think, victory is certain only on having a large army. The enemy can ensure the defeat of a powerful but imprudent king by skilfully exploiting his faults. You have not thought of the consequences of your grave act of the deceitful abduction of Sītā. You are fortunate, you have not been killed by Rāma then and there. Though you have started this war by your unjust act, even then I am giving the word, I shall kill your enemy with all my might. On Rāma's death Sītā will submit to you."

Rāvaṇa became very angry at the reproof of Kumbhakarṇa; but he remained silent. Understanding his mind, *rākṣasa* hero Mahāpārśva said, "O great King, the abduction of Sītā has been a correct act on your part. Because it is utter foolishness on the part of any person who on finding honey in the deep forest, does not drink it. Even if the abduction of Sītā is considered unjust, there is none who can punish you as you are the god yourself. With no hesitation, you may get sexually united with Sītā. Along with Kumbhakarṇa and Indrajit, we can resist even Indra, not to speak of the humans and the *vānaras*. I think only those who are weak, try to achieve their objectives by applying the principles of *sāma, dāma* and *bheda* of the *Nītiśāstra.* But we are not weak. We shall achieve our objectives only by applying the fourth principle of *daṇḍa.* We are capable of destroying the enemy even if they arrive at our door-step."

The words of Mahāpārśva were to the liking of Rāvaṇa. Praising him Rāvaṇa said, "Mahāpārśva, you have spoken the correct thing. But I am telling you about a secret story. Previously I sexually enjoyed by force one beautiful heavenly damsel while she was going to the abode of Lord Brahmā. On getting this information Lord Brahmā cursed me, my head would be torn into hundred pieces if I forcibly assault any other woman in future. Out of fear of this curse of Lord Brahmā I have refrained from applying any force against Sītā. Mahāpārśva, Rāma is not aware of my power and strength. This is why he has dared to attack my kingdom."

23

Vibhīṣaṇa's Surrender before Rāma

On hearing the conversation between Rāvaṇa and Mahāpārśva, Vibhīṣaṇa said, "O king, Sītā is a dangerous snake. You have been bound by her. Please hand over Sītā to Rāma before the arrival of the *vānara*s at Laṅkā. None of your *rākṣasa* heroes including even Indrajit and Kumbhakarṇa will be able to withstand the attack of Rāma. You too shall not escape from the hands of Rāma."

Denouncing Vibhīṣaṇa as timid, Indrajit said, "You are unnecessarily trying to spread panic among the people. Only one *rākṣasa* is capable of destroying these two princes. I have humbled the pride of the gods. It is insignificant on my part to destroy Rāma and Lakṣmaṇa."

Sharply rebuking Indrajit, Vibhīṣaṇa said, "Son, you are still immature. You have no idea as to what should be done or should not done. By giving wrong advice to the *rākṣasa* king, you as his son are actually working as his enemy. You are approving his wrong actions under delusion despite the fact he is in grave danger. You are evil-minded. You are fit to be killed. And he who has given you a place in the cabinet, is also fit to be killed. None of the *rākṣasa*s will be able to stand against the infallible arrows of Rāma and Lakṣmaṇa." Later addressing Rāvaṇa, Vibhīṣaṇa said, "O King, you please hand over Sītā to Rāma with money, jewels and divine clothes. Let us live in Laṅkā without any anxiety."

Rāvaṇa was so long silently listening to everybody's words. The suggestion of Vibhīṣaṇa to hand over Sītā to Rāma, was intolerable to him. Denouncing Vibhīṣaṇa as a jealous blood-enemy, Rāvaṇa harshly told him, "Vibhīṣaṇa, I am denying with contempt any friendship with a wicked person like you. Fie on you! You are my own brother. Had anybody else uttered such words, I would have killed him immediately."

Angry at the scolding of Rāvaṇa, Vibhīṣaṇa with mace in hand immediately rose to the sky accompanied by four of his companions and said, "O King, sweet-tongued persons are always available; but both the speakers and listeners of beneficial but unpleasant words, are difficult to obtain. You have ignored my honest advice. You are bound to suffer for this. I am taking leave of you. When the lifetime ends, the people do not listen to the good words of the friends — this proverb is going to be true."

Vibhīṣaṇa accompanied by his companions reached by the aerial path above the army encampment of Rāma when Sugrīva first came to notice them. Hanumān and other *vānara* heroes on being informed prayed for the death sentence of the *rākṣasas*. Vibhīṣaṇa while hovering in the sky, said, "O *vānaras*, I am Vibhīṣaṇa, the youngest brother of the *rākṣasa* king Rāvaṇa. I requested Rāvaṇa time and again to return Sītā to Rāma; but he had rejected my advice. On the other hand I was insulted and scolded by Rāvaṇa. Leaving behind my wife, children, servants and the courtiers, I am now the seeker of Rāma's protection. Please inform Rāma about my decision to surrender before him."

On hearing Vibhīṣaṇa's words, Sugrīva appeared before Rāma and said, "O Lord, some enemy soldiers have stealthily entered into our camp. They shall certainly kill us at an opportune moment. You may kindly take steps to protect our troops by arranging the line of battle, engaging spies and by the application of the principles of *Nītiśāstra* on proper consultations. These *rākṣasas* are probably the spies of Rāvaṇa. They are five in number. One of them claims to be Vibhīṣaṇa, the youngest brother of Rāvaṇa. They have come to surrender before you; but how would you understand whether Rāvaṇa has not sent them to you with some ulterior motive? The *māyāvī rākṣasas* have no dearth of evil designs. It is not impossible, they may even kill you after gaining your confidence."

After hearing Sugrīva, Rāma wanted to know the opinion of other *vānara* leaders. Aṅgada said, "O Lord, Vibhīṣaṇa has come from the enemies. It should not be desirable to trust him straightway. After proper evaluation of his faults and virtues, we shall have to decide whether we shall accept him or not. If his faults are more, we must discard him. If, on the other hand, his virtues are more, we may accept him without any hesitation. You may get the entire matter enquired into by a sharp-witted *vānara* spy to find out the truth and then take a decision." Counsellor Jāmavanta (Jāṁbavān) said, "Vibhīṣaṇa ḥas appeared before you to surrender after deserting his own brother when he is in great danger. This naturally gives rise to suspicion, the sinful Rāvaṇa himself has sent him here. For this there is certainly some danger from him if his surrender is accepted." *Vānara* commander Mainda said, "We may take a decision after ascertaining the mind of Vibhīṣaṇa by engaging spies."

Lastly Hanumān said, "O Lord, I do not think, the suggestions of Aṅgada and the other *vānara* leaders regarding prior enquires to ascertain the faults and virtues of Vibhīṣaṇa before acceptance of his surrender, are correct. Specially in the present circumstances it is not possible to conduct such enquires. I believe, Vibhīṣaṇa being disgusted at the oppressive activities of Rāvaṇa and on knowing your power and strength, has come to seek your protection. This actually proves his prudence. I have not marked any evil motive in his mind on seeing him. There is also no sign of cruelty on his face. I do not apprehend any danger from Vibhīṣaṇa. At the news of your war preparations, death of Vālī, Sugrīva's ascendancy to the throne of Kiṣkindhā and on Rāvaṇa's sinful activities,

Vibhīṣaṇa has sought your protection to obtain the kingdom of Laṅkā. It should be proper to give him protection without rejecting him."

After hearing everybody's opinion, Rāma said, "I cannot reject a person who seeks my protection as a friend, whatever might be his faults. I shall not be blamed by the society of the virtuous people if such a person is given protection." The words of Rāma were not to the liking of Sugrīva. He said, "Vibhīṣaṇa has deserted his own brother when he is in danger. At the opportune moment he may also desert any other person."

Rāma then told Lakṣmaṇa, "Brother, Sugrīva has rightly mentioned about the wrong action of Vibhīṣaṇa in deserting his own brother. But in this regard there are other finer aspects which deserve deliberation. The kinsfolk and other relations as also the neighbouring kings are mainly considered to be the enemies of a king. At the time of danger, it is they who at the opportune time, seek to evict him from his kingdom. This Vibhīṣaṇa has come to me for the realization of his own interests. Even the well-wishing kinsfolk may be a threat to the king. But Vibhīṣaṇa is no relation of us. For this it is unthinkable of him to try to gain our kingdom after destroying us. Vibhīṣaṇa has sought our protection to gain the kingdom of Laṅkā by having killed his brother Rāvaṇa with our help. Even the *rākṣasas* are also intelligent enough in the matter of gain and loss. Therefore in my opinion, it will be correct to receive Vibhīṣaṇa. You may say our brother Bharata is not envious of his brothers with no desire to usurp our kingdom. But brother, the example of the noble-minded Bharata is not applicable in respect of all other brothers. In the world brothers like saintly Bharata, the faithful keeper of promise given to the father like me and a friendly and faithful brother like you, are indeed rare."

Sugrīva still remained unconvinced. He respectfully said, "It is my strong conviction, this *rākṣasa* is actually a spy of Rāvaṇa. He has come here on the orders of Rāvaṇa. The

Rākṣasas are crooked beyond imagination. He will kill us after gaining our confidence. Without further consideration we should kill all of them."

Rāma after thinking for some time said, "Sugrīva, this *rākṣasa,* good or bad, will not be able to cause any harm to me. Not to speak of Vibhīṣaṇa, I can destroy, with the tip of my finger, all the *daityas, dānavas, yakṣas* and *rākṣasas* of the world." Later referring to the various mythological stories, Rāma said, "Even at the cost of his own life, it is incumbent on every virtuous person to give protection to those who seek his shelter. Otherwise he will be blamed in the society for having committed a sinful act. The person who will pray for my help seeking my protection, must be given shelter by me. This visitor Vibhīṣaṇa has been assured of safety by me. Even the sinful Rāvaṇa will be given shelter if he seeks my protection. You may immediately produce Vibhīṣaṇa before me."

Sugrīva now understood the truth of Rāma's words. He said, "Rāma, you are virtuous, powerful and the jewel of all kings. Your decision following the tenets of religion has been entirely justified. After examining Vibhīṣaṇa I have also found him to be a person of pure heart. On receiving the learned Vibhīṣaṇa, you may enter into a bond of friendship with him."

Thereafter on Sugrīva's direction, Vibhīṣaṇa along with his companions alighted to the ground from the sky and fell at the feet of Rāma. On assurance of protection by Rāma, he said, "O Lord, I am the youngest brother of Rāvaṇa. On being humiliated by the eldest brother I have come to you after leaving behind everything to seek your protection. My kingdom, life and happiness are all now under your control." After consoling Vibhīṣaṇa in sweet words, Rāma asked him to give details of the power and strength of the *rākṣasas*.

Vibhīṣaṇa said in reply, "O Prince, on the boon of Lord Brahmā, Rāvaṇa is unconquerable by *devas, gandharvas* and others. My other brother Kumbhakarṇa is highly spirited and powerful. In war he is a rival to *devarāja* Indra. Indrajit, Rāvaṇa's son is a gallant warrior. He fights in bare body holding the *aṅguṣṭhānā* (metal covering for the finger-tip) with his bow and the arrows. When necessary, he destroys the enemy after becoming invisible. Mahodara, Mahāpārśva and Akampana are Rāvaṇa's principal commanders. They are all great warriors. Countless powerful *rākṣasa* troops are under them. Rāvaṇa has conquered all the kings with their help."

Rāma being satisfied on hearing the details of the power and strength of Rāvaṇa and his army said, "Vibhīṣaṇa, I am taking the vow, after destroying Rāvaṇa along with Indrajit and other *rākṣasa* commanders, I shall make you the king of Laṅkā. Even if Rāvaṇa takes shelter under Lord Brahmā, he will not escape from me. I am taking the vow in the name of my three brothers, I shall not return to Ayodhyā without destroying Rāvaṇa and the *rākṣasa* clan."

Later, on Rāma's orders, Lakṣmaṇa in the presence of the *vānara* leaders installed Vibhīṣaṇa as the king of Laṅkā after sprinkling sea-water on him. After the ceremony, Hanumān and Sugrīva asked Vibhīṣaṇa about the means to cross the sea. Vibhīṣaṇa in reply said, "Let Rāma seek the help of the Sea God. Rāma's forefather King Sagara excavated this vast sea. On the prayer of Rāma, a scion of King Sagara, the Sea God will certainly help him in this work." As suggested by Vibhīṣaṇa, Rāma began his prayer at the sea shore invoking the blessings of the Sea God.

The question may arise why Rāma gave protection to Vibhīṣaṇa, the brother of his arch enemy Rāvaṇa only on the suggestion of Hanumān without any verification of his faults and virtues. We know *rākṣasī* Trijaṭā was a well-wisher of Sītā. She told Sītā in the presence of the other *rākṣasīs* of her dream about the downfall of Rāvaṇa along with the *rākṣasa* warriors and the destruction of Laṅkā. There were also indications in the dream that only Vibhīṣaṇa with four of his companions would remain alive with honour. Hanumān on listening to the narration of the dream from behind a tree, could realize Vibhīṣaṇa, despite being the brother of the sinful Rāvaṇa, was a person of different character. During his stay at Laṅkā he must have heard about his serious differences with Rāvaṇa with regard to Sītā's abduction. Rāma got from Hanumān all these details, which helped him to form a clear idea about Vibhīṣaṇa. When Vibhīṣaṇa sought his protection, Rāma with his power of anticipation understood his purpose was to gain the kingdom of Laṅkā with his help. This was why he did not hesitate to receive with honour his enemy's enemy Vibhīṣaṇa in adherence to the principles of *Nītiśāstra*. He actually got in Vibhīṣaṇa an insider in the Rāvaṇa's inner circle to obtain information on many matters he badly required in his campaign against Laṅkā. In this regard Vibhīṣaṇa was actually a prize catch for him obtained rather unexpectedly. As no suspicion arose about him during the talks, Rāma became sanguine, no harm would come to him if Vibhīṣaṇa was given protection. In power and strength, Rāma was second to none. He also possessed divine powers. He had full confidence in himself. In the circumstances he was confident none including Vibhīṣaṇa would be able to cause any harm to him even if he turns hostile.

Rāma being a virtuous person with high moral principles, was ever ready to receive anyone who would surrender to him and seek his protection independent of any material consideration. He was even ready to receive Rāvaṇa if he sought his protection. This moral consideration in fact outweighed other considerations in his decision to give protection to Vibhīṣaṇa. We shall see later, Rāma's decision to give protection to Vibhīṣaṇa was entirely correct. Vibhīṣaṇa played a significant role in the conquest of Laṅkā with his bravery and in furnishing Rāma various secret information about the enemy. In return Rāma as promised formally installed Vibhīṣaṇa on the throne of Laṅkā after the death of Rāvaṇa. Both Rāma and Vibhīṣaṇa were immensely benefited from their mutual friendship.

24

Collection of Intelligence by Rākṣasa Spies

IN the meantime the *rākṣasa* spy Śārdūla brought information about the mobilization of the *vānara* army on the other bank of the sea under the command of Sugrīva. Giving the details to Rāvaṇa, Śārdūla said, "O Mahārāja, Rāma's army is spread in camps over an area of ten *yojana*s and he is preparing to launch his military campaign very soon. Kindly send emissaries to ascertain Rāma's strategies and other details of the campaign. You may take recourse to one of the three principles of *sāma, dāma* and *bheda* to resist the enemy after due consideration."

On hearing Śārdūla, Rāvaṇa told Śuka, the Royal Counsellor on Economics and Politics, "You immediately proceed to Rāma's camp and convey the following message of mine to Sugrīva — O *vānara* King, you are born in a royal family. Unlimited is your power. It is of no consequence to me whether you fight against me or not. Even then you are like my brother. This is why I am telling you, you better return to Kiṣkindhā. By abducting Sītā, I have not caused any harm to you. Remember, even the *deva*s and *the gandharva*s will not be able to enter Laṅkā, not to speak of humans and the *vānara*s."

On orders from Rāvaṇa, Śuka in the form of a bird flew by the aerial path above the camp of Rāma and conveyed from the sky Rāvaṇa's message to Sugrīva. Some *vānara* soldiers on seeing him went to the sky and after bringing him down, began to belabour him. Later he was produced before Rāma to whom he disclosed, he had come here on the direction of Rāvaṇa as his emissary. On being released by Rāma, he flew to the sky and asked Sugrīva to give his reply to Rāvaṇa's message. Sugrīva then asked Śuka to convey the following reply to Rāvaṇa — "O Rāvaṇa, you are not my friend; you are the enemy of Rāma. Therefore you are also my enemy. You also are fit to be killed like Vālī. Wherever you may flee for safety, you shall not escape from the hands of Rāma. We shall shortly reach Laṅkā and kill you along with your relatives. The city of Laṅkā will also be destroyed." After the message was conveyed, Aṅgada told Sugrīva, "This *rākṣasa* is suspected to be the spy of Rāvaṇa. He seems to be ascertaining the strength of our army. It would not be correct to allow him to return to Laṅkā." On Sugrīva's orders, *rākṣasa* Śuka was then brought down from the sky and again subjected to torture in various ways. Later, on Rāma's orders he was saved from further torture and kept as a captive. In this way Rāvaṇa's efforts to drive a wedge between Rāma and Sugrīva ended in failure.

25

Vānara Soldiers build Bridge across Sea

MEANWHILE, the Sea God despite being worshipped by Rāma, remained unseen. Rāma being enraged severely disturbed the seawater by incessant shower of arrows. The fish and other aquatic animals whirling about began to groan in fear. All efforts of Lakṣmaṇa to pacify Rāma failed. The Sea God even then did not respond. Rāma then attached his *brahmāstra* to his bow and was about to discharge it in order to dry up the seawater. All around there developed a terribly threatening atmosphere. The entire world was shrouded in darkness. The mountains began to fall in pieces. All the living creatures raised a piteous cry. With the swelling of water all sides were flooded. In this situation, the Sea God appeared before Rāma with folded hands and said, "My Lord Rāmacandra, the earth, the air, space, light and the other elements of nature from time memorial have been performing their respective duties according to their own nature. That I am unfathomable and impassable, is also due to the same laws of nature. Only in absence of this nature I can turn different. But that is not possible for me. Even then I am telling you the means by which you can cross the sea. I shall indicate a particular land route for the movement of the *vānara* army. Along this path my aquatic animals will cause no disturbance to the *vānara* army."

On the promise of the Sea God Rāma was pacified. He then discharged the infallible arrow to the land of the non-Aryans by name Drumkulya in the north. Gradually the seawater became calm.

Thereafter, *vānara* hero Nala, son of Viśvakarmā with the help of the *vānara* army built a 10-*yojana* wide and 100-*yojana* long bridge along the land route across the sea earmarked by the Sea God with stone boulders and tree trunks. [It may be mentioned, the US space agency NASA in their various photographs on Palk Strait between India and Sri Lanka taken from their spacecraft (2 September 2006) found a 30-km long bridge near the sea shore on the Indian side. This bridge is believed to be a segment of the old bridge built by Rāma. Of course, this fact is known to the people since long. The bridge associated with the name of Rāma, is revered by the vast sections of devout Hindus. The present demand raised in some quarters to destroy this Rāma-setu to facilitate easy navigability along the Palk Strait, has naturally caused widespread condemnation amongst them as it would deeply hurt their religious sentiments.]

On completion of the bridge, Rāma and Lakṣmaṇa riding ahead of the *vānara* army on the back of Hanumān and Aṅgada respectively safely reached Laṅkā. Many *vānara* soldiers also reached Laṅkā by the aerial path. After the crossing of the entire *vānara* army, Sugrīva mobilized them in an area which had plenty of water and fruits and roots. The same day they reached the outskirts of the city. Rāma in adherence to the military strategy, grouped the army into several divisions and placed them under valiant commanders. Soon trenches were dug around the camping area. Rāma himself along with Lakṣmaṇa remained in the front of the army.

26

Spy Śuka Reports to Rāvaṇa

AFTER Rāma was fully prepared to launch the attack, *rākṣasa* Śuka was released on his orders. Śuka without any loss of time appeared before Rāvaṇa and after conveying various details of the *vānara* army including his persecution at the hands of the *vānaras*, said, "Mahārāja, the *vānara* army has built a bridge across the sea and by this bridge Rāma with his vast *vānara* army has crossed the sea. The *vānara* army has now been mobilized on the outskirts of the city. The attack on the city is imminent. In this situation, you may either seek a settlement with Rāma after handing over Sītā to him or you may go in for war against the *vānara* army."

On hearing Śuka, Rāvaṇa flew into a rage and said, "I shall not return Sītā even if the *devas*, *dānavas* and the *gandharvas* as also the entire people of the three worlds wage war against me. Rāma is not aware of my power and strength. This is why he is preparing to start a war against me. Śuka, I am as swift as the sea and as strong as the wind. None including Indra, Varuṇa, Yama or Kubera will be able to defeat me."

27

Rāvaṇa Deputes More Spies to Collect Information about Vānara Army

AFTER dismissing Śuka, Rāvaṇa summoned his two ministers — one also named Śuka and the other named Sārana — before him. As they arrived, Rāvaṇa told them, "Rāma has built a bridge across the sea and by this bridge the entire *vānara* army has crossed the impassable sea. This is indeed an unprecedented incident. Whatever it might be, you two immediately enter into Rāma's camp unseen by others and bring back all information about the *vānara* army, their power and strength, names of the principal warriors, details of Rāma's ministers, Sugrīva's companions, the method of the bridge construction across the sea, the line of battle, the mode of operation of Rāma and Lakṣmaṇa, the particulars of the commander-in-chief of the *vānara* army and other connected details."

Śuka and Sārana immediately assumed the form of monkey and entered into the camp of the *vānara* army. They, however, got frightened on seeing the innumerable *vānara* soldiers all around. It was not possible for them to count their number. As they were moving in the camp, Vibhīṣaṇa recognizing them, took them into custody.

Later Vibhīṣaṇa produced Śuka and Sārana before Rāma and said, "Mahārāja, these two *rākṣasa*s in disguise have entered into our camp and are collecting information about our army." On interrogation they admitted their guilt. On their speaking the truth, Rāma released them treating them to be the emissaries. He asked them to convey to Rāvaṇa that the *rākṣasa* army and the city of Laṅkā would be destroyed by his shower of arrows by the next morning.

On being released, Śuka and Sārana appeared before Rāvaṇa and after narrating the incident, told him, "Mahārāja, it appears, Rāma, Lakṣmaṇa, Vibhīṣaṇa and Sugrīva — these four lions of men — are themselves capable of uprooting the entire city of Laṅkā without any help of the *vānara* army. It is evident from the unusual and terrible weapons of Rāma, he will alone destroy the city. Rāma, Lakṣmaṇa and Sugrīva are defending the *vānara* army. The *deva*s and the *dānava*s, it appears, even unitedly will not be able to cause any harm to them. The *vānara* soldiers are all skilled warriors. They are eagerly waiting to go in for war with great enthusiasm. In the circumstances you better establish peace with Rāma after returning Sītā."

Rāvaṇa angrily rejecting the peace proposal, climbed to the top of the highest palace building along with Śuka and Sārana and saw with his own eyes the vast assembly of the *vānara* army. On being asked by Rāvaṇa, Sārana said, "Mahārāja, see there! Thousands of Vānara soldiers looking at the city, are roaring like lion. See that side! Prince Aṅgada of Kiṣkindhā, a great hero, is moving around in steady steps with terrible roars frequently swelling his tail. Aṅgada is the son of Vālī. He is as powerful as his father. He is challenging you for a fight. Inspired by the counsel of this Aṅgada Hanumān came to Laṅkā and met with Sītā. Aṅgada is the chief of innumerable *vānara* leaders."

In this way Sārana brought to the notice of Rāvaṇa about the power and strength of the various *vānara* leaders, their weapons and their locations on the ground. Thereafter, Sārana drew Rāvaṇa's attention to a certain direction and said, "Mahārāja, see there! Hanumān whom you have seen earlier, is standing in the midst of the *vānara* army. He is the son of the Wind God. You have already got a taste of his prowess.

The lotus-eyed warrior with darkish beautiful colour whom you are seeing close to Hanumān, is Rāma, the great hero of the Ikṣvāku dynasty. His glorious activities are well known throughout the world. His skill in archery is incomparable. He also possesses *brahmāstra.* He is capable of piercing the earth and the sky. He is as angry as death and as powerful as Indra. The warrior with a large chest and bright copper-like colour whom you see by his side is Lakṣmaṇa, Rāma's valiant younger brother. He is always engaged in the service of Rāma. He is well-versed in the principles of ethics and in the art of warfare. He is ever ready to sacrifice his life for the sake of Rāma. The great hero Lakṣmaṇa is determined to destroy the entire *rākṣasa* clan alone. The hero whom you see standing surrounded by four *rākṣasa*s, is your brother Vibhīṣaṇa. Rāma has installed him as the king of Laṅkā. He is angrily waiting with the desire to have a fight with you. Mahārāja, see there! The hero whom you see standing in the midst of the *vānara* warriors like an unshaken mountain, is the *vānara* king Sugrīva of indomitable valour. After killing Vālī, Rāma has given the *vānara* kingdom to Sugrīva. With crores of *vānara* soldiers, Vibhīṣaṇa and the valiant *vānara* warriors are determined to have a fight with you. Mahārāja, you have seen before your eyes the lightning-like enemy army. Now you kindly take suitable steps to win the war so that the people of Laṅkā do not suffer in any way."

In the minute description of the *vānara* army, we find evidence of unprecedented competence of Śuka and Sārana in the matter of intelligence collection. Their achievement even surpasses that of the experienced intelligence operators of the modern days. Wonderful is their power of observation. As ministers they had full background knowledge of the personal particulars of Rāma and other principal warriors of the *vānara* army and this made the narration cogent and complete in all details. The collection of so much information in such a short time of their stay in the *vānara* camp, is indeed rare and we are wonder-struck by their achievement. This incident further confirms the existence of a well-organized intelligence set-up under Rāvaṇa. There was no doubt the information collected by Śuka and Sārana proved extremely useful to Rāvaṇa in determining his war strategy. Had Śuka and Sārana been kept confined in the *vānara* camp as correctly suggested by Vibhīṣaṇana who knew them from before and suspected them to be the *rākṣasa* spies, Rāvaṇa would have been deprived of this valuable information. Why then did Rāma order their release only on the ground they admitted their guilt treating them as emissaries of Rāvaṇa? It appears Rāma did this with some clear purpose in mind. His intention was to send a clear message to Rāvaṇa through Śuka and Sārana that his *vānara* army under the command of Sugrīva, Aṅgada, Vibhīṣaṇa, Hanumān, Lakṣmaṇa and himself, is invincible and that Rāvaṇa along with his *rākṣasa* army and the city of Laṅkā would be destroyed on their assault. Truly Rāvaṇa was disheartened on getting the details of the *vānara* army and became doubtful about his victory. This indicates Rāma's decision to release Śuka and Sārana was completely justified. Rāma had an uncanny sense of judgement. This time also his judgement did not fail him. His purpose was served in demoralizing Rāvaṇa before the start of the war.

The unusual emphasis by Sārana about the invincibility of the *vānara* army was somewhat strange and suspicious. Were Śuka and Sārana won over by Rāma with his magnanimity? There would be no surprise as no spies were expected to speak with such eulogy about the enemy before their own king. Though Rāvaṇa was initially worried on hearing the details of the *vānara* army, he immediately flew into a rage. Sharply chastising Śuka and Sārana, he said, "You showed extreme height of impertinence in praising Rāma, the arch enemy of your king. I am surprised, you had no fear to speak such harsh and unpleasant words before me. Death is the proper punishment for seditious people like you. But I am not taking any action against you for your good work in the past."

After dismissing Śuka and Sārana, Rāvaṇa summoned four of his trusted spies including Śārdūla before him. On their arrival, he told them, "You immediately enter into Rāma's camp and ascertain the activities of Rāma and his ministers. Ascertain all details as to how and where they sleep, what activities they perform when they are not asleep, etc. and inform me. I believe, I shall be able to destroy the enemy on the basis of your information."

The spies on entering into the *vānara* camp were overwhelmed with fear to see the vast army. Shortly on being recognised by Vibhīṣaṇa they were subjected to torture by the *vānara* soldiers. Later, on being released by Rāma, they returned to the city and reported the incident to Rāvaṇa. The spy chief Śārdūla said, "On ordering our release, Rāma has taken shelter inside the well-arranged line of battle constructed by the *vānara* army in the shape of *garuḍa* (king of birds). It appears, he will shortly mount an attack on the city. In the situation you may either establish peace with Rāma on returning Sītā or wage war against the *vānara* army." Rāvaṇa said, "I shall not return Sītā in any circumstances. Śārdūla, you may give me details of the strength of *vānara* army and its power. All these details are urgently needed by me."

Śārdūla said in reply," Mahārāja, there is no comparison to the power and strength of Rāma, son of King Daśaratha. At Janasthāna he has alone destroyed the entire *rākṣasa* army along with the valiant commanders Khara and Dūṣaṇa. In power and strength Lakṣmaṇa, brother of Rāma is also not inferior to anyone. He is capable of fighting with Indra. Your valiant brother Vibhīṣaṇa, now a faithful ally of Rāma, is helping him in various ways. Mahārāja, it is not possible to make an estimate of the countless *vānara* soldiers. The *vānara* army is presently camping in Subela mountains. This is all the information we could collect during our stay in the *vānara* camp. Now you may decide what you think best."

It would be seen, there were no discrepancies in the reports of Śārdūla and Sārana on the *vānara* army. Apparently Rāvaṇa in pursuance of the principles of intelligence collection, deputed separate groups of spies to collect information about the power and strength of the *vānara* army in order to be fully sure of its veracity. All the groups did their job successfully in extremely trying circumstances. This time Rāvaṇa did not chastise Śārdūla for mentioning the valour of Rāma and Lakṣmaṇa as in the case of Sārana. It appears Rāvaṇa was now fully aware of the dangerous reality he was faced with and accordingly remained concerned more with the thought of defending Laṅkā and winning over Sītā. All other matters were now insignificant to him.

28

Rāvaṇa Devises a Novel Plan to Win over Sītā

Rāvaṇa, thereafter, devised a novel plan to win over Sītā in consultation with his council of ministers. On his orders *māyāvī* Vidyut-Jihvā by dint of his *māyā* power created an artificial head of Rāma and his bow and arrows. Rāvaṇa then along with Vidyut-Jihvā appeared before Sītā at Aśoka Vāṭikā and audaciously said, "O good lady, your husband has been killed in the battle. I have humbled your pride. Now all your hopes and confidence are gone. You have now no other alternative but to accept me as your husband. Not only Rāma, but also all other *vānara* leaders like Sugrīva and Hanumān, have been killed by the *rākṣasa* army. At the disaster of the *vānara* army, many *vānara* soldiers have fled secretly and taken shelter on the trees, in the hill-tops and at the shore of the ocean. I have brought the severed blood-stained head of Rāma for your observation." Vidyut-Jihvā then on Rāvaṇa's orders, produced the severed head of Rāma with his bow and arrows to him and immediately left the place. Placing them before Sītā, Rāvaṇa asked her to accept him as her husband without any hesitation. On seeing the severed head of Rāma and his great bow, Sītā went into lamentation in grief. At this time Rāvaṇa on receipt of an urgent message left the place and immediately Rāma's head with the bow and the arrows, vanished. On returning to the palace, Rāvaṇa heard the news of attack on the city by the *vānara* army and ordered mobilization of the *rākṣasa* forces. Rāvaṇa's plan to win over Sītā thus proved of no avail.

Among the *rākṣasīs* engaged in guarding Sītā, there was one *rākṣasī* by name Sarama who was kind and helpful. Soon friendship developed between Sītā and Sarama. Assuring Sītā, Sarama said, "The severed head and the bow which Rāvaṇa had shown you, were all created with *māyā* power; Rāma, Lakṣmaṇa and all others are well. Give up your grief. Your good time has come. Rāma with a vast *vānara* army has reached Laṅkā after crossing the sea. Rāvaṇa is now engaged in consultations with his ministers to deal with the crisis." At the assuring words of Sarama, peace returned to the mind of Sītā. On her direction, Sarama after collecting details of the discussions in the council of ministers, said, "Janakanandinī, Rāvaṇa's wife Mandodarī and another old minister have asked him to immediately hand over you to Rāma and make peace with him. But Rāvaṇa remained adamant and chose the path of war. Friend, you have nothing to worry. I am certain, Rāma will soon return to Ayodhyā with you after destroying Rāvaṇa." Immediately there arose huge sounds of war drums and blowing of conch-shells of the *vānara* army outside. On hearing the sounds, the citizens of Laṅkā became panic-stricken apprehending a serious calamity.

29

Rāvaṇa Rejects Last-Minute Advice of his Well-wishers to have Peace with Rāma

DURING discussions in the council of ministers, some members praised the power and strength of Rāma. Rāvaṇa immediately silenced them by sharply rebuking them. Then Rāvaṇa's wise paternal grandfather, Mālyavāna said, "O King, the abduction of Sītā is the cause of this war. You should hand over Sītā to Rāma and make peace with him. The *devas*, *gandharvas* and the sages are all praying for the victory of Rāma. Therefore it would not be proper for you to get involved in any hostility with him. During the conquest of the world, you have accumulated a lot of sin by committing irreligious acts. For this your enemies have become strong. Being addicted to worldly pursuits, you have become a cause of concern to the noble-minded sages. On the boon of Prajāpati (The Creator) Brahmā, you are immune from death only from the hands of *devas*, *dānavas*, *gandharvas* and the *yakṣas*; but the humans, monkeys and the bears are presently roaring on reaching your city of Laṅkā. It appears, the entire *rākṣasa* clan is now on the verge of annihilation. Various bad omens are being seen in the different directions. O King, I am also reminding you of another matter. The all-powerful Rāma who has built such a wonderful bridge across the sea, is not an ordinary person. I think, he has actually descended on earth in human form as an incarnation of the Supreme God Viṣṇu. Considering all these facts you may have peace with Rāma for the sake of good for the people of Laṅkā.

Boastfully rejecting the good advice of Mālyavāna, Rāvaṇa declared, he would not hand over Sītā to Rāma in any circumstances. He expressed firm confidence, Rāma would certainly be defeated in this war. Mālyavāna out of disgust did not enter into further arguments with Rāvaṇa and left the assembly hall wishing him victory.

Thereafter, Rāvaṇa in consultations with his council of ministers deployed the *rākṣasa* army under different commanders at all strategic locations and decided he would himself remain at the northern gateway with a strong contingent of *rākṣasa* army. In this way after arranging the defences of the city, Rāvaṇa departed to the inner apartments.

30

Battle between Rākṣasa and Vānara Armies

Soon the four *rākṣasa* companions of Vibhīṣaṇa assuming the form of bird, collected all the details of Rāvaṇa's defences. In the assembly of the *vānara* leaders presided over by Rāma, Vibhīṣaṇa after giving this information, said, "According to the estimate of my companions, more or less ten thousand elephants, ten thousand chariots, twenty thousand horses and more than one crore armed very powerful *rākṣasa* soldiers, have been deployed for the defence of the city of Laṅkā. Rāma, I am also bringing to your notice another information. In the war against our brother Kubera, Rāvaṇa had with him sixty lakh *rākṣasa* soldiers who were together equal to him in force, prowess, strength, pride and might. Do not get angry with me; I am not frightening you. Only to strengthen your anger against the enemy, I am giving you all these details about the *rākṣasa* army. When angry, you are capable of defeating even the *deva*s. I have no doubt about your invincibility."

Rāma heard Vibhīṣaṇa patiently. Here we find the deep characteristic differences between Rāma and Rāvaṇa. Rāvaṇa being impatient was about to execute Śuka and Sārana for mentioning the power and strength of Rāma, Lakṣmaṇa and other *vānara* leaders which was true though unpleasant. He was intoxicated with his own power and pride and had no mind to understand the importance of the information collected by his own spies about the enemies. On the other hand, Rāma was mentally calm and composed and he fully understood the importance of the information brought by Vibhīṣaṇa to help him in the preparation of his war strategy.

On the basis of the information brought by Vibhīṣaṇa, Rāma deployed the *vānara* army for the attack. Commander Nīla with the *vānara* troops was stationed in front of the eastern gateway to engage the *rākṣasa* hero Prahasta. Prince Aṅgada with his troops was directed to fight the *rākṣasa* army under Mahāpārśva and Mahodara as his rivals. Hanumān with a large army was assigned the task of attacking the western gateway. Rāma himself with Lakṣmaṇa took the responsibility of attacking the northern gateway. Sugrīva, Jāmavanta (Jāṁbavān) and Vibhīṣaṇa with troops were kept as reserves in the middle. The *vānaras* were all instructed not to assume human form during the fight. Only Rāma, Lakṣmaṇa and Vibhīṣaṇa with his four companions, it was decided, would fight in human form.

After issuing the battle order, Rāma, calm and composed with the determination to destroy the enemies, marched in steady steps towards the city of Laṅkā with the vast *vānara* army. That night the *vānara* army took rest in Subela mountains. The next morning, Rāma along with Lakṣmaṇa, Sugrīva and some other *vānara* leaders climbed to the top of the mountains and looked at the beautiful city of Laṅkā on the nearby Trikūṭ hills built by *Deva Sthapati* (architect) Viśvakarmā. On seeing Rāvaṇa at the outer gateway, Sugrīva suddenly jumped on his head throwing to the ground his multi-coloured crown. Immediately there ensued a serious wrestling between Rāvaṇa and Sugrīva and it continued for quite some time. At one time Rāvaṇa having failed to come out of Sugrīva's firm embrace, decided to invoke the *māyā* power to release himself. Understanding the intention of Rāvaṇa, the victorious Sugrīva immediately jumped to the sky and appeared before Rāma. On being oppressed and cheated by Sugrīva, Rāvaṇa remained standing at the same place dumbfounded. The *vānara* leaders congratulated Sugrīva for his victory.

Rāma embraced Sugrīva and said, "Friend, you have accomplished such a daring act without consulting me. No king ever embarks on such a dangerous mission. In future do not venture out on such similar missions. Had there been further delay in your return, I would have killed Rāvaṇa and installed Vibhīṣaṇa on the throne of Laṅkā. Thereafter, I would have given up my life after handing over the kingdom of Ayodhyā to Bharata."

Sugrīva humbly said, "*Raghunandana,* I proceeded on this work fully realizing my own strength. How can I forgive Rāvaṇa who has carried away your wife?" Satisfied with the words of Sugrīva, Rāma warmly congratulated him.

Rāma then arranged the *vānara* army in battle order and at the auspicious moment declared the start of the war. He with his bow and the arrows soon after proceeded towards the city of Laṅkā surrounded by his army. Lakṣmaṇa, Sugrīva, Aṅgada, Hanumān, Jāmavanta (Jāṁbavān), Nala and Nīla followed him. Reaching near the city, the *vānara* army on Rāma's order began the attack. Rāma and Lakṣmaṇa with a large force lay seige to the northern gateway which was being defended by Rāvaṇa himself. As decided earlier, commander Nīla, Aṅgada and Hanumān with their troops lay seige to the eastern, southern and the western gateways respectively while protecting the attacking *vānara* army. Sugrīva who was stationed with his troops in the middle, savagely attacked the city causing extensive damage. There were confused noises and shouts of the *vānara* army all around. At the sudden attack on the well-fortified city of Laṅkā, the *rākṣasa*s were utterly surprised.

In a hurriedly held meeting of the ministers, Rāma told Aṅgada, "You immediately meet Rāvaṇa and convey to him the following message of mine — O *niśācara* (one who is active at night), you shall soon realize the consequences of your sin. I have appeared at your door-step like Yama to kill you. If you do not appear before me with Sītā and seek my protection, the entire *rākṣasa* clan will be destroyed by my sharp arrows. On your death I shall make Vibhīṣaṇa the king of Laṅkā."

Aṅgada flying to the city by the aerial path, conveyed Rāma's message to Rāvaṇa, who without giving any reply angrily ordered his immediate execution. On Rāvaṇa's orders as four terrible-looking *rākṣasa*s came forward to bind him with a rope, Aṅgada, firmly holding them, at once rose to the sky and sat on the top of a palace-building. The four *rākṣasa*s while on the aerial path, fell down and were seriously wounded. Aṅgada then after destroying the building with the kick of his feet, safely returned by the sky to their camp and appeared before Rāma. On hearing all details Rāma issued necessary directions to the *vānara* army with full determination to destroy the enemy.

On Rāma's orders, countless *vānara*s and *valluka*s entered inside the city after breaking the gateways and the ramparts by striking with their fists and tails. The senior *vānara* commanders were protecting them. On witnessing the rampage and destruction caused by the enemy troops, Rāvaṇa ordered counter-attack by the *rākṣasa* troops when a fierce battle ensued between the two armies. With the blood and the flesh of the rival troops the battle field turned muddy.

Then began single combats between the rival *vānara* and the *rākṣasa* heroes. As Indrajit threw his thunder-bolt-like mace towards Aṅgada, he with that mace itself attacked Indrajit, killed his charioteer and the horses and destroyed the chariot. The *rākṣasa* hero Jambūmāli was killed at the slap of Hanumān. The *vānara* hero Nala plucked both the eyes of the *rākṣasa* hero Pratāpana. At the beating of Sugrīva, the *rākṣasa* hero Praghasa lost his life. As Agniketu and three other *rākṣasa*s attacked Rāma, he immediately severed their heads with arrows. The *vānara* hero Suṣena killed the *rākṣasa* hero Vidyunmāli with a rock. Despite being oppressed and humiliated, the *rākṣasa* army regrouped itself and continued the fight.

31

Death of Kumbhakarṇa

TAKING his seat in his divine royal throne, Rāvaṇa told the assembled *rākṣasa* heroes with regret, "It appears, all my severe austerities have gone in vain because, even after defeating Devarāja Indra, I have been oppressed by a mere human. At the time of bestowing the boon, I was warned by Lord Brahmā, my fear would come from a human. Now actually the same has happened. My prayer was that *devas*, *dānavas*, *gandharvas*, *yakṣas* and serpents will not be able to kill me and Lord Brahmā was pleased to bestow me the same boon. The human from whom fear would come to me, as predicted by Lord Brahmā, now seems to be no other than Rāma, son of King Daśaratha. King Anaraṇya of the Ikṣvāku dynasty told me long back, I would be killed by a scion of their family. I was cursed by a woman by name Vedavatī on being outraged by me. It is my belief, the same Vedavatī has been born as Sītā, daughter of King Janaka. I have on me innumerable curses from the innocent women and the sages. These curses are not likely to go in vain. Understanding the situation, you may decide for me suitable remedial measures. Let the *rākṣasas* be stationed at all strategic points. You also immediately rouse Kumbhakarṇa from sleep. He is now in deep sleep on the boon of Lord Brahmā. He remains asleep continuously even up to ten months together. Later he wakes up from sleep. Kumbhakarṇa is the greatest warrior amongst the entire *rākṣasa* clan. He will easily be able to destroy Rāma, Lakṣmaṇa and the Vānaras."

As ordered by Rāma, a group of *rākṣasas* with a huge

quantity of foodstuff, went to the palace of Kumbhakarṇa. But they could not first enter inside in the face of the terrible force of his breathing. Later with great difficulty they managed to remain steady and entered inside. On entrance they found Kumbhakarṇa lying in deep sleep on a huge gem-studded bedstead. He is ugly-looking with a massive body. Many nearby animals were found swirling around in the air due to the force of his breathing like that of a poisonous snake. In their effort to rouse him from sleep, the *rākṣasa*s first placed near Kumbhakarṇa a huge quantity of meat- , rice- and blood-filled big pitchers. Then they anointed Kumbhakarṇa with sandal paste and placed fragrant flower garlands on his body. They also sprinkled on his body a variety of perfumes. Thereafter, they began to sing in praise of Kumbhakarṇa. But there was no break in his sleep. Kumbhakarṇa even remained unaffected by the sounds of hundreds of conch-shells, shouting and beating of the drums. The *rākṣasa*s then in desperation began to beat him with hammers, cudgels, etc. and even struck him with large rocks. All this also proved of no avail. Meanwhile, it became difficult for the *rākṣasa*s to carry on their work in the face of the force of Kumbhakarṇa's terrible breathing. Finding no other alternative, the *rākṣasa*s by exciting camels, mules and the elephants, drove them on the body of Kumbhakarṇa. Simultaneously continued the terrible sounding of drums, blowing of conch-shells and trumpets and playing on the various musical instruments. Even then Kumbhakarṇa remained asleep as before. The *rākṣasa*s on being disgusted then began to oppress his body in various ways. Some of them started pulling his hair, some were biting his ears, while many of them began to pour water into the ears. Some of the strong *rākṣasa*s began to strike Kumbhakarṇa with hammers on his chest, head and the body. They also bound his body with rope and began to pull it mechanically in opposite directions. But Kumbhakarṇa could not be roused from sleep. Later when the *rākṣasa*s drove thousands of elephants on his body, Kumbhakarṇa had a feeling of discomfort and woke up from sleep. He became calm after consuming the meat and other foodstuff and asked the *rākṣasas* why he had been roused from sleep untimely.

As the *rākṣasas* explained the danger to Laṅkā following the attack of the *vānara* army, Kumbhakarṇa declared, he would first destroy Rāma and Lakṣmaṇa along with the *vānara* army and then meet Rāvaṇa. On the request of commander Mahodara who was with the *rākṣasas*, Kumbhakarṇa changed his decision and appeared before Rāvaṇa. The *vānara* commanders were terrified on seeing Kumbhakarṇa with his huge body like a mountain, on his way to Rāvaṇa's assembly hall. Many *vānara* soldiers lay down on the ground out of fear. Many even fled from the battlefield in panic.

Rāma on seeing Kumbhakarṇa asked Vibhīṣaṇa about his background. Explaining Kumbhakarṇa's characteristic details and his power and strength, Vibhīṣaṇa said he had come out of his palace to devour the *vānaras*. On hearing everything, Rāma arranged the *vānara* army in battle order and deployed Aṅgada and the other *vānara* heroes at every gateway of the Laṅkā city. Being assured by Rāma, the *vānara* soldiers regrouped themselves and became ready to destroy the enemy.

At the assembly hall, Kumbhakarṇa heard Rāvaṇa's lamentation over his humiliation at the hands of Rāma and said with laughter, "O King, the danger about which we talked earlier, has now all come true. You are now in the midst of the same danger. Your present danger is entirely due to your refusal to listen to our honest advice. O King, you have not judged the consequences of your actions because of your arrogance for power and strength. The person who, blinded by his pride of wealth, does his first work last and the last work first, is bound to suffer. The king who with due regard to his own gain and loss and having proper assessment of his power and strength, takes decision in adherence to the principles of *sāma, dāma, bheda* and *daṇḍa* after proper consultations with his ministers, is known to be versed in ethics and politics. The king should always hold consultations with those ministers who are wise and knowledgeable. The advice of those who are ministers only in name, talkative and devoid of knowledge of the scriptures, is never acceptable. You have landed yourself in this dangerous situation only on the evil counsel of some of your unscrupulous ministers. You have ignored the honest advice of Queen Mandodarī and brother Vibhīṣaṇa. There is still time. Do what you think best."

At the words of Kumbhakarṇa, Rāvaṇa angrily said, "You are giving advice in vain. It is unnecessary to mention my past mistakes. Think about our duty in the present situation. The fearful situation which has been created by my unjust acts, must be remedied only by prowess. If the path of war as decided by me is to your liking, you may take action accordingly. No virtuous person ever forsakes his friend even if he deviates from the path of virtue."

Kumbhakarṇa realized, Rāvaṇa had been angry with him. He then said in sweet words, "O King, I think I should give you good counsel in all circumstances. Out of brotherly feeling and as a friend, I have spoken these words to you. However, I am taking the vow, I shall devour the principal *vānara* leaders after killing Rāma and Lakṣmaṇa. On Rāma's death Sītā will surrender to you in no time."

Rākṣasa Mahodara rebuked Kumbhakarṇa and said, "Despite your birth in a great clan, traits of impudence, mean-mindedness and pride still persist in you. This is why you have no idea as to your duty in a particular situation. Because of your bad intention, you had the audacity to speak such things to the face of the king. The *rākṣasa* king is fully conversant with the principles of justice and righteousness. He is aware of the country's situation, his own interest and of the enemy's power and weakness. Out of ignorance you have brought various allegations against him. Work is the originator of religion, wealth and desire. These are not mutually antagonistic. Great happiness comes from the fulfilment of the desire. It is my firm belief, we should wholeheartedly follow the path enunciated by the *rākṣasa* king.

"Kumbhakarṇa, I am warning you on another matter. Your decision to destroy the enemy alone is foolish. We have already got an idea of Rāma's power and strength in Janasthāna. In force and anger, Rāma is terrible. To face him is like embracing death. I am strongly against your going to war alone."

Addressing Rāvaṇa, Mahodara said, "O King, I have got a plan by which you shall easily gain Sītā without war. Kindly listen to me. You may publicize in the city that five of your valiant warriors have destroyed the *vānara* army along with Rāma and Lakṣmaṇa in the battle with arrows engraved with Rāma's name and devoured their bodies. You shall also in great satisfaction then start distributing various presents to your servants and slaves, employees and the soldiers. This information of death of Rāma and Lakṣmaṇa will soon reach Sītā. You shall at the proper moment appear before Sītā and console her in her bereavement. You may then try to allure her with jewelleries and other costly presents. On being dejected at the death of her husband, Sītā will then certainly surrender to you. O King, by this plan of mine you shall easily gain Sītā without any war. You shall have then no need of facing Rāma in the battle."

Kumbhakarṇa sharply rebuked Mahodara for his childish plan. Turning to Rāvaṇa he said, "O King, you may rest assured I shall rescue you from this danger by killing Rāma in the battle. You may know, those who are real heroes do never roar in vain. You shall witness the success of my roar in the battlefield."

Kumbhakarṇa then told Mahodara, "O Mahodara, your cowardly words can only be liked by a foolish, weak and pedantic king. Only for a few cowards and sycophants like you, our king is now placed in such a great danger. You are all friends only in name; in work you are all his enemies. Taking advantage of his pliability, you are getting everything done by the king according to your own wishes. This is why in Laṅkā only the king exists at present; all his manpower and wealth are lost. I am immediately proceeding to fight to counteract your misdeeds."

On hearing Kumbhakarṇa, Rāvaṇa said with a smile, "Brother, Mahodara has no interest in war as he is afraid of facing Rāma in the battle. In power and strength you are second to none. You proceed to war to destroy the enemy. I believe, the *vānara*s will start fleeing away on only seeing you. And Rāma and Lakṣmaṇa too in their minds will be shaken with fear."

Kumbhakarṇa, thereafter, in full battle dress proceeded to fight in his chariot with his terrible spear in hand after paying obeisance to his elder brother Rāvaṇa. Innumerable *rākṣasa*s blowing conch-shell and beating wardrums followed Kumbhakarṇa. He told the *rākṣasa*s, Rāma and Lakṣmaṇa were responsible for the seige of Laṅkā. This was why he was determined to kill them. On coming out of the city, Kumbhakarṇa raised a terrible war cry trembling all around. But bad omens were noticed in all directions. Kumbhakarṇa's left eyes quivered and his left hand began to tremble. He felt discomfort in breathing. Disregarding all this, Kumbhakarṇa proceeded ahead. On seeing him, many *vānara* soldiers began to flee. On the efforts of Aṅgada and other *vānara* heroes, the *vānara* soldiers regrouped and attacked Kumbhakarṇa with trees. But at the counter-attack of Kumbhakarṇa, the *vānara* soldiers were routed and they began to flee in different directions. Aṅgada with great efforts brought them back when a fierce battle started between Kumbhakarṇa and the *vānara* army. At the strike of Kumbhakarṇa's mace, innumerable *vānara* soldiers lost their lives. Many also perished at the kicking of his feet. He then began to devour the *vānara*s by putting them into his mouth. At this time *vānara* hero Dvivida uprooted a mountain and threw it towards Kumbhakarṇa destroying his horses, chariot, elephants and a number of *rākṣasas* accompanying him. At this the *rākṣasas* became furious and they started devouring the *vānara* soldiers indiscriminately. On seeing the disaster in their army ranks, Hanumān flew to the sky and hurled on the head of Kumbhakarṇa many mountain-peaks, rocks and trees. Kumbhakarṇa, however, cut all of them into pieces with his trident. Then a fierce battle started between Hanumān and Kumbhakarṇa. On being pierced by the trident, Hanumān started vomiting blood. Then Nala appeared at the battlefield and struck Kumbhakarṇa with a mountain-peak. Kumbhakarṇa immediately broke it into pieces with his arrow. Nala and some other *vānara* soldiers, thereafter, simultaneously attacked Kumbhakarṇa. Many of them began to vomit blood on being embraced by Kumbhakarṇa with his arms. Aṅgada and Kumbhakarṇa were again locked in a serious combat. At the blow of Aṅgada, Kumbhakarṇa for a while became unconscious. Kumbhakarṇa on regaining consciousness struck a heavy blow on Aṅgada making him unconscious. Meanwhile, the mountain-peak hurled on Kumbhakarṇa by Sugrīva broke into several pieces on falling on his chest. Kumbhakarṇa then became furious and hurled his sharp trident on Sugrīva. Hanumān instantly held the spear in his two arms and broke it. At this the *vānara* soldiers with great delight raised a loud war cry. The *rākṣasas* out of fear retreated from the battlefield. At the breaking of his trident, Kumbhakarṇa in a rage suddenly held Sugrīva and made him a captive after making him unconscious with a mountain-peak. The *rākṣasas* wildly applauded Kumbhakarṇa for his prompt action. The *vānaras* raised a cry of distress. Assuring the *vānaras*, Hanumān regrouped them in battle order.

Kumbhakarṇa returned to the city carrying Sugrīva with him. On regaining consciousness, Sugrīva began to think how to free himself from captivity. Suddenly he cut Kumbhakarṇa's nose and ears with his sharp nails and teeth. With the nails of his feet, Sugrīva caused deep wounds at the two sides of Kumbhakarṇa's body. With his body smeared with blood, Kumbhakarṇa began to trample him on the ground. The *rākṣasa*s also started beating him. Sugrīva then assuming the form of a *kanduka* (round-shaped piece of wood) suddenly freed himself from the clutches of Kumbhakarṇa, flew to the sky and then appeared before Rāma. Kumbhakarṇa became furious at this deception of Sugrīva and left the city holding a big hammer. On reaching the battlefield, he started devouring the *vānara*s. Lakṣmaṇa tried to resist him with his shower of arrows, but failed. Kumbhakarṇa leaving Lakṣmaṇa, ran towards Rāma when a fierce battle started between the two. Rāma thrust innumerable arrows on the chest of Kumbhakarṇa. At one time all the weapons of Kumbhakarṇa fell down on the ground. Even without any arms, Kumbhakarṇa with his kicks and blows began to destroy the *vānara*s. He broke a mountain-peak and hurled it towards Rāma, who promptly destroyed it with seven arrows.

Lakṣmaṇa thought over the means to kill Kumbhakarṇa and told Rāma, "O Aryan, this Kumbhakarṇa is a peculiar hero. He is bereft of any sense of distinction between the *vānara*s and the *rākṣasa*s. Look, he is devouring the soldiers of both the sides. There is a means to kill him. Let our *vānara* leaders and the other large *vānara*s climb the body of Kumbhakarṇa from different sides. Being thus repressed with heavy weight, he would not be able to move about in the battlefield freely and devour our *vānara* soldiers. Then it would be easy to kill him."

As suggested by Lakṣmaṇa, the *vānara*s began to climb the body of Kumbhakarṇa. Angry Kumbhakarṇa then gave a big jerk to his body and violently threw the *vānara*s on the ground. Rāma, thereafter, advanced towards Kumbhakarṇa and saw him searching out the *vānara*s while licking with his tongue his own blood. Meanwhile, Rāma continued to oppress Kumbhakarṇa with his shower of arrows. Kumbhakarṇa to the best of his ability tried to thwart the impact of the arrows. Rāma at this time severed one of the arms of Kumbhakarṇa holding the hammer with his *vāyavāstra*. The severed arm of Kumbhakarṇa fell on the *vānara* soldiers and killed many of them. Kumbhakarṇa holding a *śāla* tree then advanced towards Rāma with a high speed. Rāma severed with his *svarṇapaṅkha bāṇa* this arm of Kumbhakarṇa also. Even after severance of both the arms, Kumbhakarṇa raising a vicious war cry continued his advance towards Rāma. Then Rāma with his *ardhacandra bāṇa* severed both the legs of Kumbhakarṇa. At the sound of the fall of Kumbhakarṇa's two severed legs, mountain caves, sea, city of Laṅkā and the *vānara*s and the *rākṣasa*s severely trembled.

Even without the hands and the legs, Kumbhakarṇa with a terrible roar continued his advance towards Rāma, who then with his *svarṇapaṅkha bāṇa* filled the cavity of his mouth making him speechless. Rāma, thereafter, with another sharp dazzling arrow inlaid with gold, severed the great head of Kumbhakarṇa decorated with earrings and resembling the mountain-peak. At the impact of the fall of his severed head, Laṅkā's high ramparts and the ornamental gateways were destroyed. As the huge body of Kumbhakarṇa fell in the sea, the aquatic animals, fish, and the serpents within the water were badly stricken. At the death of Kumbhakarṇa, the *deva*s delightfully raised a big roar. The *vānara* soldiers were also very much delighted. The *rākṣasa* soldiers were deeply hurt and they on seeing Rāma, began to scream loudly. Like Indra on the death of Vitrāsura, Rāma was delighted on the death of Kumbhakarṇa, the conqueror of the *deva*s who was never before defeated in any war.

In power and strength, Kumbhakarṇa was second to none among the *rākṣasa*s. He, without any accompanying fighting forces, appeared in the battle against the vast *vānara* army led by Rāma who was himself armed with all divine weapons. This was indeed an unequal war. Despite all this, Kumbhakarṇa single-handedly routed the *vānara* army and defeated warriors like Lakṣmaṇa and other valiant *vānara* heroes in the battle. This is no mean achievement. Kumbhakarṇa was not simply a warrior of exceptional strength and courage, he was also a person of very high moral principles. He did not hesitate to criticize Rāvaṇa's action in abducting Sītā by deceitful means. He advised Rāvaṇa to establish peace with Rāma by handing over Sītā to him. He squarely blamed Rāvaṇa for this catastrophic war threatening the destruction of Laṅkā and the entire *rākṣasa* clan he strongly denounced the role of his sycophant ministers who led him astray by giving him wrong advice. Explaining *rājadharma,* he advised Rāvaṇa to take his decisions only on the advice of the wise and knowledgeable ministers. Rāvaṇa, we know, did not like such unpleasant truths spoken by Kumbhakarṇa. Despite being an ardent critic of Rāvaṇa's actions, he did not hesitate to go to war on his order and give his life fighting to the last. His supreme sacrifice underlines his deep sense of patriotism. His differences with Rāvaṇa did not in any way interfere with his duty towards the country when it was in extreme danger following the foreign invasion. Kumbhakarṇa's sacrifice will no doubt inspire all right-thinking and patriotic people.

Kumbhakarṇa's role is in sharp contrast to that of his brother Vibhīṣaṇa. Both of them were strong critics of Rāvaṇa's actions. Both urged Rāvaṇa to have peace with Rāma on releazing Sītā. They were both critical of Rāvaṇa's sycophant ministers. Vibhīṣaṇa, we know, on being insulted by Rāvaṇa joined the invading army of Rāma realizing Rāvaṇa's sure defeat in the war. His motive was to gain the kingdom of Laṅkā with Rāma's help. Rāma readily welcomed him and gave him protection. He straightway installed him as the future king of Laṅkā. In return, Vibhīṣaṇa provided Rāma vital secrets about the strength and weaknesses of Rāvaṇa and his *rākṣasa* army which proved immensely helpful to Rāma in winning the war. Whatever may be the support of the Rāma-devotees behind Vibhīṣaṇa's role, it remains a fact, the people at large look upon him with contempt as a hated betrayer of his country and the king. "Country's enemy (*rājadrohī*), Vibhīṣaṇa" — this epithet now stands deeply ingrained in people's mind. No parents out of abhorrence for him give the name "Vibhīṣaṇa" to their male children. The sacrifice of Kumbhakarṇa for the country's independence is indeed a contemptuous ridicule of Vibhīṣaṇa's ascendancy to the throne of Laṅkā by his act of betrayal to his own brother and the king. Was Vibhīṣaṇa happy in his life? The *Rāmāyaṇa* is silent in the matter. We know, Sugrīva felt a deep remorse at the unethical death at his instance of his brother Vālī at the hands of Rāma and even wanted to give up his life on the burning pyre to atone his sin. In the context of the ugly betrayals of Sugrīva and Vibhīṣaṇa against their own brothers, stands, as a dazzling example, the wonderful devotion and loyalty shown to Rāma by his own brothers.

32

Death of Indrajit

RĀVAṆA, meanwhile, at the news of Kumbhakarṇa's death, fell down unconscious with a heavy heart. Later, on regaining consciousness, he went into lamentation mentioning Kumbhakarṇa's manifold qualities. Seeing Rāvaṇa in the state of lamentation, son Triśira told him, "O King, your influence is spread over the entire world. Why are you so distressed at the death of Kumbhakarṇa? Even now you have the divine amulet gifted by Lord Brahmā, you have your bow and the arrows, you have thousands of chariots. Besides, we your valiant sons are all alive. You have defeated the gods and the demons many times. It is not at all difficult for you to destroy an ordinary person like Rāma. You may take rest. I myself shall alone destroy the enemies." At the words of Triśira, Rāvaṇa was assured as if he had gained a new life.

Thereafter, Rāvaṇa's four sons Triśira, Atikāya, Devāntaka, Narāntaka and his two step-brothers, Mahodara and Mahāpārśva went out of the city with a large force and attacked the *vānara* army. Unable to withstand Narāntaka's shower of arrows, the *vānara* soldiers raised a piteous cry. On the orders of Sugrīva, Aṅgada advanced towards Narāntaka and killed him with a blow on his head after first wounding his horses. Then ensued a fierce battle between Devāntaka and Aṅgada. In the battle both of them were wounded. At last Devāntaka was killed at the hands of Hanumān. Later, Hanumān snatched away the sword of Triśira and with that sword severed all his three heads. Mahodara's head was torn into pieces with a rock thrown by the *vānara* hero Nīla.

Mahāpārśva lost his life when *vānara* hero Hṛṣava struck him on the chest with the mace snatched away from his hands. The *rākṣasas* then were gripped in great panic and they began to flee in different directions. Thereafter, Rāvaṇa's valiant son Atikāya who earlier destroyed *devas* and *asuras* on the boon of Lord Brahmā joined the war and started destroying the *vānara* soldiers. As Lakṣmaṇa appeared in defence of the *vānara* soldiers, a fierce battle started between the two. At last on the advice of Hanumān, Lakṣmaṇa killed Atikāya with his *brahmāstra*.

At the news of the death of his sons and brothers, Rāvaṇa began to shed tears in grief. Later, he remained in deep thought for some time. At this time, son Indrajit told Rāvaṇa, "Father, your son Indrajit is still alive. It does not look nice of you if you remain stricken in grief. Listen to my firm vow; today I shall without fail kill Rāma and Lakṣmaṇa in the battle."

With the approval of Rāvaṇa, Indrajit went out in the chariot with a large *rākṣasa* force. On the way he appeared at Nikumbhila (place for sacrificial rites) and offered oblation of fire. Later, as he made the offering of a live goat to the sacrificial fire, the accumulated flame emanated brightly indicating his victory. Indrajit then with his sanctified weapons, chariot and the horses, rose to the sky and became invisible. On his orders, the *rākṣasa* soldiers began to destroy the *vānaras* on the ground. Indrajit routing the *vānara* army from the sky by his shower of arrows, severely oppressed Sugrīva, Hanumān, Aṅgada and other *vānara* heroes. Thereafter, Indrajit by his arrows sanctified with *mantra*, wearied even Rāma and Lakṣmaṇa, who lost all the spirit of fighting. At this time, Rāma told Lakṣmaṇa, "Look, Indrajit has again drawn out his great weapon. Blessed with the boon of Lord Brahmā, he is extremely powerful and by dint of his *māyā* power, he has kept his body concealed. This is why we are unable to see him. It appears, Lord Brahmā Himself is behind his weapons. In the circumstances we have no other alternative than to bear with this shower of arrows in deference to the Self-born (Lord Brahmā). The *vānara* army is completely routed. All our principal warriors are lying prostrate on the ground. Now we shall remain lying on the ground feigning to be unconscious so that Indrajit may think, we have been defeated. He will then stop the fighting and depart to the city." Accordingly Rāma and Lakṣmaṇa along with the *vānara* army, on being oppressed by Indrajit's arrows, remained lying on the ground. Indrajit, thereafter, left the battlefield to give Rāvaṇa the news of the defeat of the *vānara* army.

In the terrible battle of that day, according to the narration in the *Rāmāyaṇa*, a total of 67 (sixty-seven) crore of *vānara* soldiers were killed. Countless more were wounded. As the battle stopped, Sugrīva and Hanumān, despite being wounded, went out in search of the *vānara* soldiers lying scattered in the battlefield. Soon they came across wounded old Jāmavanta (Jāṁbavān) and gave him the news of the battle. Jāmavanta (Jāṁbavān) then told Hanumān, "Hanumān, now you are the only person who is capable of saving the *vānaras*. You immediately proceed to the Himalayas by the aerial path. At the peak of the Himalayas you shall find four medicinal plants by name *mṛtasañjīvanī, viśalyakaraṇī, suvalakaraṇī* and *sandhānakaraṇī.* You bring those medicinal plants as quickly as possible and bring the *vānaras* back to life."

As directed by Jāmavanta (Jāṁbavān), Hanumān reached the Himalayas by the aerial path after crossing a distance of thousand *yojanas*; but he did not find the medicinal plants. In the situation, he angrily uprooted the entire mountain containing the medicinal plants and brought it to Laṅkā. At the sweet smell of the plants, Rāma and Lakṣmaṇa came round very soon. The dead *vānaras* also got back their lives The *rākṣasas* who died in the battle, did not, however, get any benefit from the smell of the medicinal plants as their bodies were thrown to the sea in order to keep the number of their casualties concealed from the enemy on the orders of Rāvaṇa. At the end of the work, Hanumān as before proceeding by the aerial path, kept the mountain with the medicinal plants at the same place in the Himalayas.

On getting back their lives, the *vānara* soldiers, on the direction of Sugrīva, destroyed by fire that night itself the main gateway, the royal path, assembly halls, palaces, buildings, etc. of the city of Laṅkā. In the meantime Rāma on getting round, began to destroy the *rākṣasa* soldiers by continuous shower of arrows.

At the sudden calamity of Laṅkā, Yupākṣa, Śoṇitākṣa and some other *rākṣasa* heroes went to the battle and got killed one by one. Later Indrajit's two sons Kumbha and Nikumbha were also killed at the hands of the *vānara* army. Afterwards, *rākṣasa* hero Makarākṣa fell upon the *vānara* army with all ferocity with a large force, when a terrible battle started between the two armies. At last Makarākṣa was killed at the hands of Rāma. The remaining *rākṣasa*s then fled towards the city.

Thereafter, Indrajit on offering his usual oblation of fire, again began his fight remaining invisible in the sky. His arrows pierced both Rāma and Lakṣmaṇa. None of their arrows could touch invisible Indrajit. The *vānara* army was on the verge of destruction at the shower of arrows of Indrajit. Finding no other alternative, Rāma angrily decided to apply his *brahmāstra*. Understanding Rāma's intention, Indrajit stopped the fighting and returned to the city.

Soon after, he came out of the city. Behind him was a large *rākṣasa* force. Finding Rāma and Lakṣmaṇa standing some distance away, Indrajit created by *māyā* power a living image of Sītā. He placed this Māyā-Sītā on the chariot and declared, he would immediately kill her. The *vānara* soldiers on being enraged attacked Indrajit. There was also a serious altercation between Indrajit and Hanumān. Later Indrajit with his sword severed the head of Māyā-Sītā and raised a loud roar. The *vānara* soldiers started retreating. Hanumān at the "death" of Sītā became depressed and stopped fighting. Rāma being overwhelmed with grief, fell down on the ground. Consoling Rāma, Lakṣmaṇa said, "O hero, please get up. I shall avenge the hateful act of Indrajit. I shall immediately destroy the entire city of Laṅkā by my shower of arrows."

Intervening with Lakṣmaṇa, Vibhīṣaṇa told Rāma, "O King, I do not find any reason behind this news of "death" of Sītā. We know the attitude of Rāvaṇa towards Sītā. He will never kill her. We also know, it is not possible for anyone else to meet with Sītā even by applying the principles of *sāma, dāma* or *bheda.* In the circumstances it is not clear how Indrajit could bring Sītā in his chariot to the battlefield. It is my strong belief, Indrajit has deceived the *vānaras;* the Sītā he has killed is only a Māyā-Sītā. You may rest assured, your Sītā is safe and sound at the Aśoka Vāṭikā. O King, I am telling you another very important matter. Indrajit today will perform a special rite of the sacrificial fire at Nikumbhila. After the performance of this rite, it will be impossible even for Indra to defeat him. It is the ordainment of Lord Brahmā, Indrajit will be killed, if he goes to the battle without completing the sacrificial rite. This is the most opportune moment to kill him. You send Lakṣmaṇa to kill Indrajit after nullifying his performance of the sacrificial rite.

On the orders of Rāma, Lakṣmaṇa wearing his armour and the amulet and armed with various weapons, then with a large force proceeded to Nikumbhila accompanied by Vibhīṣaṇa, Sugrīva and the other *vānara* heroes. On the way, Vibhīṣaṇa told Lakṣmaṇa "O hero, before the completion of oblation of fire by Indrajit, you will have to kill him after driving away the enemy forces by the shower of arrows. Please keep in mind, Indrajit is cruel-hearted, wicked and *māyāvī* (one who knows sorcery). No work is impossible for him."

On approaching Nikumbhila, Lakṣmaṇa struck the *rākṣasa* soldiers with his shower of arrows. Simultaneously the *vānara* army also attacked them, when a serious battle started between them. At last the *rākṣasa*s out of fear retreated.

Indrajit had just then started his oblation of fire. On getting the news of reverses in the *rākṣasa* army, he left the place of worship without completing his oblation of fire and proceeded to resist the attacking *vānara* army in his chariot. On seeing Indrajit coming out, the *rākṣasa* soldiers regrouped and advanced towards Lakṣmaṇa. Hanumān then began to destroy the *rākṣasa*s by hurling the uprooted trees. Indrajit initially could not cause him any harm. At last Indrajit attached a very powerful arrow to his bow in order to kill Hanumān. In this situation, Vibhīṣaṇa asked Lakṣmaṇa to kill Indrajit without any delay. As Lakṣmaṇa's sight fell on Indrajit, Vibhīṣaṇa hurriedly took him to the nearest forest. There were many banyan trees in that area. Showing those trees to Lakṣmaṇa, Vibhīṣaṇa told him, "Indrajit goes to the battle after offering oblation to all created beings (ghosts) underneath these banyan trees. With the power obtained from this performance of rites, Indrajit destroys his enemies remaining invisible from others. Please kill Indrajit before he comes near these trees."

As Indrajit approached the banyan trees, Lakṣmaṇa challenged him for a fight. Indrajit first did not give any reply. Finding Vibhīṣaṇa standing nearby, Indrajit told him in a manly voice, "O *rākṣasa,* you are my father's own brother. You are born in a *rākṣasa* clan. You are my uncle. I am your son. Why are you opposing me? O Evil-minded devil, birth, religion, bond of friendship — you have all sacrificed. You have become a servant of the foreigners forsaking your own people. For this, you stand insulted and hated before all pious people. Forsaking your friends and relatives, you have taken refuge under the sinful enemies. Your intelligence has become placid. This is why you are not in a position to understand the distinction between your own relatives and the enemies. Even the relatives devoid of any excellence are better than others possessing the highest excellence. A foreigner is always a foreigner. He can never be a real friend. He who serves the enemy, ultimately gets killed by the same enemy after his own relatives are destroyed. O *niśācara*, such a heart-less behaviour is possible only from a traitor uncle like you."

Without being in any way perturbed at the scolding of Indrajit, Vibhīṣaṇa said in reply, "O *rākṣasa*, fully knowing my nature, you are denouncing me unnecessarily like an ignorant person. Even being born in the cruel *rākṣasa* clan, honesty and morality which are the best attributes of the humans and which are totally absent in the *rākṣasa*s, are my special virtues. I have never been involved in any irreligious acts. The nature of our two brothers is not the same. Because of this difference in our nature, he (Rāvaṇa) has forsaken me. You shall gain nothing in blaming me. Plunder of others' wealth, oppression of others' women and the persecution of the well-wishers are the principal reasons responsible for the present danger to your father's life. In addition, killing of pious sages, antagonizing the gods and unusual pride, anger, animosity and enmity, all these also have come to threaten the life of your father. As the moral downfall of your father was intolerable to me, I have left the city of Laṅkā and joined the great Rāma. This city of Laṅkā will soon be destroyed along with your father and all others. You are a vainglorious boy. That is why you had the audacity to insult me in this way. Know it for certain, despite all your efforts, you shall not be able to enter into the foot of the banyan trees. Now depart to the abode of Yama on being killed by Lakṣmaṇa, brother of Rāma. Let the gods be happy."

After this, a terrible sanguinary battle started between Lakṣmaṇa and Indrajit. At their shower of arrows, bodies of both of them were pierced; but none was subdued. At this time, Vibhīṣaṇa came forward and began to oppress the *rākṣasa* soldiers by continuous shower of arrows. The four *rākṣasa* companions of Vibhīṣaṇa also attacked the *rākṣasa* soldiers. Innumerable *rākṣasas* were killed. In order to enthuse the *vānara* army, Vibhīṣaṇa said, "O *vānaras*, this boy Indrajit is the last resort of the *rākṣasas*. The number of *rākṣasa* soldiers who are still alive, is also limited. Advance against these few *rākṣasa* soldiers with all your might. This Indrajit is like my son. Even then for the good of Rāma I have been ready to kill him. But my two eyes are getting closed with tears. Accordingly I have refrained from committing this sinful act. Lakṣmaṇa himself will complete this task of killing Indrajit."

On being enthused by Vibhīṣaṇa, the *vānara* soldiers with a renewed vigour fell upon the *rākṣasas*. After having a fierce battle with uncle Vibhīṣaṇa, Indrajit advanced towards Lakṣmaṇa, when again a terrible battle started between the two. All sides were cast in darkness. With blood of the dead soldiers, the battlefield turned into rivers of blood. The animals and the birds began to scream in fear. At this time Lakṣmaṇa's arrows severed the head of the charioteer of Indrajit. Some of his horses were also killed. Indrajit then himself became his charioteer and continued to shoot arrows at Lakṣmaṇa. Lakṣmaṇa's shower of arrows also continued unabated. At the opportune moment, four *vānara* heroes with their feet trampled down into pieces the remaining four horses of Indrajit. Without the chariot, horses and the charioteer, Indrajit fought gallantly for some time and then suddenly entered into the city hoodwinking the *vānara* soldiers. Soon he returned to the battlefield on a new attractive chariot. A huge *rākṣasa* army accompanied him. The new charioteer is learned and experienced about horses.

Indrajit starting the battle with renewed vigour, killed innumerable *vānara* soldiers. Lakṣmaṇa then destroyed the bow of Indrajit and thrust five arrows on his chest. Despite being seriously wounded with blood oozing out of his mouth, Indrajit held a strong new bow and continued to shoot at Lakṣmaṇa. Resisting Indrajit's shower of arrows, Lakṣmaṇa severed the head of his new charioteer with an arrow. Surprisingly even without the charioteer, he continued to drive the chariot. At this time, Indrajit in a rage pierced Vibhīṣaṇa and other *vānara* heroes with arrows. In retaliation, Vibhīṣaṇa angrily destroyed all the new horses of Indrajit with kicks. Indrajit from his chariot without the charioteer and the horses, hurled a *śakti-astra* towards Vibhīṣaṇa. Lakṣmaṇa immediately cut it into pieces with an arrow. Vibhīṣaṇa was thus saved from the inevitable death. Failing to kill Indrajit with so many arrows, Lakṣmaṇa at last severed Indrajit's crown-decorated beautiful head from his body with a terrible arrow by name *supatra* and *suparva*. At the death of Indrajit, the *rākṣasa* soldiers fled in different directions out of fear. Vibhīṣaṇa and the other *vānara* heroes congratulated Lakṣmaṇa. The battlefield resounded with the cries of jubilation raised by the *vānara*s. The gods alighted to the battlefield and expressed happiness at the performance of such an incredible act by Lakṣmaṇa. Rāma with a happy mind embraced Lakṣmaṇa. On Rāma's orders, *vaidya* Suṣeṇa brought round Lakṣmaṇa and the other wounded *vānara*s by treatment.

33

Death of Rāvaṇa

In the city Rāvaṇa on getting the news of Indrajit's death, fainted and on regaining consciousness soon after, while lamenting, said in a state of violent rage, "On satisfying self-born Lord Brahmā with my worship for thousands of years, I have been blessed with the boon, I have no fear from *deva*s or *dānava*s. Lord Brahmā even gave me a wonderful armour. In the battle against the *deva*s and the *dānava*s even the Brahmā Śakti could cause no harm to this armour. I shall go to the battle wearing this armour. On being happy at my valour in the battle between the *deva*s and the *asura*s, Lord Brahmā handed over to me the most powerful bow and arrows. I shall use this bow and the arrows to kill Lakṣmaṇa." Saying this, Rāvaṇa directed the *rākṣasa*s to immediately produce this terrible bow before him.

Rāvaṇa, thereafter, decided, he would not keep Sītā alive any longer. He accordingly with a sword in hand proceeded towards Aśoka Vāṭikā. To see angry Rāvaṇa coming with a sword, Sītā began to tremble out of fear. On seeing Sītā bewildered with fright, Supārśva, Rāvaṇa's wise and virtuous minister, in an effort to desist him from committing such a heinous act, told Rāvaṇa, "Daśānana, even being a virtuous king, you are going to kill a woman! Leave Sītā alone and show your anger on going to the battle against Rāma. You are valorous, wise and known to be the most competent warrior. We firmly believe, you shall certainly gain Sītā after killing Rāma in the battle." At the just words of Supārśva, Rāvaṇa changed his earlier decision and returned to his assembly hall.

On Rāvaṇa's orders, his commanders then left for the battle with a large force of elephants, horses, chariots and foot-soldiers; when a fierce battle started with the *vānara* soldiers. Rāma alone routed most of the *rākṣasa* army. The remnants of the *rākṣasa* army retreated to the city in panic. At the reverses of the *rākṣasa* soldiers, the *rākṣasīs* went into lamentation for fear of their own lives.

At the death of his commanders, Rāvaṇa flew into a rage and declared, he would himself go to the battle. Accordingly, on his orders, four *rākṣasa* commanders mobilized one *nijuta* (10 lakh, i.e. 1 million) chariots, 3 *nijuta* elephants, 60 crore donkeys, camels and horses along with countless foot-soldiers. On completion of the mobilization, Rāvaṇa armed with various weapons left the city of Laṅkā in his divine chariot driven by his charioteer towards the battlefield. On the way various bad omens indicating death were noticed. Rāvaṇa ignored them all. At the sight of the *vānara* soldiers he started killing them indiscriminately.

Engaging *vānara* hero Suṣeṇa in protecting the retreating *vānara* soldiers, Sugrīva along with the other *vānara* heroes attacked the *rākṣasa* army. In the attack many *rākṣasa* soldiers were killed. In this situation *rākṣasa* hero Virūpākṣa attacked the *vānara* soldiers when a serious battle started between Sugrīva and Virūpākṣa. At last Virūpākṣa was killed at the hands of Sugrīva.

On Virūpākṣa's death, on Rāvaṇa's orders, *rākṣasa* hero Mahodara appeared at the battle and destroyed a number of *vānara* soldiers. Sugrīva then destroyed with his hammer Mahodara's horses. The mace hurled by Mahodara fell down on the ground on being obstructed by Sugrīva's hammer. Sugrīva then hurled eight iron hammers towards Mahodara. The hammers broke into pieces on being struck by the mace of Mahodara. At last Sugrīva severed the head of Mahodara with his sword. On his death, the *rākṣasa* soldiers began to flee from the battlefield.

Rākṣasa hero Mahāpārśva (Mahodara and Mahāpārśva mentioned here are Rāvaṇa's ministers. The other two *rākṣasa* heroes of the same name had been killed earlier) then ferociously attacked the *vānara* soldiers and started annihilating them. Then a serious fight with bows and arrows ensued between Mahāpārśva and Aṅgada. Later, Aṅgada's arrows pierced Mahāpārśva's chest and he fell down dead.

On the death of these three great *rākṣasa* heroes, Rāvaṇa, furious and trembling, rushed towards Rāma in his chariot. On the way he destroyed innumerable *vānara* soldiers. At the huge sound of the force of Rāvaṇa's shower of arrows and of the twang of Rāma's bowstring, a large number of *vānara* soldiers lay prostrate on the ground. It was Lakṣmaṇa who first shot his arrows towards Rāvaṇa. Repelling Lakṣmaṇa's arrows, Rāvaṇa appeared before Rāma and discharged a shower of arrows on him. A horrible fight with bows and arrows then started between the two great heroes. The innumerable arrows discharged by them covered the entire sky when darkness descended all around. None of them relented in any way. The two heroes destroyed each other's arrows in the sky. Rāvaṇa then discharged a *nachar* (a large arrow made of iron) weapon towards Rāma and Lakṣmaṇa. Rāma easily bore the impact of this terrible weapon and then discharged an arrow sanctified by *mantra* towards Rāvaṇa. But the arrow aborted on falling on his impenetrable armour. Many other terrible *asurāstras* like *kaṅkamukha, kākamukha*, etc. discharged by Rāvaṇa were also foiled by Rāma with his divine weapons. On the failure of the arrows discharged by Rāvaṇa, Sugrīva and the other *vānara* warriors began to rejoice surrounding Rāma.

On his own weapons being baffled, Rāvaṇa angrily became ready to discharge a terrible weapon made by Maya Dānava towards Rāma, when spear, mace, hammer, etc. started coming out of his bow. Rāma destroyed them into pieces with his *gandharva* weapons. As Rāvaṇa discharged his solar weapon, innumerable burning terrible *cakras* (wheel-shaped missile) emanated from his bow. But at the arrows of Rāma, all these weapons were destroyed. This time Rāvaṇa pierced Rāma's heart with ten terrible arrows. But Rāma remained unmoved and his arrows pierced Rāvaṇa's body.

In the meantime, Lakṣmaṇa with his arrows cut into pieces the flag of Rāvaṇa's chariot. The head of Rāvaṇa's charioteer was also severed. Lakṣmaṇa with five sharp arrows also broke into pieces Rāvaṇa's huge bow. His horses were too killed by Lakṣmaṇa's arrows. Rāvaṇa then got down from his chariot and being maddened with anger, hurled a *śakti-astra* towards his brother Vibhīṣaṇa. But Lakṣmaṇa promptly destroyed it before it struck Vibhīṣaṇa, who thus was saved from sure death. Another arrow discharged towards Vibhīṣaṇa by Rāvaṇa was also destroyed by Lakṣmaṇa. Rāvaṇa then angrily discharged a terrible *śatrughātinī śakti-astra* towards Lakṣmaṇa. This *astra* got embedded into the heart of Lakṣmaṇa and he fell down on the ground unconscious.

On seeing Lakṣmaṇa lying unconscious on the ground, Rāma, out of love for his brother, was stricken with grief. The *vānara* soldiers tried to destroy Rāvaṇa's *śakti-astra,* but failed. Rāma then alone angrily lifted this terrible *astra* with his two hands and broke it into pieces. Meanwhile, Rāvaṇa's shower of arrows continued unabated. With one of his very powerful arrows, Rāma's body was pierced. But Rāma ignored it completely. Asking the *vānara* soldiers to guard the body of Lakṣmaṇa, Rāma declared, "The sinful Rāvaṇa is within my sight; he will never be able to save his life." Saying this, Rāma with seven sharp arrows seriously wounded Rāvaṇa. In reply Rāvaṇa hurled a long spear and a hammer towards Rāma. A terrible sound was created at the collision of the weapons of the two heroes. Being oppressed by Rāma's continuous shower of arrows, Rāvaṇa retreated to the city.

Casting his sight at Lakṣmaṇa lying on the ground as a

dead person, Rāma went into a deep lamentation. Consoling Rāma, *vānara* hero Suṣeṇa said, "O the greatest of the men, please be composed. Give up your mental depression. Remain certain, Lakṣmaṇa is alive. Look, his face and the eyes are bright. No dead man's face and the eyes are like this. His chest is moving indicating he is breathing inside."

At the words of Suṣeṇa, Rāma felt considerably assured. On the orders of Rāma, as suggested by Suṣeṇa, Hanumān, for the revival of Lakṣmaṇa, as before, immediately brought from the Himalayas the whole mountain containing the four medicinal plants named *viśalyakaraṇī, sāranyakaraṇī, sañjīvakaraṇī* and *sandhānakaraṇī*. As Suṣeṇa placed the powder of the medicinal plants at his nostrils, Lakṣmaṇa got up in healthy body. Rāma embracing Lakṣmaṇa said, "Lakṣmaṇa, in your absence, victory in the war, rescue of Sītā or my living existence, would have all gone in vain." Lakṣmaṇa in a sorrowful mind said in reply, "O Aryan, you are all-powerful and true to your vow. For my sake, you completely forgot your vow of killing Rāvaṇa and rescuing Sītā. This does not behove well with you. Please keep your vow by killing Rāvaṇa today itself. I wish, the sinful Rāvaṇa be killed before the sun-set."

In the meantime, Rāvaṇa began to destroy the *vānara* soldiers with his shower of arrows on returning to the battle-field on another chariot. Immediately a terrible battle with bows and arrows started between the two. Rāma was standing on the ground, while Rāvaṇa was on his chariot. On getting the news of the battle, Devarāja Indra despatched for the use of Rāma his own golden chariot with charioteer Mātali. Placing the chariot before Rāma, Mātali said, "O great warrior, the Devarāja in order to ensure your victory, has despatched this chariot. Along with the chariot, he has also sent his huge bow, fire-like armour, arrows radiant like sunshine and the infallible *śakti-astra* as also his own *brahmāstra*, for the defeat of the enemy. You may kindly mount the chariot and destroy the *rākṣasa* clan as Devarāja Indra had repressed the *dānavas*."

As Rāma mounted the chariot of Indra, all sides were illuminated with the radiance of his body. Soon an unprecedented hair-raising terrible battle started between Rāma and Rāvaṇa. Rāma baffled Rāvaṇa's *gandharva-astra* with his *gandharva-astra* and7 the divine-*astra* with his divine-*astra*. Rāma destroyed Rāvaṇa's *paññaga-astra* (the arrow which brings forth poisonous snakes) with his *garuḍa-astra*. At this Rāvaṇa flew into a rage and pierced Rāma and charioteer Mātali. With thousand arrows Rāvaṇa destroyed Rāma's golden flag-staff and wounded his horses. Rāma himself being wounded failed to find suitable arrows to strike at Rāvaṇa again. Rāma's eyes reddened with anger. As a result of his terrible rage, there developed severe calamities all around. Even Rāvaṇa was struck with fear. The results of the war remaining undecided, the gods and the demons declared both Rāma and Rāvaṇa victorious.

In this situation, Rāvaṇa hurled towards Rāma a burning spear destroying almost all his arrows. Rāma then with Indra's *śakti-astra* first restrained the force of Rāvaṇa's spear and then cut it into pieces. Later, Rāma with his arrows killed all the horses of Rāvaṇa and pierced his whole body. Blood started oozing out of his body continuously. Rāma and Rāvaṇa were both terribly excited with anger. Showers of arrows continued unabated towards each other. In the midst of the battle, Rāma told Rāvaṇa, he would kill him (Rāvaṇa) that day itself. Meanwhile, the prowess, strength of the weapons and the enthusiasm of Rāma doubly increased. The weapon-gods appearing before Rāma assured him of uninterrupted supply of weapons.

Rāvaṇa was severely wounded by the arrows of Rāma and as such he was unable to lift his bow and shoot the arrows. He soon became unconscious. On seeing Rāvaṇa's condition, Rāma stopped the battle. At this opportunity, Rāvaṇa's charioteer took him out of the battlefield. Soon after, he regained his consciousness and scolded the charioteer for leaving the battlefield. On his orders the charioteer turned the chariot and brought him back to the battlefield. Rāvaṇa on reaching the battlefield, began to prepare his fight anew. Meanwhile, Rāma too was tired and worried. At this time Sage Agastya appeared before Rāma and advised him to recite the *Ādityahṛdaya mantra.* As Rāma recited the *mantra,* he became free from all worries and he was ready to kill Rāvaṇa.

Again a serious battle started between Rāma and Rāvaṇa; but victory or defeat remained uncertain even after a long battle. Charioteer Mātali then advised Rāma to take recourse to Indra's *brahmāstra* to kill Rāvaṇa. He said, "Lord Brahmā made this infallible *astra* for Devarāja Indra. In the battle the *brahmāstra* was like veritable Yama."

Rāma as prescribed in the Vedas, after sanctifying with *mantra,* attached the *brahmāstra* to his bow. All the living creatures then became terrified; the earth began to tremble. The *brahmāstra* on being discharged by Rāma, pierced the chest of Rāvaṇa and then entered the earth with terrible speed. The *Brahmāstra* returned back to his quiver. At the strike of the *Brahmāstra,* Rāvaṇa's lifeless body fell down on the ground. The remaining *rākṣasa* soldiers panicked and fled in different directions.

The news of death of Rāvaṇa and the victory of Rāma immediately spread in all places. The gods raised a loud sound of war-drums in joy. Sweet-scented breeze started blowing. There were showers of flowers on the chariot of Rāma. On the death of sinful Rāvaṇa, the gods and the celestial singers were happy. Sugrīva, Vibhīṣaṇa, Aṅgada and the other *vānara* leaders along with Lakṣmaṇa in exultation for victory, praised Rāma with devotion.

On seeing Rāvaṇa lying dead on the ground, brother Vibhīṣaṇa burst into lamentation in grief uttering, "You were a great hero with profound knowledge in ethics and politics. How have you fallen into the jaws of death? On being intoxicated with lust, you disregarded my honest advice and the result is this unfortunate death of yours. In your death the sound base of religion and power is now destroyed. The *rākṣasa*s who have been left behind, will be weakened."

Consoling Vibhīṣaṇa, Rāma said, "Rāvaṇa has sacrificed his life in the battlefield fighting for victory. For this great self-sacrifice of Rāvaṇa, a true kṣatriya, in performance of his duties and obligations, you should not grieve at all." After asking him to perform Rāvaṇa's last rites, Rāma said, "Vibhīṣaṇa, Rāvaṇa continued to be our enemy till his death. On Rāvaṇa's death, our importance for him is over. Now the dead Rāvaṇa is a friend of mine as of yours."

The *rākṣasa* womenfolk on seeing Rāvaṇa's dead body then began to lament. "O Lord, you unfortunate death is due to the abduction of Sītā on being intoxicated with lust, disregarding the honest advice of your well-wishers. Had you handed over Sītā to Rāma and sought peace as advised by Vibhīṣaṇa, everybody would have been happy and the war could have been avoided. We too would have been saved from this intolerable widowhood. Again, we think, you are not at fault; due to providence so many *rākṣasa*s and the *vānara*s have lost their lives in the war. You too have lost your life. Wealth, greed, prowess or authority — nothing, it appears, can avoid the inevitability of providence."

The senior-most Queen Mandodarī said in lamentation, "O King, even Indra could not stand up before you when you are angry. The *gandharva*s and the others who are skilled in the art of warfare, used to flee away at your sight. You despite being such an unrivalled hero, have been killed at the hands of a mere forest-dweller human! This sorrow is intolerable for me. I think, Rāma is not a human. He is *Sanātana Puruṣa* (eternal being); he is the Supreme Soul. He is greater than even the greatest. He is the all-powerful God Viṣṇu. That Viṣṇu for the good of mankind, has assumed the human form. And the gods have appeared in the form of *vānara*s in order to destroy the *rākṣasas*. Immediately on getting the news of death of Khara and Dooshana at Janasthana at the hands of Rāma, I was certain, Rāma is not an ordinary human being. At the news of Hanumān's easy entry into the city of Laṅkā which is impenetrable even to the gods, I could understand, our city was in grave danger. I then requested you to settle all disputes with Rāma and have peace with him. Your present fate is entirely due to your refusal to accept my advice. Sītā is devoted to her husband. She is beautiful in all respects. She is more patient than even the earth. She is the embodiment of Goddess Lakṣmī. You have done a great sin by abducting that Sītā. Your desire to gain her has not been fulfilled. You have now been burned down in the sacred wild fire of her purity."

Continuing her lamentation, Queen Mandodarī said, "That the outcome of good and bad work is different, is evident from the examples of Vibhīṣaṇa and of you. Now you are immersed in deep sorrow on embracing death. Vibhīṣaṇa, on the other hand, is going to be installed on the throne of Laṅkā as the friend of the great-souled Rāma. In your inner apartments, there is no dearth of beautiful women. But due to intoxication with lust, you could not understand this reality. In beauty, noble qualities, family prestige and generosity, Sītā is no way superior to me. Even then maddened with lust you were attracted to her. The abduction of Sītā is the cause of your death. On being released from captivity, Sītā will now wander with pleasure in the company of her husband, while I am immersed in deep sorrow on losing my husband."

In the midst of piteous lamentation, Queen Mandodarī fell unconscious on the dead body of Rāvaṇa. The other lamenting *rākṣasa* women while trying to console Mandodarī, said, "O Devī, you are not unaware, life is impermanent and the abode of Goddess Lakṣmī is ever changeable with reverses of fortune. Today this has happened in the sky of the fate of

Laṅkā." Queen Mandodarī began to cry in grief more loudly on hearing the words of the co-wives of her husband.

As Rāma asked him to perform the last rites of his brother Rāvaṇa, Vibhīṣaṇa said, "Though Rāvaṇa is my eldest brother, he is not fit to receive any worship from me as he is guilty of committing various sinful acts including abduction of women of other persons. It is true, the people will denounce me as cruel if I do not perform his last rites; but they will later praise me when they will come to know all about his sinful activities."

Pleased at the words of Vibhīṣaṇa, Rāma said, "O great *rākṣasa*, there is no comparison for your contribution in this great victory of mine. This is why I think it to be my duty to give you the just advice. Though Rāvaṇa was despotic, he showed great force, power and strength in the battlefield. In the war against the *deva*s, he was never defeated. Rāvaṇa was my enemy when he was alive. With his death, this enmity has ended. He is now a friend of mine as he is yours. Be famous by performing his last rites as prescribed in the scriptures."

At the words of Rāma, Vibhīṣaṇa performed the prescribed worship and then cremated the dead body of Rāvaṇa. At the annihilation of the enemy, Rāma's long-cherished anger subsided. After casting off the terrible bow and the arrows, amulet and anger, Rāma assumed his normal calm and dignified appearance.

We have noticed what terrible resistance Rāma's *vānara* army had to face from the Rāvaṇa's *rākṣasa* army. In the devastating war, all the principal *rākṣasa* warriors including Rāvaṇa, the conqueror of the three worlds, Indrajit, his valiant son who earlier defeated Devarāja Indra, and Kumbhakarṇa, his brother who was the most powerful warrior amongst the *rākṣasa*s, lost their lives fighting to the last. The formidable *rākṣasa* army of horses, elephants, chariots and the foot soldiers, was completely routed with unbearable losses. Amongst the *rākṣasa*s, only five who are worth mentioning namely Vibhīṣaṇa and his four companions, were alive as they sided with the invading army. Some of the *rākṣasa* warriors particularly Kumbhakarṇa were critical of the actions and policies of Rāvaṇa. Even then they did not desert Rāvaṇa following the example of Vibhīṣaṇa. In fact, almost the entire *rākṣasa* clan with the exception of only Vibhīṣaṇa and his four companions, remained firmly united behind Rāvaṇa in the fight against the *vānara* army. The *rākṣasa* army showed rare courage, determination and valour for the defence of their country's independence, which would ever inspire all the independence-loving people. The lesson to be learnt is that no internal differences should be allowed to interfere in organizing united resistance against foreign aggression.

The *rākṣasa* warriors had the belief, it would be no problem for Rāvaṇa, who had defeated the *deva*s and the *gandharva*s, and his son Indrajit who had defeated Devarāja Indra, to vanquish Rāma and Lakṣmaṇa along with their *vānara* army. They had great confidence in their own power and strength. Swayed by this confidence, they fought to the last and died. Rāvaṇa later realized, Rāma was not an ordinary person; he is the incarnation of Supreme God Viṣṇu with divine power. Even then under the intoxication of his own power and pride, he disregarded the advice of his well-wishers to have peace with Rāma preferring the path of war. Rāvaṇa's death at the hands of Rāma was predestined. In fact, he himself, as was subsequently known, preferred to die at the hands of virtuous Rāma, to attain salvation. This also explains his persistent refusal to have peace with Rāma. In any case, as depicted in the *Rāmāyaṇa*, Rāvaṇa's cup of sin was full with the abduction of Sītā and he died at the hands of Rāma. *Dharma*, as the poet wanted to establish in his great epic, thus triumphed over *adharma*.

It is worth mentioning, Rāma did not take recourse to any deceit or falsehood to ensure his victory. He conducted the war in full conformity with the established principles. We have noticed, Rāma saved the spies and the emissaries of Rāvaṇa from the torture of the *vānaras* and released them. In the midst of raging battle, Rāma one day got opportunity to kill Rāvaṇa; but he did not utilize this opportunity as he thought it improper to kill the battle-fatigued enemy. In the Mahābhārata war, Kṛṣṇa, however, did not hesitate to take recourse to various deceits and falsehoods in ensuring the victory of the Pāṇḍavas To mention only one incident, Karṇa's destruction by Arjuna was possible only on the promptings of Kṛṣṇa when Karṇa was in a helpless condition trying to retrieve the wheels of his chariot which got embedded in the earth. For this and other unethical actions, Kṛṣṇa is never called Maryādāpuruṣottama. Dharmarāja Yudhiṣṭhira suffered from serious repentance throughout his life on winning the war by unethical means on the advice of Kṛṣṇa. No repentance, however, ever occurred in the mind of Rāma after his victory on the destruction of Rāvaṇa and the other *rākṣasa* warriors because this war against Rāvaṇa was a real *dharmayuddha*. Under the righteous rule of Vibhīṣaṇa on the death of sinful Rāvaṇa, a period of peace, prosperity and happiness was established throughout the kingdom. On good governance, Vibhīṣaṇa faithfully followed Rāma's instructions on *rājadharma*.

Before and during the war, both the sides were active in collecting intelligence on war preparations of the rival camps. We have noticed, Rāvaṇa's spies in disguise on entering Rāma's camp collected all vital information about the *vānara* army. The identity of the spies was, however, exposed in no time by Vibhīṣaṇa who was aware of the nature of the *rākṣasas*. The other *vānara* leaders like Sugrīva, Aṅgada and Hanumān who maintained strict vigil all around could also locate them easily. The information brought by these spies who were released on Rāma's orders, proved very useful to Rāvaṇa. In this respect some omissions and commissions were also noticed on the part of Rāvaṇa. It is evident, Rāvaṇa got the information about the construction of the bridge by Rāma very late. This is indeed a big enigma. It is also not understood why Rāvaṇa did make no attempt to destroy the bridge while under construction. It took several days to construct this long bridge across the vast sea. It was an easy target of attack from the air. It was not difficult for the *rākṣasas* who were adept in *māyā* power, to delay the landing of the *vānara* army at the shore of Laṅkā, by destroying the bridge from the air. For some unknown reason, Rāvaṇa remained indifferent to this very vital matter of the construction of the bridge. Rāvaṇa did have no discussion in the council of ministers about the steps to destroy the bridge. It appears, he wilfully allowed the *vānara* army to enter Laṅkā unopposed with intention to destroy them together. That this strategy of Rāvaṇa was wrong had been proved by the outcome of the war.

Rāvaṇa's failure, despite all efforts to kill his brother Vibhīṣaṇa proved extremely costly to him. Vibhīṣaṇa was an honourable member of Rāvaṇa's cabinet with privy to all vital secrets about the defences of Laṅkā and other important matters. He knew, Indrajit, son of Rāvaṇa used to go to war after performance of *yajña* at Nikumbhila and there lay his source of power. It was a foregone conclusion that Vibhīṣaṇa would pass on all such vital details to Rāma and that he himself would take, in concert with the *vānara* leaders, all possible defensive and offensive measures to resist the attacks of the *rākṣasas*. On the last day of battle, Indrajit was prevented from performing the *yajña* at Nikumbhika at the sudden attack of the *vānara* army on the advice of Vibhīṣaṇa. As Indrajit went to the battle without completing the *yajña,* we know, he got killed at the hands of Lakṣmaṇa at the dispensation of Lord Brahmā. What's a terrible mockery of fate! The beloved nephew Indrajit lost his life due to the treachery of his own uncle Vibhīṣaṇa, foreboding the destruction of the entire *rākṣasa* clan. If the *rākṣasa* army could maintain stricter vigilance on

Vibhīṣaṇa's activities and movements and prevent the *vānara* army from interfering in the performance of the *yajña* at the instance of Vibhīṣaṇa, Indrajit perhaps could have come out victorious and the course of war could have moved in an entirely different direction. But things moved otherwise. Ultimately with Rāvaṇa's death, Rāma's victory was complete. Besides providing vital intelligence of the *rākṣasas*, Vibhīṣaṇa by advice and directly participating in the war hastened the victory of Rāma. Vibhīṣaṇa's contributions were gratefully acknowledged by Rāma.

In the application of the principles of *sāma, dāma, bheda* and *daṇḍa,* Rāvaṇa also made serious mistakes. His first and foremost mistake was his refusal to have peace with Rāma on the advice of his well-wishers. His efforts to sow discord between Rāma and Sugrīva by the application of the principle of *bheda* too ended in failure. Sugrīva who got the throne of Kiṣkindhā with Rāma's help and was firmly allied with him, scornfully rejected Rāvaṇa's proposal to desert Rāma. His application of *māyā* power in this regard also went awry. In the application of the principles of *sāma, dāma, bheda* and *daṇḍa,* there should be proper appreciation of the place, time and the persons involved. The success of these principles depends on fine judgement of the prevailing circumstances. The fickle-minded Rāvaṇa tried to apply these principles only as damage-control measures. The efforts thus naturally ended in ignominious failure.

In the midst of the war, the creation of Māyā-Sītā and *māyā*-heads of Rāma and Lakṣmaṇa only indicated the utter despondency of the *rākṣasas*. Nothing worthwhile was ultimately achieved. Rather these efforts, childish as they were, when found out to be a hoax, doubly enthused the *vānara* army.

We are aware of the contributions of Hanumān in collecting intelligence about the defences of the city of Laṅkā. Hanumān and Vibhīṣaṇa were actually the principal intelligence operators of Rāma. It appears from the circumstances, Rāma got all the vital information about the *rākṣasa*s mainly from these two trusted followers. Despite some deviations here and there, Rāvaṇa also obtained all important details about the *vānara* army from his efficient intelligence outfit. In the collection of information on war preparations of their rivals, both Rāma and Rāvaṇa showed equal competence.

In power and strength, weaponry, etc. it appears, both the *rākṣasa* and the *vānara* army were equally matched. Rāma and Rāvaṇa were both endowed with divine powers. None was inferior to the other in power and strength. During the fateful battle, it appeared both Rāma and Rāvaṇa were invincible to each other. Rāma, we have seen, killed Rāvaṇa with Indra's *brahmāstra* sent to him through his charioteer Mātali when his own weapons failed to do the needful. In the war Rāvaṇa, however, did not take any outside help. He fought only with his own weapons. In the death of sinful Rāvaṇa at the hands of Rāma, the purpose of his birth on the earth as the incarnation of Supreme God Viṣṇu to vanquish the evil, was thus fulfilled.

34

Sītā's Ordeal by Fire

FOLLOWING the death of Rāvaṇa, Lakṣmaṇa, on Rāma's orders, formally installed Vibhīṣaṇa on the throne of Laṅkā. On gaining the kingdom, Vibhīṣaṇa made a statement of peace and consolation to the people of Laṅkā, who on being happy, produced before him various articles like curd, flowers, etc. Vibhīṣaṇa in turn presented all these articles to Rāma.

Thereafter, on Rāma's direction, Hanumān went to Aśoka Vāṭikā and conveyed to Sītā the news of death of Rāvaṇa along with welfare of Rāma and Lakṣmaṇa. Sītā heartily thanked Hanumān for bringing the happy news and said, "On Rāma's victory I have the feeling as if I have gained the Svargarājya." Referring to Hanumān's contributions in the victory, Sītā said, "O Hanumān, your wisdom, strength, patience and devotion are all your own. None in the world can equal you." As she said this, tears of joy, gratitude and affection rolled down her cheeks. At the end of the talks, Hanumān looked at the *rākṣasīs* guarding Sītā and said, "Devī, these *rākṣasīs* have tortured you in various ways. Allow me, I shall destroy these oppressing *rākṣasīs*."

Sītā said in reply, "O *vānara* hero, these *rākṣasīs* are under the control of others. They acted as they were asked to do by their masters. Therefore it would not be proper to get angry with them. My fate is only responsible for my sufferings in captivity. Man's happiness and misery are due to the ordain of fate. I have already pardoned the *rākṣasīs*."

Hanumān said, "Devī, you are really the virtuous wife of great Rāmacandra. I have nothing to say on your words." On the eve of departure of Hanumān, Sītā said, "I am eager to meet my husband who is ever kind to his devotees." Hanumān assured Sītā, she would shortly meet with Rāma and Lakṣmaṇa.

On returning to the camp, Hanumān gave details of his talks with Sītā to Rāma and requested him to immediately meet with the grief-stricken Sītā. At the words of Hanumān, Rāṃa in a sorrowful mind with tears in eyes, remained silent for some time. He then directed Vibhīṣaṇa to immediately produce Sītā dressed in divine apparel before him.

Accordingly Vibhīṣaṇa along with his wives appeared before Sītā in the Aśoka Vāṭikā and said, "Devī, you may kindly mount the palanquin after having bath and proper cosmetic, and wearing excellent dress; your husband is eager to see you." "I want to meet with my husband without having any bath." As Sītā said this, Vibhīṣaṇa requested her to do as directed by Rāma.

Sītā then in proper cosmetic and wearing excellent dress and ornaments, appeared at the camp of Rāma in the palanquin escorted by the *rākṣasas* under the supervision of Vibhīṣaṇa. As Vibhīṣaṇa informed him of Sītā's arrival, Rāma simultaneously became a prey to grief, joy and anger. A serious debate arose in his mind. Rāma asked Vibhīṣaṇa to produce Sītā before him.

On Vibhīṣaṇa's orders, the *rākṣasa* guards then began to drive away the assembled crowd to clear the path for Sītā. At this, Rāma became furious and after angrily rebuking Vibhīṣaṇa said, "Without my approval your attempt to drive away the crowd in this way has been a great offence on your part. They are all like my own relatives. House, clothes, ramparts, cover or honour of the king are not the veil of the women. Their character is their real veil. Seeing women by others during indulgence in vices, sickness, war, *svayamvara, yajña* or marriage, is not offensive at all. Jānakī (Sītā) fell into danger. There is nothing wrong if she is seen by others particularly during my presence. Let Jānakī appear before me walking on foot alighting from the palanquin. Let the forest-dweller *vānaras* see her properly."

On the words of Rāma, Vibhīṣaṇa in a worrying mind went to bring Sītā. Lakṣmaṇa, Sugrīva and Hanumān were hurt on hearing the harsh words of Rāma. Sītā out of shame sunk herself into her own body. In this condition she, walking behind Vibhīṣaṇa, stood in front of Rāma. On seeing the face of Rāma, Sītā's grief subsided.

Addressing Sītā, Rāma said, "O good lady, I have rescued you after conquering the enemy. Towards the enemy my anger reached the last limit. I have restored your good name. I have destroyed both my humiliation and the enemy. Today my prowess stands fully vindicated. On the fulfilment of my vow, I have been free. Through sheer ill luck, the *rākṣasa* abducted you during my absence. As a human being, I have removed that stigma. Hanumān's crossing the sea and his burning of the city of Laṅkā, have been fruitful. Sugrīva's help, honest advice and prowess have been successful. All the efforts of Vibhīṣaṇa have also been fruitful."

On hearing the words of Rāma, Sītā began to shed tears of joy. But Rāma's mind turned asunder for fear of people's calumny. He stated in front of the assembled crowd, "O Sītā, I have done everything possible to wipe out your humiliation. In order to preserve my own honour I have killed Rāvaṇa. Do not think what I have done with the help of my friends, has been done only for you. I have done this to preserve my honour and the prestige and authority of the Ikṣvāku dynasty. Sītā, the truth is that I have been suspicious of your character. Your presence in front of me is distressing to me. You are at liberty to go anywhere you like. Your need to me has been over. No spirited person born in a noble family can take back the woman who has lived in another person's house for a long time. Rāvaṇa has forcibly made you sit on his lap and looked at you with covetous eyes. In this way he has defamed your great dynasty. How can I take you back? Now, as you like, you are free to go to Lakṣmaṇa, Bharata, Śatrughna or Sugrīva or Vibhīṣaṇa and surrender to anyone of them. I do not think, Rāvaṇa has spared you in view of your matchless beauty and charm."

Hearing her husband's rude words, Sītā in shame and grief began to tremble. Her eyes were drenched with tears in acute mental distress. Soon, Sītā regained her composure and after wiping out the tears of her eyes, said in a choked but firm voice, "O hero, why are you speaking against me in such harsh and unpleasant words befitting only a vulgar person to the non-Aryan woman? I am not what you think of me. Taking oath on my character, I would request you to repose confidence on me.

"It is improper to compare the ordinary vulgar women with the entire womankind. I am not unknown to you. You are fully aware of my character. Give up all your baseless suspicion about me from your mind. O Lord, it is true, Rāvaṇa touched my body; but I was not then under my control. That touch was not of my own volition. Fate is responsible for this. Rāvaṇa could never touch my heart. It was firmly devoted to you. I have spent so long with you. Surprisingly you have failed to understand my character. There is no place to hide this sorrow. Why did you not abandon me at the very time you sent Hanumān to Laṅkā in search of me? If that was done, you need not have to be involved in such a devastating war causing innumerable deaths.

"O Supreme Monarch, out of anger, you have only talked about my womanhood as an ordinary person. You did not try to realize the truth. I am the daughter of King Janaka only by name; I am not the legitimate child of Janaka. The earth is my mother. You did not care to judge with respect this real identity of mine. You contemptuously disregarded my marriage with you solemnized according to scriptures. You have completely forgot my devotion, loyalty and love towards you."

Then addressing Lakṣmaṇa who was standing nearby engrossed in thoughts, Sītā in a firm voice said, "O son of Sumitrā, I do not like to remain alive bearing all these false accusations. You immediately prepare a pyre. I shall depart to the path as determined by my past deeds after sacrificing my life in the burning pyre."

On hearing Sītā's orders, Lakṣmaṇa looked at his brother and after understanding Rāma's mind by his gestures and body language, prepared the pyre and set it on fire. He did not have the courage to ask Rāma any question in view of his terribly angry mood. Sītā then going round Rāma, stood in front of the burning pyre and offered obeisance to the *deva*s and the brāhmaṇas. Sītā, thereafter, addressed the Fire God saying, "My mind has never been detached from Rāma. Though I am virtuous, to Rāma I am an unchaste woman; but you are the witness of all the happenings of the three worlds. Kindly protect me." Saying this, Sītā jumped into the burning pyre. The women of the world began to condemn Rāma. The *vānara*s and *rākṣasa*s raised a cry of distress.

On hearing the heart-rending cry of the men and the women, Rāma also became worried. Tears rolled down his cheeks. At this time Yama, Rāma's forefathers, Lord Brahmā, Devarāja Indra and other celestial beings on seeing the flame of the fire, appeared before Rāma and said, "O Lord, how have you remained indifferent? Why are you forgetting your true identity? You are the Lord of the Creation, Himself the Supreme Lord. At the beginning and the end you are the only solemn presence. Why are you ignoring Sītā behaving like an ordinary human being?"

Rāma said in reply, "I know, I am the son of King Daśaratha — an ordinary human. Kindly disclose if there is any real significance of my self-consciousness."

Lord Brahmā said, "O the Preserver of Truth, kindly listen to my truthful words. He who is *Cakrapāṇi* (holder of *cakra* — the wheel-shaped invincible missile) Nārāyaṇa is you yourself. He who conquered your enemy the one-horned boar, is you yourself. He who is ever present at the beginning, the middle and the end, and happens to be the Supreme Being, is you yourself. Ṛṣikeśa, Puruṣottama, Parama Puruṣa, Ajīta, Viṣṇu, Kṛṣṇa and Bṛhatdala — all are your names. You are the originator of the three worlds. You are the resort of the saints. Your birth and dissolution are unknown. The real essence of your nature is beyond comprehension. This Sītā is the incarnation of Goddess Lakṣmī. And you are the Supreme God Viṣṇu. You assumed the human form only to destroy Rāvaṇa. Your specific work has been completed. Rāvaṇa has been destroyed. Now you shall stay on the earth in peace and happiness for some time and then return to *svarga-rājya*. All the wishes of your devotees have been fulfilled."

As Lord Brahmā completed his words, the Fire God himself holding in his arms the exquisitely beautiful unhurt Sītā resplendent with divine clothes and ornaments, came out of the burning pyre and presented her to Rāma saying, "O Rāma, this Videhanandinī (Sītā) is completely sinless. In words, mind, thought or sight, Sītā has never forgotten you. Rāvaṇa after forcibly abducting her from the desolate forest, kept her confined in the inner apartments of his capital city. She was physically weak having no power at all to resist Rāvaṇa. Even in the midst of her utter distress, Sītā's mind always remained devoted to you. Her mental firmness remained unshaken in the face of all sorts of allurement. O Rāghava, I am asking you to accept this pure-hearted sinless Sītā without any hesitation."

Happy at the words of the Fire God, Rāma said, "I have no doubt about the purity of Sītā. She lived in the house of Rāvaṇa for a long time. Had I accepted her without proper testing, the people would have censured me as lustful and foolish. I know, Sītā is devoted to me. Rāvaṇa has no power to gain Sītā who is ever pure. She is protected by her own purity. As the sun and its light are inseparable, Sītā is also not separated from me. That she remained fully concentrated in her devotion to me in the midst of her terrible distress in captivity, goes without saying. As no virtuous person can give up his glorious activities, I cannot forsake Sītā who is known to be pure in all the three worlds. It is incumbent on me to accept the just words of the celebrated personalities like you." Saying this, Rāma happily accepted Sītā. At this great reunion, all were elated with shouts of joy.

God Maheśvara then said, "O Arindama (Rāma), the terrible darkness which engulfed the three worlds as a result of Rāvaṇa's sinful activities, has been removed by you. Now after assuring Bharata, you ascend to the throne of Ayodhyā. Thereafter, you attain fame on completing the *Aśvamedha Yajña* at the proper time. Look, your father in a chariot is hovering in the sky. Pay obeisance to him along with Lakṣmaṇa."

Accordingly Rāma and Lakṣmaṇa paid obeisance to their father as he alighted on the ground. Daśaratha on seeing his beloved son Rāma said in great happiness, "Son Rāma, in your absence my stay even in *svarga-rājya* gave me no comfort. That sad incident of my sending you to the forest on the words of Kaikeyī, is still fresh in my mind. Today by embracing Lakṣmaṇa and you, I am free from all my sorrows. O Rāma, I could know, you are the incarnation of the Supreme Being. On the prayer of the *deva*s, you, unknown to others, were born as my son for the purpose of destroying Rāvaṇa. You have successfully completed your task. You may now return to Ayodhyā and get installed as the king. Your mothers and the people will be happy to see you again. You have caused happiness to the *deva*s on spending in the forest for long fourteen years for the pleasure of your father and for destroying the sinful Rāvaṇa. For this you have also earned great praise from the people at large. I pray, you live happily for long along with your brothers and others on assuming royal duties at Ayodhyā."

Rāma said in reply, "O Dharmayajña, be gracious to Kaikeyī and Bharata. 'I have deserted you with your son' — this curse of yours on Kaikeyī uttered earlier should not touch her." "Be it so" saying this, Daśaratha embraced Lakṣmaṇa and slowly said, "Son, you shall go to heaven on gaining virtue and Rāma's pleasure. Your salvation will be ensured if you remain devoted to Rāma. Indra with other gods and the sages do worship Puruṣottama Rāma. He is the Supreme Being — the *Brahman*. You have gained immense fame and virtue by rendering selfless service to Rāma and Sītā."

Addressing Sītā, Daśaratha said, "O Videhanandinī, do not be angry with Rāma. For your good this ordeal by fire was necessary. You shall remain as an example to the womankind for this ordeal. Husband is the most venerable preceptor of woman. Always look after his welfare." Giving such instructions to Rāma, Lakṣmaṇa and Sītā, Daśaratha departed to *Indraloka* by the chariot.

After the departure of Daśaratha, Devarāja Indra appeared there and asked Rāma if he had to pray for anything from him. Rāma in reply prayed for restoration to life for the dead *vānara* soldiers and location of areas with rivers having flowing water, plentiful fruits, roots and flowers for the comfortable stay of the *vānara*s. As Indra happily granted the prayer, all the dead *vānara*s came back to life assuming their former healthy bodies. Suitable areas were also earmarked for the *vānara*s. The assembled gods blessed Rāma and Lakṣmaṇa and departed.

35

Rāma Leaves Laṅkā for Ayodhyā

THE next day, Vibhīṣaṇa requested Rāma to stay in Laṅkā for a few days along with Sītā and Lakṣmaṇa to enjoy his hospitality before departing to Ayodhyā. In reply Rāma said, "O Hero, on gaining your help, I have been worshipped and entertained by you. Even then it is my duty to accept the invitation from a friend like you. But I am helpless. At Ayodhyā, brother Bharata, our mothers, the citizens and the friends are eagerly awaiting our arrival. I am also anxious to meet them. You have already entertained me profusely. I beg leave of you. Please arrange for a *vimāna* which can fly us to Ayodhyā."

As requested by Rāma, Vibhīṣaṇa immediately produced before Rāma the golden *puṣpaka vimāna* of Kubera which was capable of moving at the speed of mind. This *vimāna* was forcibly seized by Rāvaṇa from Kubera. Rāma and Lakṣmaṇa were amazed to see the wonderful *vimāna*.

Rāma then in consultation with Lakṣmaṇa, asked Vibhīṣaṇa to suitably reward the *vānara* leaders and the soldiers for their valour and enthusiasm in the war saying, "Friend, they shall be happy if you honour them for their contributions to our victory. If you show magnanimity in your victory and sincerely give and take gifts from the subjects, and distribute favours amongst them, they shall remain ever loyal to you. Always remember, the king who remains indifferent to the sufferings of his own people and frequently goes to war causing unnecessary destruction of human lives, is disowned by his army." Vibhīṣaṇa accordingly rewarded the *vānara* leaders and the soldiers.

On mounting the *puṣpaka vimāna* along with Sītā and Lakṣmaṇa, Rāma in a farewell speech said, "O great *vānaras*, you have all performed your duties befitting genuine friends; now you may depart to your respective places. O Sugrīva, you are virtuous and a true friend of mine. You have excellently completed all your duties. You may now return to Kiṣkindhā accompanied by your army. O Vibhīṣaṇa, I am giving you this kingdom of Laṅkā as a gift. You shall stay here. As you are protected by me, even Indra and the other gods will not be able to cause any harm to you. I am seeking permission from all of you to return to my own capital at Ayodhyā. I extend my invitation to you all to visit Ayodhyā."

Vibhīṣaṇa and the *vānara* leaders then expressed their desire to witness the coronation of Rāma at Ayodhyā. On Rāma's approval, they also mounted the *vimāna.* Soon after with permission of Rāma, the *puṣpaka vimāna* flew towards Ayodhyā by the aerial path.

36

Rāma's Inhuman Behaviour with Sītā on her Rescue
Some Observations

THERE are no words to condemn Rāma for his inhuman behaviour towards Sītā on her rescue from Rāvaṇa's captivity. It is rare even for an ordinary person to use such cruel words to his own wife within the hearing of such a large crowd. Sītā spent in captivity almost a year in extreme distress. For this Rāma himself was responsible. It would not have been possible for Rāvaṇa to abduct Sītā had Rāma not left the hermitage in the chase of the *māyā-mṛga* disregarding repeated warnings of Lakṣmaṇa. Was it not proper for Rāma to personally meet Sītā at the Aśoka Vāṭikā and bring her to his camp with respect and consolation? Even if it was not possible for him to do so in view of his preoccupation, he could have easily sent brother Lakṣmaṇa for the purpose. He did neither. Without doing it, he, as we know, sent Vibhīṣaṇa to bring her to his camp. Sītā wanted to meet Rāma in her old clothes; but on Rāma's orders as conveyed through Vibhīṣaṇa, she had to put on new clothes and ornaments. From this it appears, Rāma did not like to give any importance to her sufferings in captivity. Showing utter disregard to Sītā, Rāma asked Vibhīṣaṇa to bring her before him on foot from the gate of the camp through the assembled crowd as if Sītā did not have any mind, heart or feelings and was a curious object only to be seen and enjoyed by others. Even Rāvaṇa did not parade Sītā through the public streets during her captivity and humiliate her in this fashion.

Sītā's humiliation did not end there. Rāma told Sītā in clear terms, he did not wage this dangerous war only to rescue her from captivity; he went to war and killed Rāvaṇa with his own power and strength to take revenge of her abduction and to redeem the honour and prestige of his celebrated family. It appears, Sītā's rescue was rather secondary to Rāma; Rāvaṇa's sinful act, as if, only provided an opportunity to Rāma to show his prowess in destroying a formidable enemy like Rāvaṇa.

Thereafter, in completing Sītā's humiliation in the open public, we know, Rāma casting aspersions on Sītā's character in view of her long stay in Rāvaṇa's captivity, refused to accept her and asked her to go anywhere. Rāma forgetting all sense of proportion even asked her to embrace any body including even any one of his brothers she liked. The *rākṣasa*s or the *vānara*s did not make any comment on Sītā's character. In fact, such a spurious thought did not come to their mind at all. This decision was Rāma's alone. It is against the established principle that all vital decisions must be taken after consultation with wise and reliable people. It is reasonable to believe, Rāma's decision would have been different had he discussed the matter with Lakṣmaṇa, Sugrīva, Vibhīṣaṇa, Hanumān and other *vānara* leaders. It seems, Rāma's decision was due to his fear that the people of Ayodhyā would refuse to accept Sītā as their Queen in pursuance of the prevailing social custom and belief in view of her long stay in other's house. It was apparently wrong on the part of Rāma alone to take a decision on such a very important matter at Laṅkā itself. He on return to Ayodhyā in consultations with his council of ministers, own brothers and the people's representatives, could have taken a considered decision after making necessary enquiries about Sītā's character. From the secret and open enquiries it would have been proved beyond doubt that Sītā was above all suspicion. Such findings endorsed by sages like Vasiṣṭha, would have convinced the people about Sītā's purity of character. Subsequent events might have taken a different course without such painful ordeal of fire of Sītā. Even perhaps the later incident of Sītā's entry into the *pātāla*, could have been avoided.

Sītā, we know, strongly refuted the aspersions on her character and while reiterating her love and devotion to Rāma, did not hesitate to compare his disgraceful uttering with that of a low-class vile person. Claiming herself as the daughter of the earth (Goddess Lakṣmī), she proudly declared, her identity was not simply the wife of Rāmacandra; her other identity was also equally glorious. She actually meant to say, Rāma should have thought twice before casting any aspersion on the character of Goddess Lakṣmī. Sītā, as we have seen, proved her purity unhesitatingly going through the ordeal of fire with endorsements of the gods proving Rāma entirely wrong. Rāma had to admit, Sītā was pure and had remained ever devoted to him. Notwithstanding his admission and subsequent explanation of his action, Rāma ever remained condemned in the society for his harsh treatment and unjust aspersions inflicted on Sītā. It is said, Rāma ceased to be an *avatāra* with the destruction of Rāvaṇa, the main task for which he was born and became an ordinary king subject to the prevailing customs and beliefs of the time. Hence this deviant conduct of Rāma. But even a right-thinking person would have behaved in a different way than Rāma in similar circumstances.

37

Rāma Arrives at Nandīgrāma and Meets with Bharata

COMING back to the original story, Rāma while flying in the *puṣpaka vimāna* by the aerial path, began to show Sītā, on the ground below, all the places of interest such as the vast battlefield in Laṅkā, the path of the bridge built by the *vānaras* across the sea, the Maināka mountain on the sea, the place of mobilization of the *vānara* army on this side of the sea, etc. As the *vimāna* landed at Kiṣkindhā, the wives of Sugrīva boarded it as they were also eager to witness Rāma's coronation ceremony at Ayodhyā. At last the *vimāna* landed at the hermitage of Sage Bharadvāja. At the request of Rāma, on the wishes of Sage Bharadvāja, all the trees right up to Ayodhyā, bore plenty of fruits and honey for the *vānaras*. Sage Bharadvāja told Rāma, he had already come to know with his divine power all the happenings like abduction of Sītā, death of Vālī, building of the bridge across the sea, death of Rāvaṇa, rescue of Sītā, etc. Rāma that day stayed at the hermitage of Sage Bharadvāja along with the others.

On Rāma's orders, Hanumān flew by the sky to inform of Rāma's arrival to his mothers at Ayodhyā, the hunter-king Guhaka at Śṛṅgaverapura and brother Bharata at Nandīgrāma. Rāma had still doubt whether Bharata would willingly return the kingdom of Ayodhyā to him as promised. He had, therefore, instructed Hanumān to particularly find out the mental attitude of Bharata. On arrival at Nandīgrāma, Hanumān found Bharata in a sorrowful mind wearing deer-skin and having matted hair on the head like a saint. His body was thin at the grief of his brother Rāma. He was conducting the affairs of the kingdom in front of the pair of sandals of Rāma, while his army commander, priest and the ministers in dyed clothes were standing before him.

Hanumān with folded hands appeared before Bharata and said, "The person in Daṇḍakāraṇya with matted hair for whom you are grieving, that Rāmacandra has enquired about your welfare. O Deva, give up your grief. Soon you shall meet with your brother Rāma. Rāma after destroying Rāvaṇa and rescuing Sītā, is shortly arriving here along with Sītā, brother Lakṣmaṇa and the other friends."

On hearing Hanumān's words, Bharata in joy fell down unconscious on the ground and soon after regained consciousness. Happy with the good news, Bharata told Hanumān, "For bringing this excellent news, I am presenting you a gift of one lakh cows, one hundred villages, sixteen good-natured beautiful girls and many other beautiful women." Hanumān then, on the request of Bharata, narrated the incidents of Sītā's abduction by Rāvaṇa, death of Vālī, Rāma's friendship with Sugrīva, construction of the bridge across the sea, attack on Laṅkā, Rāvaṇa's death, etc. He said, "Tomorrow on the day of *Puṣyanakṣatra* with the completion of the period of his fourteen-year exile, you shall meet with Rāma."

The next day at the appropriate time Rāma along with Lakṣmaṇa, Sītā and others, landed at Nandīgrāma by the *puṣpaka vimāna*. On Rāma's wishes, Bharata entered the *vimāna* and happily paid his obeisance to him. Rāma also reciprocated by embracing him with deep affection. In this way, Rāma, Bharata, Lakṣmaṇa, Sītā, Śatrughna and the mothers met with one another and with this reunion of the family, there descended an atmosphere of happiness all around. On being introduced, Sugrīva, Vibhīṣaṇa and the *vānara* leaders on assuming human form, paid their respects to Bharata and enquired about his welfare. Embracing Sugrīva, Bharata said, "Sugrīva, by good service, man becomes a friend and by doing harm, man becomes an enemy. You are our great benefactor. Now we have become five brothers." Turning to Vibhīṣaṇa, Bharata said, "O Rākṣasa King, only with your help, it has been possible for Rāma to accomplish such a difficult job."

After the reunion, Bharata caused to put on the pair of sandals to Rāma's feet and said with folded hands, I am returning to you this vast kingdom which was kept in my custody. My wishes have been fulfilled on seeing you in royal dress. Kindly inspect your treasury, granary, palace buildings, forests and the other places. I have increased all these ten-fold."

On hearing Bharata's words, the *vānara*s began to shed tears of joy. Vibhīṣaṇa also could not control his tears. Rāma then along with Bharata and others came to the palace at Ayodhyā. On Rāma's direction, the *puṣpaka vimāna* flew northwards to the capital of Kubera.

38

Rāma's Coronation and his Establishment of a Righteous Society

THEREAFTER, under the supervision of Sage Vasiṣṭha, Rāma's coronation ceremony was solemnized with great pomp and grandeur. On the occasion of the coronation, Rāma distributed amongst the invited brāhmaṇas many cows, bulls and horses as also gold coins, clothes and ornaments. Valuable necklaces were also gifted to Sugrīva and the other *vānara* leaders. Sītā with her own hands gifted her divine apparel to Hanumān remembering his services to her. She then took out one of her most valuable necklaces and looked at Rāma and the *vānara* leaders. Understanding Sītā's intention, Rāma requested her to hand over the necklace to the person with whom she was most satisfied. Accordingly Sītā handed over the necklace to Hanumān as he was thought to be the most suitable person to receive it in view of his force, memory, fame, capability, adroitness, modesty, sense of morality, manliness, prowess, wisdom and other exemplary qualities.

At the end of the ceremony, Sugrīva having been honoured in this way, returned to Kiṣkindhā with his wives and the others. Vibhīṣaṇa too having been gifted with kingdom of Laṅkā, jewels and wealth, departed to Laṅkā.

As described in the Uttara-Kāṇḍa, though a later addition but considered to be an integral pat of the epic, Rāma on ascending the throne, began to govern the vast kingdom with justice and fair-play in cooperation with his virtuous brothers. One day Rāma called brother Lakṣmaṇa and said, "I intend to install you as the crown prince and give you the charge of the administration of the kingdom."

The grateful Lakṣmaṇa refused to accept the proposal with due modesty. Then on his wishes, Bharata was installed as the crown prince, while Rāma continued as the king. During his long 10 thousand year's reign, Rāma performed many sacrificial rites including ten *Aśvamedha Yajñas*. It is said during the benevolent rule of Rāma, no women had to suffer from the pangs of widowhood. The people were free from diseases and snake-bites. None had to suffer any unnecessary hardship on account of natural calamities or any other accidents or disasters. The protection of the good and the punishment of the bad were assured. Inspired by the noble example of the king, the citizens used to lead virtuous lives. Being free from disease and grief, the people's lifespan extended up to one thousand years. As a result of adequate rainfall, agricultural fields were full of crops and the trees covered with fruits and flowers. Sweet breeze used to blow giving immense comfort to the people.

Mahatma Gandhi, the Father of the Nation was influenced by the idea of *Rāmarājya* and favoured establishment of such a righteous regime in India to ensure the welfare of the people. This was not a system of government of any institutional religious establishment. It was an ideal secular democratic establishment, as introduced by Rāma, wedded to the welfare of all sections of people in adherence to the principles of justice and fairness. Gandhiji's dream of *Rāmarājya* remained unfulfilled on account of the prevailing adverse circumstances. Though a secular constitution is established in India, the aspirations of the people have remained unrealized due mainly to the absence of political will of the leaders and their non-adherence to the principles of *rāja-dharma* as enshrined in the great epic. The situation will improve only with rise of leaders of Rāma's stature and qualities.

The events in the Uttara-Kāṇḍa, despite being a later addition, appear to have completed the *Rāmāyaṇa* in its entirety. In fact, without the Uttara-Kāṇḍa the great epic would have remained half-finished. This *kāṇḍa* mentions, besides many relevant mythological stories, various startling events during Rāma's reign. We shall now refer to some of those events for the benefit of the readers.

39

Abandonment of Sītā

In the midst of peace and prosperity prevailing throughout the kingdom under Rāma's benevolent rule, there came the news that Sītā was pregnant causing great jubilation among the people. One day when Sītā expressed her desire to visit the *tapovanas* of the sages, Rāma readily agreed to make necessary arrangements assuring she would go for the visit the next day itself. Thereafter, Rāma was engaged in humorous discussions with some of his close friends. During the discussions, Rāma asked one of his friends named Bhadra, "What do the citizens discuss about my activities? What also is their opinion about Sītā, Bharata, Śatrughna or Kaikeyī?" Bhadra said in reply, "O King, the citizens mainly discuss about your power and strength shown in destroying Rāvaṇa." When Rāma asked him what other matters they discussed about him, Bhadra said, "They talk — after destroying Rāvaṇa, you have brought Sītā to your own house, but you are indifferent and callous to the fact that Rāvaṇa has touched Sītā during her captivity. The citizens feel, you have done this only because of your deep attachment to Sītā. Sītā had to live for a long time in the Aśoka Vāṭikā under Rāvaṇa's control; yet you do not have any hatred or anger in the matter. The citizens have the fear, they too shall have to accept in future their own women in similar circumstances because they generally follow what is done by their own king."

Rāma was stricken with sorrow on hearing the words of Bhadra. As Rāma wanted to know from the other friends about the truth or otherwise of the revelations made by Bhadra, they by shaking their heads said, "Bhadra's words are true."

After the departure of the friends, Rāma called Bharata, Lakṣmaṇa and Śatrughna, and after disclosing before them the calumny about Sītā said in tearful eyes, "I am born in the great Ikṣvāku dynasty. Sītā is born in the virtuous family of Janaka. This terrible calumny about Sītā is verily intolerable. On her rescue from Rāvaṇa's captivity, Sītā was declared as pure-hearted by the Fire God, the *deva*s and other great men in Laṅkā itself. I too knew her to be pure and have accordingly brought her to Ayodhyā. Now the people are spreading my infamy. Infamy is also condemnable in the society of the *deva*s. I am prepared to sacrifice my own life and even you all to alleviate the calumny. Should I not be able to abandon the Janakanandinī? I am now immersed in the great sea of sorrow. I am not finding any other way other than abandoning Sītā. Lakṣmaṇa, tomorrow morning itself, you shall leave Sītā in the forest near the *tapovana* of Sage Vālmīki. There must not be any disobedience of my order."

Saying this, Rāma with tears in his eyes, departed to the inner apartments with a heavy heart.

The next day Lakṣmaṇa reached the bank of the Ganges along with Sītā by the chariot driven by Sumantra. Sītā thought, she was going to meet with the sages as decided earlier. Leaving Sumantra at the river bank, Lakṣmaṇa crossed the river by boat with Sītā and immediately fainted. There were continuous tears in his eyes. Sītā was surprised at this strange behaviour of Lakṣmaṇa and as she asked him the reasons, Lakṣmaṇa in tearful eyes and looking downwards said, "Devī, you are innocent. Rāma also knows it well. Yet for fear of people's calumny, he has been compelled to abandon you. There are many beautiful *tapovana*s on this bank of the Jāhnavī. On the orders of Rāma, I shall leave you here. You may pass your days in religious meditation in the *āśrama* of Sage Vālmīki. I wish you good luck."

On hearing the cruel words of Lakṣmaṇa, Sītā lost her consciousness for a moment and fell down on the ground. In tearful eyes she said, "Lakṣmaṇa, it appears, the Almighty God has created this body of mine only to suffer pain and sorrow. Despite being pure-hearted and devoted, I have been forsaken by my husband. When the sages will ask me why I have been forsaken by the great King Rāmacandra and what irreligious act have I done, what reply would I give? I could have sacrificed my life in the waters of the Jāhnavī; but I am pregnant. On my death my husband's royal lineage will end. Because of this fear, I have given up the idea of suicide."

Lakṣmaṇa, on return to Ayodhyā, after conveying good wishes to everybody, you shall convey this message of mine to the virtuous king — "O Rāghava, Sītā is pure-hearted and entirely devoted to you. Though you are aware of this, you have abandoned me only out of the fear of people's calumny. I have fully understood this. It is also my responsibility to remove all calumny or infamy against you. Because you are my ultimate salvation. You should not bear any grudge against the citizens for spreading this calumny. Kindly treat them as you do with your own brothers. To make the subjects happy is *rājadharma*. Husband is the god of the woman. It is the duty of every woman to serve her husband even with her own life."

At the end of the talks, Lakṣmaṇa with a sorrowful mind and tears in the eyes, went round Sītā and came to the other bank after crossing the river by boat. Sītā remaining alone unprotected in the forest began to cry loudly afflicted with terrible grief. Sage Vālmīki on getting the information from the *āśrama* boys, immediately came to the river bank along with his disciples and consoled Sītā saying, "O Pativratā (woman extremely devoted to her husband), you are the daughter-in-law of King Daśaratha, the beloved Queen of Rāma and the daughter of King Janaka. I am cordially welcoming you. I have already come to know of your arrival here by dint of my spiritual power. Nothing is unknown to me. You are pure-hearted and sinless. You shall from now on live in my *āśrama*. Many women ascetics live near my *āśrama*. They shall look after you like their own child. Do not harbour any grief in your mind."

Sītā became free from worry in the *āśrama* of Sage Vālmīki.

The question may arise how far it was justified for Rāma to abandon Sītā in this way. Like the incident at Laṅkā, here also Rāma did not discuss the accusations of the citizens with his council of ministers, the representatives of the people or the sages like Vasiṣṭha. No opportunity was also given to his brothers to discuss the matter. Taking advantage of the loyalty of the brothers, he only imposed his own decision on them. The citizens no doubt maintained that Rāma had set a wrong example by taking back Sītā who lived in another person's house for such a long time and that this was done by Rāma only for his deep attachment to her. The calumny, if any, was thus against both Rāma and Ṣītā. It appears, as we have observed in the earlier incident of Sītā's ordeal of fire in Laṅkā, had the matter been discussed threadbare with the others, some ways could have been found out particularly when the accusations of the citizens were palpably false. Rāma, we feel, should have shown more patience before taking such a harsh decision unilaterally. Of course, it was not easy for Rāma to take this decision when he was himself convinced about Sītā's purity on the endorsement of the gods and the other great men. Rāma's grief, as we know, was as deep as that of Sītā. But the poet of the great epic with an entirely different objective depicted the story of *Rāmāyaṇa* in which Sītā's abandonment by Rāma and her subsequent entry into the *pātāla* (details later) constitute an integral part. This was to show Sītā, and justifiably so, as an ideal woman with all the noble qualities like love, devotion, purity and sacrifice. The poet's objective has been entirely fulfilled with his wonderful description of the events. Our comments on Rāma's action would appear to be only of academic interest.

Rāma willingly accepted this grief and sorrow by abandoning his beloved pure wife only for the sake of his subjects. Being a great king wedded to the welfare of his subjects, any personal loss, however deep it might be, was insignificant to him. In this respect, Rāma's grief appears to be even greater than that of Sītā. At least Sītā had the consolation, she was able to put an end to all calumny particularly against her virtuous and self-restrained husband by going out of the sight of the people. But Rāma remaining in the midst of his people, continued to perform his heavy duties as the king with a grief-stricken heart.

Could Rāma take any other steps to remove the grievances of the people without straightway abandoning Sītā? We can conceive of some alternatives. Rāma could have sent Sītā to her father Janaka. But in that case the people would not have considered that she had been actually abandoned — their grievances and suspicion persisting. Rather these would have increased further. Sītā was pregnant; on her delivery, Rāma naturally would be impelled to see his new-born child and make arrangements for his upbringing and training as a royal scion. This would have created fresh problems for Rāma with the people's calumny taking an ugly turn. Rāma could have also kept Sītā under the care and protection of some trusted people in the company of reliable women in a separate house far away from Ayodhyā. That also would not have solved the problem. Rāma by abandoning Sītā in the forest struck at the very root of the problem. The wishes of the people were fulfilled. Rāma knew, this forest being near the *tapovana* of Sage Vālmīki, Sītā would get protection under him. That this decision of Rāma was entirely correct was justified from subsequent events. Sītā was looked after by the women saints living near Vālmīki's *tapovana* and the twins of Sītā, when born, were brought up and trained along with other *āśrama* boys under the guidance of Sage Vālmīki (details later).

Now on return to Ayodhyā, Lakṣmaṇa finding Rāma dejected and grief-stricken, told him with tearful eyes, "O King, as directed by you, I have left Janakanandinī in the forest near the *tapovana* of Sage Vālmīki. For this you should not grieve at all. It does not look nice for a calm and composed person like you, to remain grief-stricken like this. As you are aware, time destroys everything. It is undesirable to get unduly attached to wife, son, friend or wealth. In course of time, separation is inevitable from all of them. You yourself are capable of controlling your grief and for the sake of the education of the people, you shall have to do just that. O King, if you remain always grief-stricken for Sītā, the calumny for which you have sacrificed her, would agitate and excite the people again. Therefore, control all your grief with forbearance."

Rāma on hearing the learned observations of Lakṣmaṇa expressed satisfaction and said, "Lakṣmaṇa, at your words, all my grief has subsided."

40

Death of Brāhmaṇa Boy

RĀMA remained devoted to his royal duties with undivided attention. One day an old brāhmaṇa with his dead minor son appeared before Rāma and said, "O King, it is the king's faults that cause sufferings to the people. Therefore you as the king are responsible for the untimely death of my son. Certainly in absence of good governance, unholy practices have surfaced in the kingdom. Kindly bring my dead son back to life. Otherwise along with my wife, I shall give up my life praying and fasting."

Rāma at the grief of the brāhmaṇa was himself very much perturbed and in order to decide his course of action called a meeting of the council of ministers. Narrating the incident of the untimely death of the brāhmaṇa's minor son, he requested the ministers to give their respective views. Sage Nārada who was also present in the meeting, said in reply, "O King, in the present *Tretā-yuga, tapasyā* (performance of the religious austerities) is completely forbidden for the śūdras. Even in the *Dvāpara-yuga* such performance of austerities by the śūdras would constitute a great sin. Certainly someone belonging to the śūdra caste has been engaged in religious austerities. For this irreligious act of the śūdra, the son of the brāhmaṇa has met with untimely death. You immediately stop this irreligious act after conducting necessary searches in the different parts of the kingdom. If this act is stopped, the dead son of the brāhmaṇa will come back to life."

Rāma accordingly armed with various weapons, went out in the *vimāna* and after the search of the different places of the kingdom, found a person engaged in deep *tapasyā* with his head downcast on the bank of a lake. Coming near him, Rāma said, "O *tapasa* (ascetic), I am Rāmacandra, son of King Daśaratha. Out of curiosity, I am asking you, out of the four castes, what caste do you belong to? And what is the purpose of this *āsurika tapasyā* of yours?"

The *tapasa* said in reply, "The purpose of this *āsurika tapasyā* is to attain godhood with my present body itself. My desire is to conquer the *Devaloka* (abode of the gods) and become a god myself. I belong to the śūdra caste. My name is Śambūka."

Before the *tapasa* could complete his words, Rāma severed his head with his sword. Devarāja Indra and the other gods praising Rāma for his deed, began to shower flowers on him from the sky. At the boon of the gods, the dead son of the brāhmaṇa immediately came back to life.

The present-day educated people conscious of human rights would be dumbfounded at the death of Śambūka, while performing religious austerities, at the hands of Rāma. They believe, everybody irrespective of any caste distinction should have the right to follow his religious pursuit without any hindrance. Death of a so-called low caste śūdra to serve the interest of an upper caste brāhmaṇa is apparently repugnant to them. Rāma to them was here an outright murderer when his role was to protect all sections of the people as a righteous and benevolent king. We are aware, Rāma was a person of divine power. It is not understood why he did not use this power to revive the dead boy to life. If that was not possible, he could have dissuaded Śambūka from his religious pursuit if he (Rāma) was sure, Śambūka's course of action was the cause of the boy's death. Without taking any such conciliatory step, his sudden severance of Śambūka's head was indeed a rash act unexpected of Rāma known for his self-restraint.

This incident was clearly a reflection of the then social system consisting of four main castes of brāhmaṇa, kṣatriya, vaiśya and śūdra. The death of the śūdra and the resultant revival of the dead brāhmaṇa boy was only symbolic and simply an interpolation.

It may be mentioned here, though man originates from the same source and there is no difference between one man and another; but in actual situation there arises many distinctions and differences between them. The reasons are personal and characteristic differences, family condition, prevailing environment, genetic constitution, differences in individual merit and work and a host of other factors. On the basis of these natural distinctions and differences, the Hindu religion in recognition of this unity and diversity, has evolved a system of society consisting of four classes or castes of people according to their actual profession. This social system consisting of four castes has not been forcibly imposed on the society by anybody. This is merely the recognition of what is true and natural. On the basis of quality and work, distinctive castes are in vogue in all the countries. There is no relation between the hateful and corrosive system of untouchability which has plagued the Hindu society and the caste system on the basis of man's quality and work. As the human body remains healthy on the fine co-ordination of its different organs, so the human society flourishes being based on the cooperation of the four castes. In the system of four castes, the brāhmaṇas, as explained in the beginning, are likened to the head of the human body, the kṣatriyas to the arms, the vaiśyas to the belly and the śūdras to the two feet. The authors of the Hindu Śāstras are of the view, in the co-ordination and cooperation of the religious austerities of the brāhmaṇas, the power and strength of the kṣatriyas, the production of wealth and its even distribution by the vaiśyas and the faithful services of the śūdras, lies the all-round development of the human society. In the absence of this mutual co-ordination and cooperation, the society gets plagued with evil forces causing untold sufferings to the people.

The brāhmaṇas as conceived in the Hindu Śāstras will spread moral and ethical principles among the people, the kṣatriyas will govern the country emulating the principles of justice and fairness as enunciated by the brāhmaṇas, the vaiśyas similarly under the watchful eyes of the kṣatriya rulers, will ensure the economic prosperity of the people with production and fair distribution of wealth, while the śūdras by their faithful services will ensure smooth functioning of the entire society. The kṣatriyas holding the reins of government will punish everybody including even the brāhmaṇas who deviate from their duties and responsibilities. In fact in the beginning, the Hindu society, on this system of four castes, functioned smoothly ensuring peace and happiness of all the sections of the people. Gradually with the society getting complicated with increase of population and other factors, the people belonging to the different castes, fell prey to greed and corruptions forgetting their original duties and responsibilities. Today our society is in grave danger due to the activities of the ignorant and wrathful religious leaders, the power-hungry and self-seeking ruling class, greedy and corrupt trading community and of the arrogant and the revenge-seeking downtrodden śūdras. It is easy to understand, this painful situation of our society has arisen mainly because of the various acts of omissions and commissions of the ruling class. It is rightly said, the country and the people suffer when the king or the ruling class deviates from *rājadharma* negating good governance. Sage Nārada thus thought, the untimely death of the brāhmaṇa boy in the *rāmarājya* signifying an evil omen, was certainly due to some deviations of King Rāmacandra. When Rāma found Śambūka, a śūdra by caste, observing religious austerities — a function reserved for the brāhmaṇas, he concluded, Śambūka was fit to be killed being guilty of unauthorized intrusion into other's function without any qualification. This is not to eulogize the caste system in any form. Whatever might be its justification in ancient days when the society was a simpler institution, the caste system which inhibits mobility of profession and is divisive in nature and which has facilitated the growth of hated caste distinctions and untouchability in our society, cannot be justified in any way. It is a good thing, it is on the wane.

Yet another thing deserves mention. When in reply to his queries, Śambūka revealed, the aim of his *āsurika tapasyā* was the conquest of the *devaloka*, Rāma with his knowledge of Rāvaṇa's terrifying activities on the strength of the boon of Lord Brahmā, perhaps thought, Śambūka was actually another Rāvaṇa in the making. In order to put an end to such a dangerous possibility, Rāma unhesitatingly destroyed Śambūka. Mythological stories cannot, of course, be assessed with our present-day values and ideas. The makers of the Śāstras had their own values and conviction. Two things are, however, clear. First, the king or the ruler must be just and fair and secondly, no unworthy person should be allowed to capture power. To assert this obvious truth this grotesque story was interpolated apparently by some cunning brāhmaṇa proud of his so-called superior caste. On the revival of the dead brāhmaṇa boy following the death of Śambūka, righteous rule of Rāma, as described in the *Rāmāyaṇa*, was re-established bringing peace and prosperity in the kingdom.

41

Sītā's Entry into Pātāla

MEANWHILE, in the *āśrama* of Sage Vālmīki, Sītā gave birth to male twins. Vālmīki was very happy to see the two godly strong and beautiful boys. He after performing some religious rites, gave the names Kuśa and Lava to the twins according to their actual time of birth. Thus the elder one was named Kuśa and the younger Lava. As the two boys grew in age, Vālmīki meticulously taught them the *Rāmāyaṇa* songs.

At the invitation of Rāma, Sage Vālmīki along with Lava and Kuśa arrived at Ayodhyā to attend the *Aśvamedha Yajña*, On his instructions the two boys went round singing the *Rāmāyaṇa* songs at the *āśrama*s of the sages, along public thoroughfare, in front of the royal palace, at the arena of *yajña* and in various other places. Rāma was charmed on listening to the beautiful songs.

At the end of the *yajña*, in the assembly of the invited guests in the palace which was not attended by Sage Vālmīki, as Lava and Kuśa started singing the *Rāmāyaṇa* songs to their utter delight, they all cast their careful looks at them. To them the two boys appeared to be the exact reflected image of Rāmacandra. Lava and Kuśa sang the *Rāmāyaṇa* songs beginning from the first to the twentieth cantos. As Lakṣmaṇa, on Rāma's orders, was about to offer gold coins and other gifts to the two singers, they refused to accept them. They respectfully said, "We live in the forest; we are contented with the fruits and the roots grown in the forest. What shall we do with the gold coins in the forest?"

Later, on being asked by Rāma, Lava and Kuśa said, "God Vālmīki has composed this great epic. He is our Guru (preceptor). He is now present at the place of the *yajña*."

Rāma could understand, these two boys were actually the sons of Sītā. He immediately sent a message to Sage Vālmīki saying, if Sītā was pure-hearted, she might, with his permission, provide its satisfactory evidence.

On getting the affirmative reply from Sage Vālmīki, Rāma called a meeting of the eminent sages the next day in the palace hall. Vālmīki arrived there along with Sītā at the appointed time. Addressing Rāma he said, "O Daśarathanandana Rāma, though Sītā is pure-hearted, you have forsaken her out of fear of people's calumny. Now Sītā will do something to create your confidence in order to remove your fear. Kindly give your permission. Rāma, I am telling the truth, these twin valiant boys born of Sītā, are your sons. With my divine vision, I am aware of everything."

Rāma with folded hands said, "O brāhmaṇa, you are a virtuous person. I have full belief in your words. Earlier also Sītā gave proof of her purity in the presence of the gods and that was why I brought her to my house. But the people continued to spread calumny against Sītā and me which was unbearable to me. Because of that I forsook her despite her innocence only out of fear of people's calumny. Kindly pardon me. I know, these twin boys are my own sons. Now let Sītā be the object of my love and affection by again giving proof of her purity. At this moment many gods and sages are present here. They are also eager to get the proof of her purity."

Sītā then coming forward said with folded hands, "I have never thought of any other person other than Rāma. I pray, let Goddess Vasundharā take me in her womb."

Suddenly a divine throne descended there. The all-powerful serpents were holding the throne. As Goddess Vasundharā welcoming Sītā placed her with her hands on the throne, Sītā began to enter into *pātāla* with showers of flower falling from the heaven. For her pure-hearted nature, the gods began to praise Sītā. All the assembled gods, sages and the virtuous people were struck with wonder at the incident of Sītā's entry into the *pātāla*.

Rāma watching Sītā's entry into the *pātāla* began to lament with a sad heart with downcast head. Addressing Mother Vasundharā, Rāma said, "O Mother, you kindly return Sītā to me, or alternatively, give myself a place in your womb. Be it *pātāla* or *svarga*, I want to live together with Sītā. If Sītā is not returned, I shall destroy the whole world."

At this moment Lord Brahmā appearing before Rāma along with the other gods said, "Rāma, have patience, do not grieve. I am now compelled to remind you again of the mystery of your advent to the earth. Nothing is unknown to you. Remember, you are the incarnation of the Supreme God Viṣṇu. The unblemished and pure Sītā is yours. By dint of the virtue of her devotion to the husband, Sītā is presently in the *Nāgaloka* (abode of the serpents). In the heaven you shall meet with Sītā. I am declaring in this assembly, this wonderful *Rāmāyaṇa* epic which you have heard and shall also hear in future, has all been described by the great poet Vālmīki. This first epic is established in you and you are the principal sharer of its fame. Now along with the assembled sages, you listen with attention to the remaining parts of the epic from the mouth of Sage Vālmīki."

Saying this, Lord Brahmā along with the gods left the place. The next day, Rāma listened from Sage Vālmīki to the remaining parts of the epic containing innumerable details on various subjects and was highly delighted. This part is known as Uttara-Kāṇḍa.

The *Aśvamedha Yajña* is over. Sītā has entered into the *pātāla* after giving proof of her purity. Rāma in the absence of Sītā is grief-stricken. There is no peace in his mind. He is always engrossed in the thought of Sītā.

Rāma did not marry any other woman other than Sītā. Subsequently during the religious ceremonies, a gold image of Sītā used to be installed in place of the wife. On entry into the *pātāla,* Sītā became free from all blemishes. But Rāma wedded to the welfare of his subjects, continued to carry on his obligations as the king to ensure their prosperity and happiness. Yet these subjects did not hesitate to spread all calumny against him and Sītā compelling her to go out of their sight by entering into the *pātāla* causing Rāma terrible mental anguish. Rāma forgetting everything remained at the services of his subjects. Only for the virtuous and compassionate Rāma, it was possible to show such unparalleled equanimity of mind and devotion to duties forgetting all personal sufferings.

42

The Last Journey

IN this way Rāma's righteous rule completed many years. Suddenly one day an ascetic sought the interview of Rāma introducing himself as the messenger of Maharṣi Atibala. On being asked by Rāma about the purpose of his visit, the ascetic said, "Mahārāja, I shall disclose my purpose in confidence. You first take the vow, you shall kill anyone who will hear our discussions or enter this room during the discussions." Rāma taking the vow accordingly, directed Lakṣmaṇa to remain on guard at the door so that none could enter inside during their discussions. Finding Rāma alone, the ascetic disclosing his true identity said, "O King, I am Yama. Lord Brahmā has sent me to you. He has asked me to remind you, the period of time determined for you to stay on the earth for the protection of the people, has been over. You have freed the people from fear and oppression by destroying the sinful Rāvaṇa. Now the time has come for your return to your own abode."

In reply Rāma said, "I have been born to perform my duties in all the three worlds. With the completion of the task bestowed on me, I shall now return to the place I have come from. It is my duty to partake in the works of the gods who are my kinsfolk."

Rāma and Yama were thus engaged in discussions, when Sage Durvāsā appeared at the door and in a harsh tone asked Lakṣmaṇa, "Immediately arrange for my interview with Rāma. This is extremely urgent." On paying obeisance to Sage

Durvāsā, Lakṣmaṇa respectfully said, "O Bhagavan, you may kindly tell me your need. Is it not possible for me to fulfil your need? Rāmacandra is now busy with other works. Kindly wait for a few moments."

At the words of Lakṣmaṇa, Sage Durvāsā flew into a rage and said, "Immediately convey my arrival to Rāma; otherwise you and your brothers, their children, the cities and the entire kingdom will be destroyed by my curse." On hearing these terrible words of Durvāsā, Lakṣmaṇa remembering Rāma's strict orders not to allow any body to enter inside, thought for a few moments about his duty. He then decided, his own death was preferable to the deaths of all others. He accordingly entered inside violating Rāma's orders and conveyed to him the news of Durvāsā's arrival. Rāma bidding farewell to Yama, immediately came out and respectfully asked Sage Durvāsā about his need. The sage told Rāma, "My vow of fasting for thousand years has been over. I want to eat something immediately." Rāma arranged food for him without delay. After finishing the food, Sage Durvāsā profusely praised Rāma and departed.

After his departure, Rāma remembering his vow before Yama, became restless. On seeing Rāma's condition, Lakṣmaṇa said, "O great King, do not grieve for me. Kill me without any hesitation and keep your vow. Any deviation from the vow will land you in hell."

Rāma was perturbed at the words of Lakṣmaṇa and immediately convened a meeting of his council of ministers and the priests to advise him on his course of action in the present situation. The ministers and the priests heard the details; but remained silent. After some time, Sage Vasiṣṭha said, "Rāma, with my spiritual power I have already come to know about your separation from Lakṣmaṇa and his death. The decree of fate is inviolable. Therefore, forsake Lakṣmaṇa and fulfil your promise. The religious order will be destroyed if your promise is broken."

Addessing Lakṣmaṇa, Rāma then said, "Lakṣmaṇa, it is improper to violate *dharma*. I am forsaking you. The virtuous people do not find any difference between death and the act of giving up." On hearing the words of Rāma, Lakṣmaṇa immediately rushed to the river Sarayū and gave up his life in its waters.

Overwhelmed with grief on forsaking Lakṣmaṇa who was as dear to him as his own life, Rāma declared, he would also give up his life following the path of Lakṣmaṇa after installing Bharata on the throne. But Bharata refused saying he had no desire for any kingdom or wealth leaving Rāma and declared, he would follow in Rāma's footsteps. At last on the suggestion of Bharata, Rāma installed Kuśa and Lava on the thrones of Kosala and Uttar Bhāga kingdoms respectively after dividing the vast Kosala empire. Brother Śatrughna was then at Mathurā. On being apprised of the developments at Ayodhyā by the messengers sent from the capital, he installed his two sons Subāhu and Śatrughātī on the thrones of Mathurā and Vaidiśa kingdoms respectively after dividing the main Mathurā kingdom. He then hurriedly arrived at Ayodhyā and on hearing all details, decided to follow Rāma in his last journey. The people of Ayodhyā, meanwhile, assembled in front of the palace and expressed their desire to give up their lives along with Rāma. At this time Sugrīva arrived at Ayodhyā and announced, he had installed son Aṅgada on the throne of Kiṣkindhā kingdom and had come here to follow Rāma with the others.

Later, Rāma told Vibhīṣaṇa, "O Rākṣasarāja, you shall continue to govern the kingdom of Laṅkā so long as the moon, the sun, this world and my name will survive. Do never deviate from the path of *dharma*. I have another request for you. You shall everyday worship God Jagannātha, the family deity of the Ikṣvāku dynasty."

Looking at Hanumān, Rāma said, "O Kapiśresṭha (greatest of the *vānaras*), so long as my name will remain circulated, you shall wander around happily remembering my name. Also tell Jāmavanta (Jāṁbavān), the son of Lord Brahmā similarly about my words." He then told the assembled *yakṣas* and the *vānaras*, they might also follow him if they so liked.

The next day, on completion of all arrangements for his journey to the heaven under the supervision of Sage Vasiṣṭha, Rāma in divine clothes meditated on the Supreme God and after coming out of the palace with a stem of grass in hand, proceeded in slow steps towards the River Sarayū. The arrows, the quivers and the weapons used by him, accompanied him assuming human form. The all protective Gāyatrī (Vedic prayer for the divine light to illuminate human mind), Oṁkāra (symbol representing the Supreme Being), Vaṣaṭkāra (incantation uttered during presentation of burnt offering to the deity) and the Vedas (the oldest religious texts containing hymns, incantations and rituals of ancient India) dressed as brāhmaṇas, accompanied Rāma. The virtuous sages understanding that the gates of the heaven have been opened, followed Rāma. The female inmates of the palace, slaves and the maids and the others became Rāma's companions. Bharata and Śatrughna with countless brāhmaṇas and the animals followed Rāma. On the way many *yakṣas*, *vānaras*, *rākṣasas*, citizens and the people belonging to various classes joined the last journey of Rāma. Ayodhyā turned into a deserted city.

Rāma slowly reached a sacred place on the bank of the river. Behind him there was a large crowd. At this time Lord Brahmā along with the gods appeared there. With the radiant divine force of the gods, the world assumed a beautiful appearance. Scented breeze began to blow. There were showers of flower from the heaven. At the sweet sound of hundreds of instruments, the entire atmosphere took a serene outlook. Rāma slowly descended into the water in the midst of wide cries of lamentation of the vast crowd.

Lord Brahmā then said from the sky, "O Viṣṇu, welcome, welcome. It is our fortune, you have appeared before us. Along with your virtuous brothers, you now assume the new body. O God, you are the protector of all. You are without infirmities, immortal, unfathomable and great. It is not easy to know you."

On hearing Brahmā's words, Rāma along with the brothers bodily entered into the force of Supreme God Viṣṇu. The *devas* then began to worship the all-pervading Deva of Viṣṇu. As the Supreme God Viṣṇu, Rāma told Lord Brahmā, "These countless people are all illustrious. Thy have come to give up their lives out of love for me. You may kindly determine suitable abodes for them on their death." After their death in the waters of the river Sarayū, Lord Brahmā fixed their abodes according to the consequences of their action in the previous life. On completion of his functions, Lord Brahmā happily departed to Svargapurī along with the gods. Thus ends the wonderful story of *Rāmāyaṇa* as depicted by Sage Vālmīki encompassing all the noble principles for the welfare of mankind.

Conclusion

THE accomplishments of Rāma which we have witnessed in the epic, are entirely due to the nobility of his character. Rāma was born with all the virtues. Therefore, in whatever works he laid his hands on, his success was assured. For his sweet behaviour he was dear to everybody from the very boyhood. He was ever eager to help others whatever might be the danger. In all difficult pursuits he took a leading role. His compassion knew no bounds having no regard to personal loss or gain. His sense of justice and fair-play was reflected in his governance of the kingdom and the establishment of *rāmarājya,* the main theme of which was the welfare of the people. He did not hesitate even to abandon his beloved and sinless wife Sītā in deference to the wishes of his own people. For this he caused immense pain and anguish not only to Sītā but also to himself. Yet Rāma harboured no ill feelings for his people whom he continued to serve as before with justice and fairness. In the end the people realized their folly and did not hesitate to give up their lives as if to atone their sin, in the waters of the river Sarayū along with Rāma and his virtuous brothers. We shall ever pray for the advent in India of leaders with Rāma's nobility of character to clear the debris that has accumulated in our society because of various acts of omissions and commissions of the political leaders. This calls for enlightened awakening of the civil society throwing up such leaders and workers whose main aim would be not self-aggrandizement but the selfless service of the people. In this holy land of ours, this is not an impossible dream.

Though Rāma was a simple straightforward person wedded to the welfare of the people, he did not hesitate to disregard their persistent entreaties and went to the forest gladly on the wishes of his father. He told them, under Bharata's better governance of the kingdom the people would remain ever happy and contended. Rāma's words did not go in vain. We know, during Rāma's exile in the forest, Bharata who governed the kingdom as his representative, increased the revenue and the resources of the kingdom ten times. The people were also happy under his fair administration.

Rāma, the embodiment of truth and fairness, did not hesitate, as the circumstances demanded, to ruthlessly apply principles of *daṇḍa* to destroy the wicked. He was soft as flower as also severe as thunder. In Janasthāna, we have seen, Rāma destroyed the *rākṣasa*s and later the sinful Rāvaṇa for his crime in abducting Sītā. These opposing characteristic distinctions were present in Rāma in wonderful co-ordination. He was ever ready to give protection to anyone seeking his refuge. Rāma was even willing to pardon Rāvaṇa, the perpetrator of the most heinous crime and give him protection if he had returned Sītā. This is indeed rare and had been possible only for a person of Rāma's nobility and greatness of character.

Rāma showed exemplary courage, bravery, fortitude, leadership quality and proficiency in operational planning during the successful military campaign against Laṅkā. We are aware of the efforts of Sugrīva and particularly of Hanumān in searching out Sītā in far away Laṅkā. Brother Lakṣmaṇa besides giving timely advice and guidance to Rāma in the conduct of the war, himself showed exemplary heroism in combating the enemy. This is particularly evident during his battle with valiant Indrajit who got killed at his hands. Sugrīva, Hanumān, Vibhīhṣaṇa and the other *vānara* leaders gallantly fought in the war indicating their complete loyalty to Rāma. The collection of advance information about the strength and weaknesses of the *rākṣasa*s by Hanumān and Vibhīṣaṇa was immensely helpful to Rāma. Sugrīva and Vibhīṣaṇa true to their promise gave spontaneous support and cooperation to Rāma as they were convinced of the latter's supernatural power and strength, nobility of character and various other qualities. Of course, self-interest influenced their decision. Sugrīva and Vibhīṣaṇa got Kiṣkindhā and Laṅkā kingdoms respectively on the death of their brothers at the hands of Rāma.

During exile in the forest Rāma and Lakṣmaṇa had no resources whatsoever except their own personal power and strength. For all these they primarily depended on their allies. The royal army of Ayodhyā had no role in the war against Laṅkā. It is reported, on getting the information about Sītā's abduction by Rāvaṇa, Bharata mobilized a huge army to move to Laṅkā in the aid of Rāma. Bur at the last moment Rāma reportedly sent a message to Bharata not to send any army from Ayodhyā as he would be able to accomplish the task with the help of the *vānara* army. At the end of war when Rāma returned to Ayodhyā with Sītā and Lakṣmaṇa, many kings expressed disappointment on being deprived of the privilege of participating in the great war of victory against Laṅkā under Rāma's leadership.

Rāma was prepared for both the paths of war and peace for the accomplishment of his objective of rescuing Sītā. Always he was guided by the principles of truth, justice and fair-play. Just on the eve of the full-scale war, Rāma sent Aṅgada to convey his message to Rāvaṇa to surrender. Rāvaṇa scornfully rejected Rāma's last-minute peace efforts and warning and even tried to belabour Aṅgada who, however, as we know, managed to release himself and safely returned to the *vānara* camp. Having exhausted all his peace overtures, Rāma started the full-scale war destroying Rāvaṇa and his vast *rākṣasa* army. In victory Rāma true to his nobility of character, remained magnanimous. He gave the kingdom of

Laṅkā to Vibhīṣaṇa as he had earlier installed Sugrīva on the throne of Kiṣkindhā. He did not take for himself any resources from Laṅkā or Kiṣkindhā. Everything he left for Vibhīṣaṇa and Sugrīva. To both of them he explained the principles of *rājadhrama* and advised them to govern their kingdoms with the sole objective of ensuring the welfare of their subjects.

Rāma himself on taking over the reins of the government of his own kingdom of Ayodhyā, was able to establish an ideal state where all sections of the people were happy, by faithfully following the principles of *rājadhrama*. He even did not hesitate to forsake Sītā, his beloved wife to satisfy the people. The success towards the establishment of *rāmarajya* was primarily due to his nobility of character and his sense of justice and righteousness. He understood, for the successful formulation of the state policy, he must be armed with all sorts of information — good or bad — of the kingdom. This important task he accomplished with the help of his faithful brothers and through a band of trusted agents. During the reign of his distinguished father King Daśaratha, royal army contingents as also trained secret agents were deployed at strategic locations. All these arrangements continued during Bharata's benevolent rule. On ascending the throne, it appears, Rāma completely overhauled the administration. Different departments like education, health, justice, communication, etc. received added importance. The external and internal stability was firmly established. With the rule of law and right dispensation of justice, the bad were firmly suppressed and the good protected. Under the righteous rule of Rāma different sections of the people belonging to the four castes were engaged in their respective duties and responsibilities in full cooperation with one another as prescribed by the learned sages. It was a state of peace, prosperity and happiness. As the people were bound by a strong sense of religion, they had no inclination towards any evil conduct.

Despite his controversial acts like the killing of Vālī, humiliation of Sītā at Laṅkā on her rescue, killing of Śambūka, abandonment of Sītā, etc. Rāma is held in high esteem and devotion by countless people for his nobility of character, achievements and establishment of a righteous society ensuring for all peace, prosperity and happiness. It matters little if some people of our times claiming to be free-thinkers, hold an adverse view of Rāma's various actions and of the story of *Rāmāyaṇa*. The way Rāma has been accepted by the people at large, is the most important thing. The religion, culture, customs and manners, thinking, belief and in fact the very existence of the vast sections of the Hindus, centre round the teachings of Rāma and the *Rāmāyaṇa*. Even today the influence of these teachings has not waned in any way. The same old tradition is still continuing as before.

It is possible, there are many exaggerations in the description of *rāmarājya*. From the practical point of view, the existence of such a perfect socie ty is difficult to conceive. Even then it must be admitted, if the king or the ruler guided by the lofty principles of *rājadhrama* as enshrined in the *Rāmāyaṇa*, sincerely conducts the affairs of the state, substantial improvement can be brought about in our present decadent society. We find from the other great epic *Mahābhārata*, Dharmarāja Yudhiṣṭhira was able to establish a society where the people lived in a state of peace, happiness and prosperity. Inspired by the king's exemplary character, the rebel kings, burglars and robbers, and the dishonest royal officials surrendered to him of their own accord and sought his pardon. Our present-day rulers and the politicians have to learn many things from the righteous kings of the epics.

Today the people of our country are in a state of great despair. In the absence of effective enforcement of the rule of law, the protection of the good and the suppression of the bad — the primary responsibility of the government — are hindered. Bereft of morality, a section of the people guided only by their self aggrandizement is ceaselessly engaged in the pursuit of wealth and personal prominence. We are fast forgetting the basic humane qualities like love, tolerance, conciliation, generosity, sacrifice, unity, equality and honesty of purpose. Violence in various forms has gripped the society. The political parties are shamelessly engaged in the struggle for power forgetting the interest of the nation.

It is, however, gratifying to note, democracy is firmly established in India. The publicity media is very strong. The intellectuals are ardent critics of the government's acts of omission and commission. The judiciary is quite active. The non-governmental organizations have maintained a strict vigil on the activities of the government. India now possesses human resources of a very high order. There is also no dearth of natural resources. The general people are simple, god-fearing and hard-working. Under proper leadership they are capable of doing wonders. It is our hope and prayer, India will produce leaders like Rāma and with proper exploitation of the resources we possess, our country in no distant future will occupy a glorious place in the comity of nations fulfilling the dream of the freedom fighters.

Index